Write your blessed name, O Lord, upon my heart,
There to remain so indelibly engraved that no prosperity,
That no adversity shall ever move me from your love.

Be to me a strong tower of defense,
A comforter in tribulation, a deliverer in distress,
And a faithful guide to the courts of heaven
Through the many temptations and dangers of this life,
O Jesus, my only Savior!

Write your blessed name, O Lord, upon my heart,
There to remain so indelibly engraved that no prosperity,
That no adversity shall ever move me from your love.

THOMAS À KEMPIS

Pray without Ceasing

REVITALIZING PASTORAL CARE

Deborah van Deusen Hunsinger

For April and Denis —
10-18-06
With gratitude and joy for
the companionship of our shared
journey.
And love and affection,
Deborah

William B. Eerdmans Publishing Company
Grand Rapids, Michigan / Cambridge, U.K.

© 2006 Deborah van Deusen Hunsinger

Published 2006 by
Wm. B. Eerdmans Publishing Co.
2140 Oak Industrial Drive N.E., Grand Rapids, Michigan 49505 /
P.O. Box 163, Cambridge CB3 9PU U.K.
www.eerdmans.com

Printed in the United States of America

11 10 09 08 07 06   7 6 5 4 3 2 1

Library of Congress Cataloging-in-Publication Data

Hunsinger, Deborah van Deusen.
  Pray without ceasing: revitalizing pastoral care /
  Deborah van Deusen Hunsinger.
      p.   cm.
    ISBN-10: 0-8028-4759-5 / ISBN-13: 978-0-8028-4759-1 (pbk.: alk. paper)
    1. Prayers. 2. Pastoral care. I. Title.

  BV210.3.H855 2006
  48.3′2 — dc22

                                        2006013773

Unless otherwise noted, the Scripture quotations in this publication are from the
Revised Standard Version of the Bible, copyrighted 1946, 1952 © 1971, 1973 by the
Division of Christian Education of the National Council of Churches of Christ in the
U.S.A., and used by permission.

Contents

Preface

This book had its genesis in two hospital stays. During the first, I was a student chaplain undertaking Clinical Pastoral Education (CPE). Twenty years later, I was a patient recovering from emergency surgery. In each case, a minister of the Gospel gave me the gift of prayer and pastoral care at a time of personal need. I am indebted to these two Christian ministers: the Reverend John N. Simpson, my CPE supervisor, whose insight and practical wisdom were used by God to call me into ministry; and the Reverend Deborah K. Davis, chaplain at Princeton Medical Center, whose compassionate presence and prayers sustained me.

I am also indebted to Princeton Theological Seminary for its generous sabbatical and research assistance policies. Special thanks are due to Theresa Latini, at the time a Ph.D. candidate in practical theology, who provided editorial suggestions in preparing the manuscript. I am also grateful for the opportunities I had to present this material in various stages of its development. I would like to express my appreciation for warm hospitality to the First Presbyterian Church of Myrtle Beach, South Carolina; the National Association of Presbyterian Korean Women, Seoul, Korea; Furman University's Pastors' School, Greenville, South Carolina; the Presbytery of New Brunswick, New Jersey; the Northeast Region of the American Association of Pastoral Counselors; the program in Continuing Education at Princeton Theological Seminary; and my home church, Nassau Presbyterian Church in Princeton, New Jersey. I also remember with thanks the students who have taken my course called "Prayer and Pastoral Care"; their thirst for learning has been a source of ongoing encouragement.

I would also like to acknowledge the support of the editorial staff at Eerdmans Publishing Company. I am especially indebted to my editor, Mary Hietbrink, for her clarity, skill, and attentiveness to detail. As to "William B." himself, as he is affectionately known in our home, I owe him more thanks than can be easily summarized. His inimitable style of "doing business" brings endless delight; his professional judgment, profound respect and gratitude.

Finally, I am grateful to my husband, George Hunsinger, not only for his comments in reading the manuscript, but also for thirty years of rich theological conversation. His companionship and support in our shared vocation has made my life's work a joy. This book is dedicated to him with all my love.

Introduction

Praying with those in need is at the heart of the Christian life. The New Testament urges us to bear one another's burdens (Gal. 6:2), to confess our sins and pray for one another (James 5:16), to encourage one another (1 Thess. 5:11), and to care for one another (1 Cor. 12:25). Throughout the history of the church, Christians have undertaken ministries of intercessory prayer, visitation of the sick, and small groups that share the joys and hardships of the members' common life in Christ. Such ministries of mutual edification, support, and prayer are the work of the whole church, an undertaking of "the priesthood of all believers." When individuals are upheld by one another in Christ, nurtured by the Word of God, and knit spiritually into a common body, they are blessed with vitality as they reach out to a world in need.

Pastoral care denotes first of all the theologically informed and spiritually attuned care that pastors offer their congregations in times of special need. Pastors learn how to listen to people in crisis, to discern their needs, both spoken and unspoken, and to offer intercessory prayer on their behalf. One of the aims of this book is to assist ordained ministers in these tasks. At the same time, however, it also endeavors to provide them with resources to train their congregations in ministries of mutual prayer and pastoral care so that this work might include all the people of God.

Ministers need a working theology of prayer that will foster the training of their congregations at every level. Spiritual practices need to be recovered throughout the church's common life, for they are the lifeline of its relationship with God and the heart of its fellowship in

Christ. Ordained ministers are not merely providers of pastoral care but, more importantly, those who equip their congregations to provide it. The New Testament envisions a ministry to which all are called. By virtue of their baptism, all Christians are called to bear one another's burdens, to intercede on behalf of others, and to build each other up. The Reformation teaching on "the priesthood of all believers" insists that ministry belongs first not to a clerical elite, but to the entire body of Christ. The spiritual bonds that knit a community together depend upon the work of prayer through the Holy Spirit. Ministry that begins in mutual care and common prayer leads to a common mission.

This book offers theological reflection to assist congregational leaders as they develop mutual care, accountability, and prayer in their churches. As an exercise in practical theology, it aims to build up the body of Christ. It commends organizing congregations into small groups, provides guidance for study groups in spiritual formation, and assists deacons in their ministries of visitation and prayer. It is designed to be used in a variety of teaching and training situations in the church.

Many people in the North American church today are uncomfortable in praying with others. Even those who pray privately may be averse to praying with others aloud. Few churches encourage young people to pray together except in the context of formal worship. Parents, themselves ill-equipped, may feel embarrassed about praying with their children; if they pray with them at all, it is usually confined to a memorized grace before meals or bedtime prayer. Even deacons who have taken on a ministry of visiting the sick can feel self-conscious when it comes to praying with another. The culture of many churches, especially in the mainline denominations, fosters a feeling that such "spiritual" sharing is too private and that praying together is too frighteningly intimate. Moreover, many do not know where to turn in the Bible for wisdom and guidance. Because a whole generation has been poorly equipped, many Christians find themselves unable to pray with others at the core of their need.

Until recently, many Protestant seminaries neglected teaching about prayer except as something of historical interest. Yet even with rising interest in "spirituality," rare is the course that focuses on the theoretical and practical issues of prayer and pastoral care. As a result, seminary graduates who pray do so with some uncertainty about what they are doing and why. A clearer understanding is needed. One place seminarians might receive concrete training in prayer and pastoral care is in Clinical Pastoral Education.[1] Some CPE students are encouraged by their supervisors not only to pray with their patients or parishioners but also to reflect critically on these practices. Yet in other programs, students are actively discouraged from doing so — sometimes actually forbidden to do so.

In theological education, observes Craig Dykstra, spiritual practices need to be identified, studied, and pursued. "This is especially true today," he writes, "when this task has been singularly neglected." Finding a way to lift up Christian practices, "to describe them, analyze them, interpret them, evaluate them, and aid in their reformation," is a responsibility of practical theology.[2] For the practices of the Christian community are the embodiment of its living traditions. This book offers a theological framework to guide churches in this task.

Recently efforts have been made to recover the "classical tradition of pastoral care."[3] After decades of deriving their assumptions from other disciplines, most notably the various psychotherapeutic schools, pastoral theologians are recognizing that pastoral care has its own uniqueness rooted in two thousand years of theological reflection and pastoral practice.[4] Basic Christian doctrine (e.g., the Trinity, Christology, justification, sanctification, vocation, eschatology, and ecclesiology) has profound implications for pastoral practice. Yet for more than a genera-

---

1. CPE is multifaith professional education for ministry. It teaches pastoral care in settings where ministry is practiced (e.g., churches, hospitals, universities, the military, prisons, etc.). See www.acpe.edu.

2. Craig Dykstra, "Reconceiving Practice," in *Shifting Boundaries: Contextual Approaches to the Structure of Theological Education*, ed. Barbara Wheeler and Edward Farley (Louisville: Westminster/John Knox Press, 1991), pp. 48, 47. According to Dykstra, our current understanding of "practices" is ahistorical, individualistic, and technological, something done *to* and *for* others, undergirded by a utilitarian ethic. By contrast, he argues that the practices of the Christian faith are more adequately conceived as being cooperative and communal "complex traditions of interaction," something we do *with* others. We learn the practices of Christian faith by participating in them in the community, through mentoring relationships with others who are competent "practitioners." By entering into the practices of the faith, we develop new knowledge and insight that cannot otherwise be gained.

3. Cf. Andrew Purves, *Pastoral Theology in the Classical Tradition* (Philadelphia: Westminster/John Knox Press, 2001); Thomas Oden, *Classical Pastoral Care* (Grand Rapids: Baker Books, 1994).

4. Cf. William A. Clebsch and Charles R. Jaekle, *Pastoral Care in Historical Perspective* (New York: Harper, 1964).

tion, pastoral theology has largely ignored — or simply taken for granted — this heritage as it has mined various secular disciplines for the insight offered there. While the gains should not be minimized, there also have been losses. Chief among them is confusion about what makes Christian ministry distinctive in relation to other "helping professions." When one discipline derives its presuppositions and methods from another, it loses its way. Pastoral care is no exception. In recent years, however, pastoral theologians have begun to recover the richness of Christian doctrine for their reflection on pastoral work, as Thomas Oden points out:

> Pastors . . . are rediscovering the distinctiveness of pastoral method as distinguished from other methods of inquiry (historical, philosophical, literary, psychological, etc.). Pastoral care is a unique enterprise that has its own distinctive subject-matter (care of souls); its own methodological premise (revelation); its own way of inquiring into its subject-matter (attentiveness to the revealed Word through Scripture and its consensual tradition of exegesis); its own criteria of scholarly authenticity (accountability to canonical text and tradition); its own way of knowing (listening to sacred Scripture with the historic church); its own mode of cultural analysis (with worldly powers bracketed and divine providence appreciated); and its own logic (internal consistency premised upon revealed truth).[5]

When theology is taken seriously, pastoral care recovers its distinctiveness. It locates itself anew as "faith seeking understanding." Starting from faith, it inquires about the "cure of souls." It attends to the spiritual needs of particular people in specific Christian communities:

> The cure of souls thus means in general, concern for the individual in the light of God's purpose for him, of the divine promise and claim addressed to him, of the witness specially demanded of him. God is the One who is primarily and properly concerned about souls. They are always in His hand. Yet in His service, in the ministry of witness committed to His people, there is a corresponding human concern, . . . a *mutua consolatio fratrum*.[6]

5. Thomas Oden, *Classical Pastoral Care*, p. 4.

6. See Karl Barth's discussion of "cure of souls" as a basic form of ministry in *Church Dogmatics*, IV/3 (Edinburgh: T&T Clark, 1961), p. 885.

Being instructed by Scripture, pastoral care assumes that our deepest need — which offers the vital cure — is for God and one another:

> The cure of souls understood in this special sense as the individual cure of souls means a concrete actualisation of the participation of the one in the particular past, present and future of the other, in his particular burdens and afflictions, but above all in his particular promise and hope in the singularity of his existence as created and sustained by God.[7]

From the perspective of Christian faith, God addresses each person in adversity as well as prosperity, and calls us to share both our sorrow and our joy with one another (Rom. 12:15). As we accompany one another in Christian faith, we are called to participate in one another's lives in concrete ways, sharing not only the burdens and afflictions but also the promise and hope of each life created and sustained by God. Discerning the call of God in and through every circumstance of life is impossible apart from meditating on the word of God as mediated through Scripture. In our life of faith, we rely on the leading of the Spirit in and through the biblical Word. We turn to Scripture as we seek to support one another in listening for God's guidance. We listen to each other having first listened to God. Pastoral care for others begins with seeking God.

If we are to intercede for others meaningfully, we must consider their need. Discernment of another's true need requires compassionate presence and attentive listening. Listening inwardly to our own hearts is also essential. Paradoxically, we are able to focus on another's need apart from our own pressing concerns only when we are most self-aware. In this matrix of three-dimensional listening — to God, to the other, and to our inmost selves — we pray for the Holy Spirit to give us the words we need. Our prayer, through the Spirit, binds us together with God and one another. Christian fellowship, *koinonia*, is the gift God gives to those who pray together. In prayer, Christians are knit together spiritually, joined in intimate communion with God and one another. This is the subject I explore in Chapter One.

A practical theology of prayer involves specific skills and prac-

---

7. Barth, *Church Dogmatics*, IV/3, p. 886.

tices. In Chapter Two I reconsider the ancient practice of *lectio divina*, listening to the word of God as a discipline that deepens prayer. Through Scripture, a concrete word is spoken, offering guidance, wisdom, and hope. In Chapter Three, I outline the essential skills for listening to another person in the context of faith. In Chapter Four I provide instruction in *focusing*, originally a psychotherapeutic technique devised to help persons gain inner clarity by noticing their embodied emotional responses. For our purposes, this technique will help caregivers identify those unresolved issues that impede their ability to listen. In addition, in this chapter I will argue the importance of self-empathy as a means toward continued growth as a caregiver. In these chapters I build upon the gains the field has acquired through its careful study of depth psychology and interdisciplinary reflection.[8] Pastoral theology needs to root itself in the richness of its theological heritage while using the tools it has acquired from the psychological disciplines.

In Chapters Five through Nine I go on to consider five forms of prayer: petition, intercession, confession, lament, and thanksgiving and praise. A chapter on each develops their pastoral implications in light of theological reflection. The addendum offers a variety of concrete suggestions for developing pastoral care groups in a congregation. In addition, it offers guidelines for teaching practical caregiving skills. Additional case studies and pastoral conversations are provided in the appendices for further reflection and group discussion. The book thus aims not only to reflect theoretically on the place of prayer in pastoral care, but also to provide practical guidance for those wishing to build up their congregations through this means.

What strengthens vitality in the church? When structures for a praying community are created at every level of the church's common life, the blessing of a congregation that "prays without ceasing" will enrich the whole church. Where such a process is undertaken, trust is deepened and love grows. When the community is built up in this way, it receives what it needs for pastoral care. Moreover, the community's spiritual life is renewed for the work of mission. United in Christ, the church will have the vitality it needs to serve the world that God loves.

---

8. Cf. Deborah van Deusen Hunsinger, *Theology and Pastoral Counseling: A New Interdisciplinary Approach* (Grand Rapids: Eerdmans, 1995).

One   A Theology of *Koinonia*

Pastoral care cannot be Christian unless conducted in a spirit of reverence. The work of prayer is integral to every step. If we believe that it is finally God who provides what is needed, then prayer is not optional. God bids us to pray in times of trial — "Call upon me in the day of trouble" (Ps. 50:15) — and promises his help: "Ask, and it will be given you; seek, and you will find; knock, and it will be opened to you" (Matt. 7:7). Prayer is, as John Calvin recognized, the "chief exercise of faith."[1] Through it, faith is nourished, hope is renewed, and our love for God is strengthened. Pastoral care arises from prayer and leads back to it.

Prayer in the context of pastoral care is prayer on behalf of another. It is our response to another's need, offered up to God. When we intercede for another, God draws us into communion with himself, providing the strength to face the situation at hand. We sense our complete dependence upon God, and yet we see that God uses the human community to effect his purposes. Through common prayer our spirits are knit together, giving us a foretaste of the communion of saints. By these living spiritual connections, courage is renewed, faith is deepened, and Christian fellowship is revitalized. *Koinonia* is the *telos* as well as the indispensable means of all true pastoral care.

Frank Lake, founder of the Clinical Theology movement in Great Britain, states that true pastoral dialogue is "initiated by the pastor's

---

1. John Calvin, *Institutes of the Christian Religion,* Library of Christian Classics, vols. 20-21, ed. John T. McNeill, trans. Ford Lewis Battles (Philadelphia: Westminster Press, 1960), 3.20.1.

I

willingness to listen" to the parishioner and is "concluded when both of them are listening to Jesus Christ." As the transaction of listening moves from the one plane to the other, "we have an epitome of that for which the world exists."[2] Though Lake focuses on the relationship between pastor and parishioner, his claim would apply to anyone who cares for another in Christ's name. When persons gather in this name, listen to each other in the light of faith, and express their needs in prayer, they fulfill God's purpose of *koinonia* or spiritual fellowship. This communion is the "epitome" of which Lake speaks.

The Greek noun *koinonia* (as well as related words with the same root meaning) occurs 119 times in the Bible.[3] It is variously translated into English as "communion," "community," and "fellowship." But these single nouns do not quite capture its richness or range of meaning. Biblical passages that speak of our participation *in Christ* or of our having a share in Christ point to what is meant by *koinonia*. For example, in the Eucharistic passages in First Corinthians, Paul speaks of the cup of blessing as a participation *(koinonia)* in the blood of Christ, and the bread which we break as a participation *(koinonia)* in the body of Christ. As we partake of the consecrated elements, we become members of Christ's body. We participate in Christ's life even as we take Christ's body into our own bodies. We are *in Christ* and Christ is *in us*.

Koinonia draws together the vertical dimension (our relationship with God) and the horizontal dimension (our relationship with each other) by means of our common life in Christ. In 1 John 1:2-4, the author uses the concept of *koinonia* (usually translated as "fellowship") to draw these dimensions into relationship with each other:

> . . . the life was made manifest, and we saw it, and testify to it, and proclaim to you the eternal life which was with the Father and was made manifest to us — that which we have seen and heard we proclaim also to you, so that you may have fellowship with us; and our fellowship is with the Father and with his Son Jesus Christ. And we are writing this that our joy may be complete.

2. Frank Lake, *Clinical Theology* (London: Darton, Longman & Todd, 1966), p. 15.
3. Cf. John Reumann, "Koinonia," in *The Encyclopedia of Christianity* (Grand Rapids and Leiden: Eerdmans/Brill, 2003), pp. 134-36.

Fellowship in the church *means* fellowship with the Father and the Son through the Spirit. The communion that the church shares is its communion with God in and through Jesus Christ. Our spiritual fellowship with one another connotes our common participation in Christ's suffering and comfort (2 Cor. 1:7) as well as our partnership in the Gospel (Phil. 1:5).

Further, *koinonia* points to the church's living hope that it will *participate in* or *partake of* the divine nature:

> His divine power has granted to us all things that pertain to life and godliness, through the knowledge of him who called us to his own glory and excellence, by which he has granted to us his precious and very great promises, that through these you may . . . become *partakers [koinonia]* of the divine nature. (2 Peter 1:4)

Koinonia is the word used in what may be the most familiar of all benedictions: "The grace of the Lord Jesus Christ and the love of God and the fellowship *[koinonia]* of the Holy Spirit be with you all" (2 Cor. 13:14). The *koinonia* of the Holy Spirit is the perfect fellowship the church enjoys when it is one in the Spirit, living out its unity in Christ. *Koinonia* is thus an eschatological concept, pointing toward a fulfillment not fully realized here on earth, of a true communion of saints that finds its identity and hope in Christ. This spiritual fellowship in Christ is strengthened whenever members of Christ's body gather together for prayer.

Koinonia is the fellowship that makes pastoral care possible. When *koinonia* flourishes, so does pastoral care. In this chapter, I proceed as follows. I begin by tracing the theological ground and reality of *koinonia* in the perfect fellowship of the Holy Trinity itself. The love and freedom between the Father and the Son in the Spirit become a template for understanding our relationships with each other. Jesus Christ is mediator of the fellowship not only between God and ourselves, but also in our relationships with each other. Accordingly, I then delineate the central role of Christ in mediating *koinonia*. Turning more specifically to pastoral care, I argue that *koinonia* is an end in itself, not merely a means to some other end. Prayer in the context of pastoral care draws persons into intimate fellowship with God and one another. It is God's gift to the church. We learn to pray in community, and we depend upon the community to uphold us in prayer. Since pastoral care is the work of the whole community, not simply the ordained staff, I conclude the chapter by arguing for the priesthood of all believers. All the saints need to be equipped for the work of ministry. All need to participate in ministries of intercessory prayer and pastoral care to build up the body of Christ.

Koinonia Relationships

The Christian understanding of the Trinity arose out of the church's intuition of God's perfect *koinonia*. As depicted in Scripture and affirmed in the creeds, God is not solitary but uniquely relational. The Father loves the Son, and the Son loves the Father through the Holy Spirit to all eternity. The Trinitarian fellowship they enjoy is one of mutual indwelling. Even in their irreducible differences, they remain an indivisible unity, one God. Their fellowship does not diminish but rather enhances the personal integrity of each. The Father remains the Father in all eternity, loving the Son through the Holy Spirit. The Son alone becomes incarnate, suffers, dies, and is raised from the dead. He is mediator and advocate between the Father and all humanity. The Holy Spirit is the living presence that flows eternally between the Father and the Son, not only as the bond of love between them, but also as the active agent of their love in the world. As he binds the Father and the Son in eternity, so he also binds us to the Father through the Son here on earth. Each member of the Trinity retains his particular identity, yet they are completely one in purpose, action, and essence. As the Trinitarian persons of the Godhead relate to each other in mutual love and freedom, so we are called to become fully human through loving relationships with others and with God.

The mutual indwelling that characterizes the Holy Trinity becomes a template for understanding our relationship to Jesus Christ. Christ so dwells in us that we are made members of his body, the church. We are *in Christ* and he is *in us* through the Holy Spirit. When we come to God in prayer and join one another in the Spirit through the Son, we do not lose our individual identity but find it. In our relationship with God, we are granted the freedom to be our true selves. God does not overwhelm us with his presence, but liberates and sustains our particularity by it. We discover our uniqueness in relation to God and others, not apart from them.

Our fellowship with Christ is similar in intimacy to the eternal communion of the Trinity, but different in the following respect. In ourselves and apart from Christ, we remain sinners who are unable to enter God's holy presence. But in and through Christ, we are made righteous before God and given access to the Father as adopted children. Our union with Christ becomes the ground for the grace to address the Creator of all things as *our* Father. As members of Christ's body, we are enabled to approach God with familiarity and trust. Our being *in Christ (koinonia)* allows us to claim God as our Father.

The eternal flow of love and freedom between the Father and the Son, and between Christ and the church, is also meant to characterize our relationships with one another. Human beings were created for community *(koinonia)*. "The eye cannot say to the hand, 'I have no need of you,' nor again the head to the feet, 'I have no need of you'" (1 Cor. 12:21). Paul's understanding of the church as the body of Christ (Rom. 12, 1 Cor. 12) sees it as a differentiated unity in which each part plays an indispensable role for the good of the whole. In the creation story (Gen. 2:18-25), human beings made in God's image as male and female recognize one another as true counterparts who need each other. Although irreducibly different, they are made for fellowship. Their differences are not effaced, nor are the boundaries between them blurred, yet only *together* do they form the *imago Dei:* "So God created man in his own image, in the image of God he created him; male and female he created them" (Gen. 1:27). The humanity made in God's image is thus not the male creature alone, as the tradition has sometimes implied, but only male and female together. Though all persons reflect the image of God, they cannot be fully human as isolated beings. The image of God, as Karl Barth suggests, is not an intrinsic quality in humankind, such as our rational or intellectual capacity, but rather our being created in relationship with God and one another.[4] Only as relational beings do we find our true identity as God's image.

4. Karl Barth, *Church Dogmatics,* III/2 (Edinburgh: T&T Clark, 1960), p. 324. The main point being made here is an analogy between God's differentiated unity (Father, Son, and Holy Spirit) and humanity's differentiated unity (human beings as male and female). This is not to say that one has to be married in order to reflect God's image, only that to be human means to be in relationship.

Ray Anderson comments on this truth: "To be sure, human existence is profoundly experienced in a multitude of social relations. Brother, sister, parent, child, hus-

Barth speaks of *Mitmenschlichkeit* (translated as co-humanity) to convey the interrelatedness (literally *"with-*ness") in which we are not human without the other. We become God's covenant partners together in community. Only the whole church knit together in love can become what it is: the true marriage partner of Christ (Ephesians 5). Human beings need one another in order to be human. Isolation is a sign of human misery. To deny our need of others is a defense against the pain of isolation. Human flourishing requires human community — people bonded together in mutual giving and receiving.

As Barth describes it, we are not fully human apart from (1) mutual seeing and being seen, (2) reciprocal speaking and listening, (3) granting one another mutual assistance, and (4) doing these all with gladness. First, as we allow others to see us as we truly are, neither hiding nor withholding ourselves, we affirm our common humanity. Second, as we speak and listen to one another, we seek to know the other in her uniqueness and to be known in ours. "Each fellow-man is a whole world," Barth says, "and the request which he makes of me is not merely that I should know this or that about him, but the man himself, and therefore this whole world."[5] The purpose of speech is to reveal our true self to the other and to help the other to see the world through our eyes. It is an act of self-revelation and self-interpretation that seeks to create a bridge of mutual understanding. Third, we give one another mutual assistance, thus acknowledging our need of the other and the other's need of us. None of us is self-sufficient, as Barth points out: "My humanity depends upon the fact that I am always aware, and my action is determined by the awareness, that I need the assistance of others as a fish needs water."[6] At the same time, we maintain a constant awareness of the other's need of our assistance. We recognize that we are called to assist others in order to retain our own humanity. Finally, we do all these with gladness. We are gladly open with the other, letting

---

band, wife, friend — all these are forms of co-existence and thus manifestations of true humanity. But these are all secondary, not an intrinsic order of humanity. One does not have to be a brother or sister, husband or wife, in order to be human. But one does, according to our understanding of co-humanity, have to be either male or female." See *On Being Human: Essays in Theological Anthropology* (Pasadena: Fuller Theological Seminary, 1991), p. 52.

5. Barth, *Church Dogmatics*, III/2, p. 258.
6. Barth, *Church Dogmatics*, III/2, p. 263.

ourselves see and be seen. We gladly speak and listen. We gladly receive and offer assistance. Barth calls this gladness "the secret of the whole." Each receives the other as a gift: "Human nature is man himself. But man is what he is freely and from the heart. And freely and from the heart he is what he is in the secret of the encounter with his fellow-man in which the latter is welcome and he is with him gladly."[7] As we give and receive one another gladly as incomparable gifts, we find our true humanity.

If the *imago Dei* is our being with and for one another in co-humanity, then the paradigmatic form of prayer in pastoral care will join us together in our common life in Christ. Prayer finds its basic context "wherever two or three are gathered" in the name of Christ. Pastoral care flourishes as the community prays together. Not only do we learn to pray in community, but the community is called to pray with and for each individual member of the body. Prayer as a communal activity builds up the body of Christ even as it cares for each individual member. Moreover, the prayers of each are determined by the prayers of all. They are in principle the prayers of the whole community, even as the prayers of the community are applied in practice by each believer.

Jesus Christ as the One Mediator

These relationships of love — between the Father and the Son, between Christ and the church, and among the members of the church, all in and through the Holy Spirit — are discernable in Christ's high priestly prayer. As depicted in the Gospel of John, in taking leave of his disciples, Jesus prays,

> I am praying for them . . . for they are thine; all mine are thine, and thine are mine, and I am glorified in them. . . . I do not pray for these only, but also for those who believe in me through their word, that they may all be one; even as thou, Father, art in me, and I in thee, that they also may be in us, so that the world may believe that thou hast sent me. The glory which thou hast given me I have given

7. Barth, *Church Dogmatics*, III/2, p. 264.

to them, that they may be one even as we are one, I in them and
thou in me, that they may become perfectly one, so that the world
may know that thou has sent me and hast loved them even as thou
hast loved me. (John 17:9-10, 20-23)

This passage establishes the central place of prayer in the work of pastoral care. Jesus Christ prays to the Father for the church, for its unity
throughout the ages. Though he prays first for his disciples, he also
prays for every generation that follows, for those who depend upon
their apostolic witness. The same Spirit who unites the Father and the
Son in mutual indwelling also incorporates the church into the intimacy of the divine life. When the church finds its identity in God, it
gives a credible witness to the world. The glory that the Father gives the
incarnate Son is shared with the disciples so that they might become
one. As the Father dwells in Christ through the Spirit, so Christ dwells
in the church. The church receives the glory of God as it participates in
Christ's own life and finds its identity in him. As we are "in Christ," we
receive and find our unity. Everyone who comes to him dwells in him
and is knit together into his body. When the church speaks with one
voice about who Christ is, the world receives its witness. The world recognizes God's love when it is awakened to what God has done in Christ
for the sake of the world.

Jesus Christ is the key to this whole series of interconnections. As
attested by Scripture, he is our only Mediator and Advocate. Through
him, the love and knowledge of God are communicated to us. He is the
self-revelation *of God* because he is himself fully divine, at one with the
Father. He is the actual presence of God's love *to us* because he is fully
human as well, sharing our human nature. As he mediates God to us,
he also mediates us to God. He not only reveals God's love and makes it
present to us; he also mediates our love and gratitude back to God.
When we offer prayer to God in Christ's name, we acknowledge this
mediation in both directions. James Torrance comments,

> We can only pray "in the name of Christ" because Christ has al-
> ready, in our name, offered up our desires to God and continues to
> offer them. In our name, he lived a life agreeable to the will of God,
> in our name vicariously confessed our sins and submitted to the
> verdict of guilty for us, and in our name gave thanks to God. We

pray "in the name of Christ," because of what Christ has done and is doing today in our name, on our behalf.[8]

Our love for one another likewise occurs through the mediation of Christ. Through him we have God and God has us, and through him we have one another. "We have one another only through Christ," writes Dietrich Bonhoeffer, "but through Christ we really do *have* one another. We have one another completely and for all eternity."[9] Thus Christ is the hidden center of all our relationships. Present through the Spirit in every pastoral encounter, he enables our words to bear fruit. The mediations in which Christ is at the center thus exist in three modes:

- God's love for human beings descending from heaven to earth, mediated by Christ and communicated in the power of the Holy Spirit. (This is the vertical relationship downward of God's grace and love for humanity through Christ.)
- Human love for God ascending to heaven, mediated by Christ and communicated in the power of the Holy Spirit. (This is the vertical relationship upward of the human response of love and gratitude toward God through Christ.)
- Mutual love among human beings as mediated by Christ in the power of the Holy Spirit. (These are the horizontal relationships of love and freedom between human beings, as mediated by Christ.)

God's love within the Trinity itself — the Father for the Son and the Son for the Father through the Holy Spirit, in God's own eternal and transcendent being — is the eternal ground of Christ's mediation in all its modes.

These spiritual relationships undergird the work of pastoral care. All our prayers participate in Christ and in his high priestly prayer to the Father. He is the One who mediates our prayers to God. His high priestly prayer incorporates every prayer we offer in his name. When we pray the Lord's Prayer, he adopts us as brothers and sisters into his rela-

8. James B. Torrance, *Worship, Community, and the Triune God of Grace* (Carlisle, U.K.: Paternoster Press, 1996), p. 35.

9. Dietrich Bonhoeffer, *Life Together* (Minneapolis: Augsburg/Fortress, 1996), p. 34.

tionship as Son to the Father. He makes his Father to be ours as well, so that we can utter the first word of the Lord's Prayer. If he were not the Son of the Father, on the one hand, or fully human like us, on the other, we could not participate in the mystery of adoption. And if we were not God's adopted children, we could not claim God as the One to whom we belong in life and in death. As Barth writes,

> It is he — Jesus Christ through the Spirit, the Spirit as the Spirit of Jesus Christ — who makes good that which we of ourselves cannot make good, who brings our prayer before God and therefore makes it possible as prayer, and who in so doing makes it necessary for us. For Jesus Christ is in us through his Spirit, so that for his sake, praying after him as the one who leads us in prayer, we for our part may and must pray, calling upon God as our Father.[10]

The mediation of Christ is both vertical and horizontal. It is Christ who makes it possible for us to pray at all, and also to be present to each other in his name. When he stands between us and those we seek to serve, the relationship is reconfigured. His presence determines the pastoral conversation. He is the lens through which we see another, or the light by which we glimpse another's heart. An ancient prayer of St. Patrick's that speaks of Christ's mediating presence in all our interpersonal relationships conveys this idea well:

The Eye of God
The eye of God betwixt me and each eye,
The purpose of God 'twixt me and each purpose,
The hand of God betwixt me and each hand,
The desire of God betwixt me and each desire.

I sing as I arise today
God be in every breath.
As the mist scatters on the crest of the hill,
May each ill haze clear from my soul today.

The dearness of Christ 'twixt me and each dearness,
The wish of Christ 'twixt me and each wish,

---

10. Barth, *Church Dogmatics*, III/4, p. 94.

The pain of Christ 'twixt me and each pain,
The kindness of Christ 'twixt me and each kindness.

I sing as I arise today
God be in every breath.
As I clothe my body with wool
Cover my soul with thy love, O God.

The eye of God 'twixt me and each eye,
The purpose of God 'twixt me and each purpose,
The hand of God 'twixt me and each hand,
The desire of God 'twixt me and each desire.[11]

When God's eye comes between our eye and that of another, then our mutual seeing is sanctified. When God's hand mediates our common action, then our shared work is made holy. The sanctifying presence of Christ purges our natural human desires of anything base or unworthy. Yet it must also be said that even our most noble aims need to be judged and transformed by the purposes of God. Christ's mediation reconfigures even our loftiest aspirations.

This transfiguration of desire is illustrated in John Baillie's *Diary of Private Prayer*. Though the language is archaic, Baillie portrays the shift from high aspirations to aims reconfigured by Christ:

O omnipresent One, beneath whose all-seeing eye our mortal lives are passed, grant that in all my deeds and purposes today I may behave with true courtesy and honour. Let me be just and true in all my dealings. Let no mean or low thought have a moment's place in my mind. Let my motives be transparent to all. Let my word be my bond. Let me take no unchivalrous advantage of anybody. . . .

Yet, O Lord God, let me not rest content with such an ideal of manhood as men have known apart from Christ. Rather let such a mind be in me as was in Him. Let me not rest till I come to the stature of His own fullness. . . . Let me love as He loved. Let my obedience be unto death. In leaning upon His Cross, let me not refuse my own; yet in bearing mine, let me bear it by the strength of His.[12]

11. "The Eye of God," from Kathy Eddy, *Cry of the Wild Goose: Celtic Prayers and Songs of Resurrection* (1984); original version from *Celtic Prayers*, ed. Avery Brooke (New York: Seabury Press, 1981), pp. 36-39.

12. John Baillie, *A Diary of Private Prayer* (New York: Oxford, 1936), p. 49.

The prayer calls upon God to grant a mode of conduct that has true human dignity, as it recognizes the value and dignity of others. It desires all that is gracious and honorable by the culture's highest standard. Yet, the second half of the prayer deepens the request of the first. While the first part of the prayer holds up an "ideal of manhood [true humanity]," it becomes clear that even such noble ideals are utterly transcended by Christ. Christ's mind and stature, his love and obedience far surpass even our noblest aspirations. Even our highest values are judged and transfigured by the Cross. The prayer thus stretches the imagination beyond human knowing, trusting that God's grace will be sufficient during trial or testing. It asks for something that outstrips human capability, believing that Christ will grant strength where human strength fails. It is a prayer that trusts finally in Christ's mediation.

Prayer also changes our relationship to ourselves. St. Patrick's prayer invokes Christ's intercession in human pain. Whenever Christ stands between us and our own suffering, then all that would otherwise be meaningless can be borne in and through him. When our suffering is offered to Christ, it is wholly encompassed in his. It is taken up into his Cross, which, by the power of God's mercy, redeems us. His presence gives suffering a dimension of depth that can enable us to endure. Frank Lake comments,

> No one suffers the mental pain of persecutory emptiness without [Christ's] participation. Since this is true, and God has, in Christ, reconciled the world of the persecuted to Himself through His Cross, it is of the utmost importance that we should learn how to make this fact meaningful to those who suffer like Him.[13]

The cross of Jesus Christ borne for our sakes imparts the gift of perseverance. Our communion with Christ thus reconfigures not only our desires and our actions, but also our suffering. It entrusts all our relationships — with God, with one another, and with ourselves — to Christ, having faith in his intercession. With each new petition, St. Patrick's prayer offers a glimpse into the unexpected richness of his presence.

13. Lake, *Clinical Theology*, p. 194.

Koinonia as an End in Itself

Koinonia is the central purpose of Christian pastoral care. The loving communion of persons, both human and divine, is its *telos*. Being fully present to others, listening with care, and praying for their needs are ends in themselves. They are not a means to some other end. Because psychotherapy has come to dominate the practice of pastoral care, many pastors assume that providing pastoral care means becoming a positive "agent for change." Pastoral care thus becomes a strategy, sometimes even a "treatment plan." Programs in pastoral care equip students with practical tools to help people in their marriages, their parenting, and other relationships. Interpersonal communication and developmental psychology are studied, and psychosocial systems are analyzed. Concrete skills and conceptual maps are developed. Action plans are created, delineating steps to be taken in various pastoral encounters: how to set up short-term counseling contracts, how to make a psychodynamic assessment, how to analyze pertinent social and cultural factors, how to refer people to other professionals.

When *koinonia* is seen as the purpose of pastoral care, this whole orientation is transformed. While it is not discarded, it is necessarily reconfigured. Practical strategies for change are subordinated to more basic spiritual aims. Consider a young minister in her first pastorate. After she had preached a sermon on the presence of God in the midst of trial, a man thirty years her senior approached her with a problem in his marriage. It was a complex situation, one that she had never before encountered, either in her personal life or her studies. As she cast about wondering how to help him, she panicked, feeling she had nothing to offer. Anxiety overtook her as she assumed that it was her job to bring about effective change in his life. She not only underestimated the power of her caring as it pointed toward God's own care; she also forgot that God was already at work in the midst of the crisis. The man's "problem" was not hers to solve. His whole life story was known to God, and God was at work in him, "both to will and to work for his good pleasure" (Phil. 2:13). As Bonhoeffer has written,

> Because Christ stands between me and an other, I must not long for unmediated community with that person. . . . Because Christ has long since acted decisively for other Christians, before I could

begin to act, I must allow them their freedom to be Christ's. They should encounter me only as the persons that they already are for Christ. This is the meaning of the claim that we can encounter others only through the mediation of Christ.[14]

The young pastor had taken too much responsibility for her parishioner, forgetting God's work both through her and apart from her.

John Patton makes a similar point when he defines "the presenting problem" as the *context* rather than the *focus* of pastoral care. He writes,

> If the people of God are called to care for one another through their hearing and remembering . . . then the central act of pastoral caring is not problem solving. *It is the hearing and remembering in relationship, and the human problems are the contextual background for the more important task of care.*[15]

Koinonia does not negate the value of other frameworks that reflect on the human condition. It includes them, for such knowledge is often useful in the fulfilling of God's purposes. The point here is that though pastoral care is informed by other disciplines, it uses their insights in the service of spiritual aims. The minister I described took her presence and caring for granted, without perceiving their centrality to the task of pastoral care. By seeing "the problem" as the *context* rather than the *focus* of her time with her parishioner, the pastor would see her task differently. She would see his psychological issues in theological perspective. Matters of empathic connection and spiritual discernment would be more prominent than psychological diagnosis or cure. How might she best hear the substance of his needs at that time? Had his faith been strengthened or undermined by the trials he faced? What had enabled him to reach out to her for help? What did he need, and how did he understand where God was leading him? Their conversation would be shaped more by the common faith they shared, as informed by God's word, than by any assumed cultural, psychological, or sociological commonality.

14. Bonhoeffer, *Life Together,* p. 44.

15. John Patton, *Pastoral Care in Context* (Louisville: Westminster/John Knox Press, 1993), p. 40; italics added.

The Church Community: Where We Learn to Pray

All Christian prayer is first the prayer of Jesus Christ, then the prayer of the community, and last of all our own individual prayer. As we have seen, even our most personal prayers belong to the community before we give them voice. We never pray as isolated individuals, but always as members of the body of Christ. Christ sanctifies our prayers by incorporating them into his own. He accepts, elevates, and corrects them. Through the Spirit, he discerns the core longings of our hearts and mediates them to the Father. In a similar way, our individual prayers are shaped and sanctified as they are incorporated into the historic prayers of the church.

In our common life of worship, we gather together with a church that prays without ceasing. As we "join our voices with angels and archangels and with all the company of heaven" in the great prayer of thanksgiving (such as the Eucharistic Prayer from *The Book of Common Prayer*), we are connected to the saints throughout the ages. Our theological imaginations are shaped by theirs. The great hymns, liturgies, and prayers of the church deepen our understanding of the God to whom we pray. Prayer is thus never an individualistic act, even though it is undertaken by individuals. Karl Barth writes,

> But as he prays in community, he does so in anticipation with and for all other human beings. He does as an individual what they all can and should do. Hence he does not merely represent himself, or the community in the world, but humankind and the world as a whole before God. His asking as an individual thus acquires a genuinely universal character.[16]

In prayer we cannot separate ourselves from the members to whom we are joined. The "we" who prays to "our" Father prays for and on behalf of the whole world, which also belongs to Jesus Christ, even when the world does not know it.

---

16. Barth, *Church Dogmatics,* III/4, p. 103.

Pastoral Care as the Work of the Whole Community

Like prayer, pastoral care is the work of the entire community. It is not something that only pastors do. All Christians are called to care for one another, just as they intercede for others, both inside and outside the church. This vocation is conferred not by ordination but by baptism. In baptism, every Christian is called to live out the priesthood that belongs to the whole church.

The "priesthood of all believers," so important to the Reformation, has been lost in large segments of the contemporary church. The clericalism of the Middle Ages that Luther deplored has been replaced by "professionalism." Only "professional" Christians, those set apart by education, training, and ordination, are now the "real" Christians. Ordinary believers lack the mystique of such a caste. Only professionals can interpret the Bible or pray in a given situation. The dignity of the faithful is thus lost.

If we were to retrieve the dignity of every Christian's calling, what would be entailed? In his book *The Church,* Hans Küng comments that this doctrine makes sense only "if every member of the community really does exercise priestly rights and functions."[17] In pastoral care, every "priestly" function has significant concrete content. Küng lists these functions as (1) direct access to God, (2) spiritual sacrifices, (3) the preaching of the Word, (4) baptism, the Lord's Supper, and the forgiveness of sins, and (5) mediating functions. Because all these functions are rich with implications for pastoral care, it is important to consider each in turn.

First, all Christians have direct access to God. Jesus Christ as the one mediator gives access to all who call upon him in faith. In the Old Testament, a special cadre of priests alone could enter the Holy of Holies. The coming of Christ brought such priestly mediation to an end because his unique sacrifice was a perfect offering that needed no repetition or renewal. It sufficed to make human fellowship with God possible, reconciling us to God in spite of our sin and uncleanness. The letter to the Hebrews contrasts the sacrifices of the high priests of Judaism with Christ's perfect and unrepeatable sacrifice:

17. Hans Küng, *The Church* (New York: Sheed & Ward, 1967), p. 372.

And by that will we have been sanctified through the offering of the body of Jesus Christ once for all. And every priest stands daily at his service, offering repeatedly the same sacrifices, which can never take away sins. But when Christ had offered for all time a single sacrifice for sins, he sat down at the right hand of God. . . . For by a single offering he has perfected for all time those who are sanctified. (Heb. 10:10-14)

Unlike the priests of the Old Testament, Jesus Christ offers himself once for all. His perfect sacrifice accomplishes what nothing else could ever accomplish: the forgiveness of sins. In faith, through baptism and by the power of the Holy Spirit, all who participate in Christ's self-offering are given access to the Father. There is no longer a barrier that separates us from God, but rather a fellowship that joins us with God through Christ. Küng writes,

> Every believer, as a member of the community . . . has an ultimately direct relationship with God, which no human being . . . can take away from him. . . . It is in this most intimate personal sphere that ultimate decisions between an individual and God are taken, as also between an individual and his fellow men. This is where God's grace makes direct contact with man, God's Spirit guides him. This is where he finds his ultimate freedom and his ultimate responsibility. No one can judge, control or command the decisions which are made in this sphere of direct contact between God and men.[18]

The inviolable sphere in which each person stands before God with her own responsibility needs to be respected. Each person is accountable for her own choices; here no one can take responsibility for another — neither spouse nor parents nor pastor. Each person finally answers directly to God for the choices she has made. Each is called into the obedience of a specific calling and is answerable to God in a unique relationship of love and trust. As we recognize each person's unique relationship to God, we are able to focus more on our own responsibility and less on that of others. An attitude that respects this sacred sphere respects God's mysterious work in every individual life. Pas-

18. Küng, *The Church*, p. 373.

toral caregivers will acknowledge that primary relationship with God in all that they do and say.

Second, all Christians are called to make spiritual sacrifices as "priests" of God. Because Christ's sacrifice is sufficient, we are not required to atone for our sins, nor could we possibly do so. As people who discover our forgiveness in Christ, the sacrifices we offer are those of praise and thanksgiving. When we offer ourselves as a living sacrifice to God, we do so with praise to God for the gift of salvation received in faith. As Paul writes in his letter to the Romans, "I appeal to you therefore, brethren, by the mercies of God, to present your bodies as a living sacrifice, holy and acceptable to God, which is your spiritual worship" (Rom. 12:1). Our prayers and praise to God, as well as our service of love toward others, are our spiritual sacrifices to God through Jesus Christ.

Some of the most painful and consequential choices of our lives are efforts to balance out the moral ledgers of the past, as we seek to atone for our own sins or perhaps those of our forebears. However, these misguided efforts cannot succeed. We act as if Christ had not come when we try, of ourselves, to redeem the past. Children who attempt to atone for the choices of their parents, for example, become entangled in a history for which they are not responsible and thus suffer greatly. Bert Hellinger provides an example of such spiritual entanglement:

> A doctor once told a group that his father had been a doctor for the SS and had supervised many human experiments in the concentration camps. . . . The son's question was, "What shall I do about my father?" I said to him, "In the moment your father impregnated your mother, he wasn't acting as an SS officer. The two things are different, and you can and must keep them separate."
>
> Like this doctor, it's possible for a child to acknowledge his or her father *as a father* without assuming responsibility for the father's actions. Children in such situations must not minimize or excuse their father's actions, but they can say, "What you did is your responsibility. Still you are my father. Whatever you have done, we're related. I'm glad that you gave me life. Even when what you did was horrible, I'm your son, not your judge."[19]

19. Bert Hellinger, *Love's Hidden Symmetry* (Phoenix: Zeig Tucker & Co., 1998), p. 99.

It requires discernment to know one's true responsibility and to allow others their own. In addition, it requires courage to take responsibility for one's own misdeeds, and faith to accept the atonement of the Gospel. The work of atonement — the overcoming and undoing of our guilty past — belongs to Christ alone. Christ won an actual atonement that our futile efforts attempt but by definition cannot effect, since none of us is Savior or Judge. Yet each of us can offer praise and thanksgiving for the reconciliation accomplished in him. Thanks and praise are integral to the work of prayer in pastoral care, particularly in situations of remorse and repentance. (See Chapter Eight.)

Third, all Christians are called to bear witness to the Word of God. "You are . . . a royal priesthood . . . that you may declare the wonderful deeds of him who called you out of darkness into his marvelous light" (1 Peter 2:9). "Preaching the message of salvation" is the "primary command which Jesus gives to his disciples," which is why there are so many different terms (about thirty) to describe this activity.[20] The Word is entrusted to all believers, not simply to an educated elite. The whole community, and each person within it, serves the world by bearing witness to Christ and to the salvation of the world effected through him. In pastoral care this means that each person is called to give his or her unique witness. While in some quarters of the church there is a regular forum for such witness, others lack an institutional means for personal testimony. Particularly in mainline churches there is a reluctance to give one's own witness. Could it be that the ability to interpret one's life through the lens of faith is disappearing from sectors of the church?

A major factor in the explosive impact of the Reformation was the translation of the Bible into the language of the people. This gave previously unheard-of access to the Gospel. Eventually, millions of Christians were able to read Scripture themselves. But with the advent of the historical-critical study of the Bible, many came to believe that interpreting their lives in light of the biblical witness was a specialized skill that only experts could tackle. As something essentially beyond their ken, the Bible was no longer perceived as a book through which God's Spirit spoke to ordinary people. Habits of reading and study that had developed over generations began to decline, and biblical illiteracy be-

20. Küng, *The Church,* p. 375.

came widespread in a relatively short span of time. As a result, many persons ceased to do the ongoing work of interpretation essential to the life of faith. Scripture became little more than a collection of odd historical data, rather than a sacred text giving shape to history, personal identity, and destiny. This problem continues today. As George Lindbeck writes, "The use of Scripture is not part of people's lives, and thus reading and hearing it (when they do read and hear it) has little impact."[21]

In the priesthood of all believers, every person is to offer her own witness to the grace of God. While not all are called to preach on Sunday morning, all *are* called to give their personal testimony. No one can speak for another in such an act. The varied richness of the entire community's witness is edifying to the church and has power to speak to the world. "When you come together, each one has a hymn, a lesson, a revelation, a tongue, or an interpretation. Let all things be done for edification" (1 Cor. 14:26). Every member of the community is called to "account for the hope that is in you" (1 Peter 3:15) — to preach, persuade, or testify according to the faith they hold.

Fourth, the community is called to baptize, to forgive sin, and to celebrate the Lord's Supper. When Jesus' disciples are instructed to "make disciples of all nations, baptizing them in the name of the Father and of the Son and of the Holy Spirit" (Matt. 28:19), they are doing so as representatives of the whole church and not as a specialized class.[22] Similarly, Jesus' words about loosing and binding sin (Matt. 18:18) are addressed to the church as a whole, not to a clerical elite. Jesus' command to the disciples to drink the cup and break the bread in remembrance of him is also to be enacted by the whole church for the sake of all. While certain individuals are set apart by ordination to perform these functions, they do so on behalf of the community and not as private individuals. Pastoral care not only enacts the sacramental significance of baptism as it reaches out to people in need; it also extends the forgiveness of God in the Lord's Supper. Moreover, the work of pastoral care is itself sacramental. By virtue of their baptism, pastoral caregivers take on a representative role, interceding for others and offering Christ's forgiveness in return. Eucharistic celebrations at the

---

21. George Lindbeck, "Scripture, Consensus, and Community," in *Biblical Interpretation in Crisis,* ed. Richard John Neuhaus (Grand Rapids: Eerdmans, 1989), p. 75.

22. Küng, *The Church,* pp. 379-80.

end of life, as family and friends gather round hospital beds, are especially rich in meaning, giving spiritual depth to mutual forgiveness. Though churches set apart ordained ministers to consecrate the elements, all Christians are called to partake.

Fifth, all Christians are called to pray for others, thus mediating in a secondary way between God and the world. While there is only one Mediator, Jesus Christ, every Christian is called to mediate between God and the world insofar as he or she intercedes on behalf of others. Bonhoeffer makes this point:

> All Christians have their own circle of those who have requested them to intercede on their behalf, or people for whom for various reasons they know they have been called upon to pray. First of all, this circle will include those with whom they must live every day. . . . A Christian community either lives by the intercessory prayers of its members for one another, or the community will be destroyed.[23]

In prayer we know the dignity of a calling to stand with those who suffer, to bear their burdens with them, to support them in times of trial, and to comfort them with the comfort of God, with which we ourselves have been comforted (2 Cor. 1:4). As those redeemed by Christ, we are to live not for ourselves but for the sake of all for whom Christ died.

God wills to include every person in the working out of his purposes. Our sense of identity as well as our deepest joy arise from an understanding of this vocation. Barth writes, "[God] tells [man] that he needs him in a definite and concrete respect, that he has a use for him. He is not to pass his short span of life in vain."[24] To be given an essential part in God's purposes is the source of our human dignity, honor, and worth. Since it is an honor that God confers upon us, we cannot disown it, whatever our personal struggles. By calling us to be his witnesses and to do works of service in the world, God confers upon us the greatest possible significance:

> [Man] has his honor before God and from God. . . . Not circumstances and no man can increase or diminish it, can give it to him

23. Bonhoeffer, *Life Together,* p. 90.
24. Barth, *Church Dogmatics,* III/4, p. 657.

or take it from him. Even he himself cannot do this. God alone is competent to decide his dignity and worth.[25]

Equipping the Saints for Ministry

How are we to be equipped for this vocation? Where do we find the confidence to carry out these ministries of prayer and pastoral care? If our common priesthood has been neglected by the church, how can we reclaim it? The task is daunting only if we forget that God has already given us the gifts we need. Just as the saints of the church refer to all those sanctified by Christ, so the gifts of the Holy Spirit are lavished upon the whole church and not upon a single elite. These gifts are not "exceptional, miraculous or sensational."[26] Nor are they intrinsically connected with ordination. Though such misconceptions are widespread, the gifts of God are completely ordinary. Seldom are they characterized by extraordinary signs and wonders. Saint Paul labors to refute the view that the unusual gift of ecstatic speech is the only gift to be esteemed. On the contrary, he insists that interpretation is even more desirable than tongues, for whatever is edifying to the congregation is of the greatest value. Küng states, "[Paul] emphatically reduces in importance this sensational gift, by insisting that it is nothing compared with the charism of interpretation; it is not of itself edifying for the community, nor does it clarify the understanding of the [one] who prays."[27]

The criterion by which we are to judge the value of any gift is its power to build up the community. Yet such gifts are everyday phenomena in the life of the church, both in the early church and in the church today. Küng lists several examples with their scriptural reference: exhortation, acts of mercy, service, teaching, utterances of wisdom and knowledge, faith, discernment, helping, administration, and the most common gift of all, love, which is above all the others.

Such gifts obviously are not given only to ordained leaders. On the contrary, they are bestowed on all members of the church to meet the needs not only of the community but also of the world around it.

25. Barth, *Church Dogmatics*, III/4, p. 678.
26. Küng, *The Church*, p. 181.
27. Küng, *The Church*, p.181.

Thus any natural talent may be a potential charism. When brought into the service of Christ, our gifts are transformed by the Holy Spirit to be used for the good of all. In a point that is especially pertinent to pastoral care, Küng notes that even our suffering might be a charism to strengthen the faith of others, citing Paul's words in Colossians 1:24: "Now I rejoice in my sufferings for your sake, and in my flesh I complete what is lacking in Christ's afflictions for the sake of his body, that is, the church." If even our capacity for suffering could be edifying for the church, then whatever befalls us can be used by God. Our afflictions, borne in patience and hope and given over into Christ's keeping, would thereby serve a worthy end. Such an insight points toward the essentially mutual nature of all Christian ministry. For even those who are homebound, even the utterly incapacitated, have a gift to offer the community. Suffering borne in faith can function as a powerful witness to the sufficiency of God's grace and build up the body of Christ.

All Christians, therefore — not just those with spectacular gifts — enable the church to fulfill its call. Ordinary but indispensable gifts are spread throughout the community and are not by any means limited to those in ordained leadership. Nor are they limited to just a small group. Saint Paul asks, "Are all apostles? Are all prophets? Are all teachers? Do all work miracles? Do all possess gifts of healing?" (1 Cor. 12:29-30). The varied gifts of God spread among the people cannot function in isolation from each other. On the contrary, each of us needs the others in order to function properly as a whole. Here again, *koinonia,* our mutual partnership in Christ, is the mysterious gift of the Spirit that enables the church to carry out its work. One with the gift of ecstatic speech, for instance, needs another with the gift of interpretation.

As Saint Paul develops the idea of the church as the body of Christ, he shows the indispensability of each part to the whole:

> For the body does not consist of one member but of many. . . . If the ear should say, "Because I am not an eye, I do not belong to the body," that would not make it any less a part of the body. If the whole body were an eye, where would be the hearing? If the whole body were an ear, where would be the sense of smell? (1 Cor. 12:14, 16-17)

Each member of the body has at least a small but essential part to play for the good of the whole. No one can say that she does not belong simply because she is unable to do something that another member can do with ease. None of us is to judge or to undervalue the particular gift that we have been given. Rather, we are to develop and use it to the greatest extent possible. Those who are tempted in this way would do well to meditate on the parable of the talents (Luke 19). For we will be judged not by the standard set for our neighbor, who may have been given many talents and used them well, but rather by what we have done with the single talent given us.

Given the wealth of the community's gifts, how are they to be developed? James Fenhagen has argued that "it is more important for the ordained ministers in a congregation to enable others to identify and carry out their ministries than to do it themselves."[28] While clergy need to know how to offer prayer and pastoral care themselves, it is even more crucial for them to nurture such gifts in their congregation. As they develop their capacity for discerning their congregation's gifts, they also need to offer encouragement so that those gifts can be claimed and cultivated. Equipping the saints for ministry entails a scope of preaching and teaching that cannot be overemphasized. The whole congregation needs to be called forth week after week with continual opportunities for service, witness, and prayer.

All persons need help in discovering their gifts. All need help in developing them for the mission of the church. The church loses something of its distinctive identity when it sees its task merely to be one of finding the right "volunteers" for various committees. Instead, constant discernment is required to identify and call forth the entire range of gifts that lie nascent within the community. Even this is not the exclusive work of the clergy, but rather that of the whole body. While the ordained pastor might model such a process, all members need to observe and encourage the gifts of others. This is part of what it means to live in the mutual relationships that characterize our partnership (koinonia) in Christ.

The ordained pastor's role is to hold up a vision that not only values the gifts of all but also requires the congregation's participation in discerning and eliciting those gifts. Such a task is clearly the work of many individuals over time. The Holy Spirit uses the wisdom of others to call specific individuals in particular ways. A person discovers the

---

28. James C. Fenhagen, *Mutual Ministry* (New York: Seabury Press, 1977), p. 105.

uniqueness of his vocation by hearing what others see in him, especially when that seeing has been clarified by prayer. One man confided to me his "rule of thumb" in spiritual discernment. If three persons who didn't know each other called his attention to a particular gift of his, he seriously pondered it as a matter of utmost importance. He subjected the matter to prayer, believing in the power of the Holy Spirit to communicate through these ordinary means.

In a time of personal crisis, the care of the community makes the grace of God palpable. Few would single out the ordained minister, no matter how essential her role, as the only one through whom God's grace operates. Rather, it is the ongoing care of the whole people of God that makes one feel loved by God. The cards, letters, casseroles, flowers, phone calls, and offers of help that pour in from the community during a time of illness or loss speak far more eloquently of God's compassion than any single official pastoral visit could. Don Browning states this obvious but frequently overlooked point: "The minister's pastoral care is only a small part of the total care of a congregation."[29] After studying a number of congregations in terms of their actual patterns of care, Browning and his colleagues concluded that the corporate acts of caring done by the congregation as a whole, as well as by various important subgroups in it, were far more meaningful to its members than anything that the ordained pastor did alone. Browning goes on to say that this finding does not devalue the importance of an official pastoral visit, especially during a life crisis or major life transition, but rather places such visits in perspective. Ordained ministers, he argues, should consider their task to be more nearly one of facilitating "natural patterns of care" that already exist than of seeing themselves as providing all the pastoral care needed. Especially since loneliness was the greatest single problem cited, it would be much more valuable for pastors to use whatever skills they might have to build bridges between people rather than to try to be "all things to all people" themselves.

If the work of prayer and pastoral care is truly to be the work of the whole congregation, then equipping the saints for ministry happens as every member takes responsibility for calling forth others as

---

29. Don Browning, "Pastoral Care and the Study of the Congregation," in *Beyond Clericalism,* ed. J. Hough and B. Wheeler (Atlanta: Scholars Press, 1988), p. 117.

members of Christ's body. Churches need to understand that pastoral care is not the "job" of the pastor but rather the task of the entire community. As Browning suggests, when we fail to understand our vocation as "agents" and not just "recipients" of care, we are in danger of perceiving the pastor as a hired "professional" Christian who is doing the work of the community rather than facilitating and enabling the work that all are called to do.

Churches who do such equipping provide guidance in listening to others with compassion, in interpreting Scripture as the Word of God, in praying with those in need, in hearing another's confession and offering Christ's forgiveness, and in blessing God in every circumstance of life. These are not esoteric matters about which only the professionally initiated need to know. Rather, they are common, everyday matters that show what it means to be a Christian.

Conclusion

Whether one's church is in a more rooted, rural culture or in a more mobile, urban culture, few churches are immune to the societal patterns that make loneliness such a primary source of suffering in the United States today. With institutions and cultural patterns that schedule every hour into some kind of programmed activity, allowing scant time for ordinary interaction, people find themselves cut off from each other. The impact of replacing communal forms of recreation and entertainment with television and electronic media should not be underestimated.[30] With so many persons both inside and out-

---

30. Cf. Patsy Rodenburg, *The Need for Words* (New York: Routledge, 1993), p. 38. Rodenburg describes the losses incurred with the advent of television: "I remember witnessing the introduction of TV into a small village in Portugal in the late 1970s. The first set appeared in a workers' café, a local gathering place where gossip was exchanged and stories told. It was an exciting place to visit because it was so alive with talk, especially in the summer, when words would drift far into the night. It was also a place where every level of society and age mixed. Children would listen to elders and become part of an ongoing story which was that village and those people. Then the television set arrived. Gradually the place fell silent. Watching replaced talking. . . . Rather than remaining a tightly knit group of speakers, speaking for themselves, the people in the village surrendered to the patterned speakers beamed in from Lisbon."

side the church feeling emotionally and spiritually isolated, the rich vision of God's fellowship where all can share their heart's longing, and where each has a needed gift to offer, can be both healing and renewing. It is precisely into a world such as this that relationships of trust, mutual sharing, and prayer are most needed.

The New Testament assumed churches that were small, interdependent units, where each person was needed for the community to thrive or sometimes even survive. Though the intense interdependence of the New Testament church (cf. the book of Acts) is rarely feasible today outside of particular sect groups, church communities today can, by God's grace and with clear intentionality and accountability, achieve a proximate form of interdependence that will enable genuine spiritual growth in the Christian life. Indeed, it is difficult to imagine how even basic spiritual sustenance can take place apart from intentional small groups designed to nurture spiritual vitality. For there is no growth in faith apart from the mutual edification of those in community. The kind of upbuilding described in the New Testament is a matter of the heart, the emotional, intellectual, and spiritual core of the human being; and to share from the heart is to give of ourselves with the whole of who we are.

The spiritual fellowship to which we are called invites us into intimate communion *(koinonia)* with God and with one another. Life in the church is meant to mirror the mutual indwelling of the Holy Trinity. Since we are fallen creatures, such mutual love and freedom is merely glimpsed and not fully grasped. Nevertheless, a vision of mutuality has been given to us as part of the Gospel's treasure. Our unity in Christ, our dependence upon Christ, and our willingness to offer and receive help from one another are all part of this rich vision. In pastoral care, real interdependence becomes a reality when we reach out to one another in love. Only as we consent to open our inner lives to each other will we grow in trust. Only as we take steps to pray together will we find the unity we are called to realize. Each of us is called to listen to and intercede for others on the basis of their true need. Each of us is called to give witness to the One who sustains and renews our lives. Each of us is responsible for exercising the gifts we have been given for the good of all.

Two Listening to God

We do not undertake prayer on our own, but as a response to God's initiative in our lives. Prayer is a human activity that acknowledges the prevenience of grace. It does not occur without the prior activity of the Spirit, as Scripture tells us: "God's love has been poured into our hearts through the Holy Spirit" (Rom. 5:5); "The Spirit helps us in our weakness; for we do not know how to pray as we ought" (Rom. 8:26). Scripture also instructs us to bring all our needs to God. We are to submit our concerns to him in prayer, and it pleases God when we do so: "Ask, and it will be given you" (Matt. 7:7); "The prayer of the upright is his delight" (Prov. 15:8). We honor God as our Creator and Provider when we turn to him with our needs, both our own and those of the ones for whom we care (Luke 11:9-13). "Cast all your anxieties on him, for he cares about you" (1 Peter 5:7). "Pray for one another, that you may be healed" (James 5:16).

Just as Scripture is the means by which God speaks to the church, so prayer is the means by which we respond. Through Scripture God draws near to us. Through prayer, we draw near to God. We acknowledge what we have received through the Word. Therefore, in order to pray, we first need to hear God's Word. Who God is for our lives comes to us by meditating on Scripture. Certainly God may communicate with us through a medium outside the Word (e.g., through the kindness of a stranger, the beauty of the natural world, or the solace of music). But we cannot know it as a message from God apart from its interpretation by means of Scripture. As the New Presbyterian Catechism states, "As the wind blows where it will, so may the Spirit speak or work in people's lives in unexpected or indirect ways, yet always according to the Word, never contradicting or diluting it."[1]

Pastoral caregivers listen for what God might be saying in each situation to which they are called. They lend their ears to another who is seeking God. They place their discernment in the service of that seeking. James Torrance comments on the "first task" in this circumstance:

> It seems to me that in a pastoral situation, our first task is not to throw people back on themselves with exhortations and instructions as to what to do and how to do it, but to direct people to the Gospel of grace — to Jesus Christ, that they might look to him to lead them, open their hearts in faith and in prayer.[2]

After listening to the other's story, they turn to God in prayer, directing everything that has been shared toward God. As they lift up the other to God's light, they ponder his or her needs, explicitly or implicitly stated, as they are illumined by Scripture. By taking those needs to God, they witness to the One who alone can finally meet them.

The Language of Scripture Shapes the Language of Prayer

Whenever we meditate on Scripture, we are at the same time learning to pray. For the language that God uses forms in us the habits of mind needed for our response. Not only the church but also the people of Israel were trained to pray through the words, images, and cadences of the Psalms, the prayerbook of the Bible. The Psalms offer the entire range of human response before God, teaching us to call upon God in trouble, to lament in times of trial, to praise God for life's blessings, to confess the sin that tempts us to despair, and to bow before God's majesty and holiness.

Pastoral caregivers who immerse themselves in the Psalms will have words of hope "on their lips and in their hearts" (Rom. 10:8). In times of crisis, when their sympathy seems faltering and inadequate,

---

1. *The Study Catechism: Full Version* (Louisville: Witherspoon Press, Office of the General Assembly, PCUSA, 1998), Question 59, p. 37.

2. James Torrance, *Worship, Community, and the Triune God of Grace* (Carlisle, U.K.: Paternoster Press, 1996), p. 34.

when their words of encouragement sound hollow, or when they are simply overcome with grief, Scripture is able to comfort those giving care as well as those who receive it. Because it is the Word of God, Scripture orients them constantly toward the fundamental issues of life and death, judgment and grace, forgiveness and hope, and love and truth. When it comes alive *as* the Word of God, Scripture has a way of piercing the human heart. Pastoral caregivers guided by Scripture hear and respond to the other's need at the same time that their own most fundamental longings are addressed.

There is no substitute for daily meditation on Scripture as the means by which we can begin to embody the language of prayer. As in learning any language, daily immersion yields the greatest facility in use. Studying Scripture affords us the opportunity to learn the vocabulary and grammar of prayer. But we also need active conversation, offering back to God the words of Scripture in our own voice as we respond to our particular situation. Thus praying with Scripture — where God's own word can be heard through our efforts to articulate our needs — is the daily exercise that enables God to tutor us in prayer.

The weekly liturgy also shapes us in specific ways. Worship forms in us certain habits of mind. It shapes our theological imagination. Here we are given specific words and postures of prayer, expanding the range of our vocabulary. Phrases known by those who pray with the *Book of Common Prayer,* for example, may find their way into situations of pastoral care. A familiar petition from the Eucharistic liturgy — that we might "feed on Christ in our hearts with faith by thanksgiving" — when embedded in the context of personal trial, gives unexpected strength, reminding the believer of Christ's Eucharistic presence. The powerful rhythms integral to African-American preaching may buoy us up with hope. As we hear the preacher's ardent call to God for deliverance and are caught up in the congregation's contagious joy, we believe anew in God's passionate activity on behalf of the oppressed: "The Lord works vindication and justice for all who are oppressed" (Ps. 103:6). Christians suffering persecution around the globe offer us a glimpse of faith tested as through fire. Joining them in prayer can be both humbling and edifying when we know something of the challenges they face.

The language of prayer cannot be internalized simply by reading about it. As with any language, active communal practice is needed. We learn the words and cadences of prayer in and through the community of faith as it has been shaped by a biblical imagination and lived out in diverse cultures throughout the world.

Prayer Is Relationship with God, Not a Pastoral Resource

Recent writings in pastoral theology look upon Scripture and prayer as "resources" for pastoral care. After decades of ignoring our theological heritage, pastoral theologians seem to be rediscovering the Bible. They have turned anew to parable, prophecy, and proverb for insight into human emotions and interpersonal relationships, the entanglements of sin, and our most fundamental sources of hope. Prayer is seen as an essential tool for achieving our goals of reconciliation with those from whom we are estranged, or for overcoming fear and meeting life's challenges, or for finding peace and healing. Empirical studies have sought to correlate prayer and reduced levels of stress, enabling bodily organs to function more efficiently. It is argued that prayer enhances both physical and emotional health.[3]

Yet this approach to prayer distorts the Christian faith. Scripture and prayer are not expedients for Christians to meet their self-determined goals. Even when the goals are worthwhile, prayer must not be reduced merely to an instrumental value. Prayer is not a tool that we manipulate in order to handle various crises. Consider this comment by a contemporary pastoral theologian: "The only legitimate function that any methodology, including spiritual practices, can serve in a counseling situation is to alleviate distress and enhance adaptation to the culture in which a person chooses to live."[4] "Spiritual practices" in a coun-

---

3. Studies have proliferated during the past decade linking strong religious commitment with a lower incidence of depression, less tobacco and alcohol consumption, fewer medical complications during childbirth, increased median survival times after contracting cancer, improved coping with breast cancer, higher self-esteem, lower blood pressure, reduced stress, and a healthier cardiovascular system. See "Benefits of Prayer," available from http://www.1stholistic.com/Prayer/hol_prayer_Benefits.htm; Internet; accessed 29 May 2006.

4. Newton Maloney, "Review of *Psychology, Theology, and Spirituality in Christian Counseling* by Mark McMinn (Deerfield, Ill.: Tyndale Publishers, 1996)," *Journal of Pastoral Care* 51, no. 1 (Spring 1997): 119.

seling situation are said to be for "alleviation of distress" and "adaptation to culture." Prayer, then, is no longer seen as an end in itself. It becomes the means to ends other than communion and communication with God. These ends have become higher goods to which even God is subordinated. Whenever our self-determined goals come first, however laudable they may be, God and our love for God are displaced from the center. A prevailing danger in our culture is that of subordinating everything, even our faith, to therapeutic and pragmatic values.[5]

Forgiveness is increasingly commended for its therapeutic value. As Gregory Jones has noted, "Practices and conceptions of Christian forgiveness are radically transmuted and distorted in a therapeutic context — even when well-meaning Christians are the ones doing the transmuting and distorting."[6] Forgiveness is distorted when subordinated to other goals. The God of the Bible is a jealous God who wants no other gods before him, not even the much-lauded contemporary gods of physical and emotional health.[7]

---

5. The worst forms are blatantly self-serving, such as the 2000 best seller *The Prayer of Jabez: Breaking Through to the Blessed Life* by Bruce Wilkinson (Sisters, Ore.: Multnomah Publishers, 2000), which had sold more than nine million copies by February 2001. Wilkinson lifts two otherwise obscure verses from First Chronicles (4:9-10) in which a man named Jabez prayed for God's blessing and protection. The author exhorts his readers to recite Jabez's prayer every day for thirty days, promising that they will experience life-transforming effects, including freedom from suffering, vocational success, and financial prosperity. One has only to study 2 Corinthians to see the parallels to the false apostles excoriated by Paul.

6. Gregory Jones, *Embodying Forgiveness: A Theological Analysis* (Grand Rapids: Eerdmans, 1995), p. 49.

7. See, for instance, "The Forgiveness Factor: Social Scientists Discover the Power of a Christian Value," *Christianity Today*, 10 January 2000, available from http://www.christianitytoday.com/ct/2000/001/1.38.html; Internet; accessed 15 July 2003. The article discusses how psychologists, sociologists, and even politicians are increasingly recognizing the healing power of forgiveness in families, groups, and nations. Three studies are cited: (1) an examination of college students who considered themselves deprived of parental love, who, after participating in a forgiveness program, demonstrated improved overall psychological health, including greater self-esteem and lowered anxiety; (2) a study of elderly women participating in a forgiveness program who experienced a significant decrease in depression; and (3) a study based on the experiences of persons in Yugoslavia, Rwanda, and most especially South Africa, leading to the conclusion that forgiveness, "not retaliation, represents the most strategic intervention in reducing violence in our society."

Scripture and prayer are the means by which we come into communion with God. They need to be valued for their own sake, not simply for what they can do for us. Communion with God — enjoying, knowing, and loving God, witnessing to God, and participating in God's work in the world — is the central purpose of human life. The first question of the Westminster Catechism puts it succinctly: "What is the chief end of man? To glorify God and enjoy him forever." God is to be loved for God's own sake and not merely for the sake of his benefits. Commenting on God's promise to Abram, that God himself will be sufficient for all his needs (Gen. 15:1), Calvin writes, "In God alone we have the highest and complete perfection of all good things."[8] Prayer is not a "resource" at our disposal. It is the gracious means through which we may draw near to God on the basis of his word of promise. Scripture, as the written Word of God, is the vehicle by which God addresses our daily need. Through Scripture, God grants us the encouragement, judgment, grace, and forgiveness that we lack apart from an encounter with him.

Referring to Scripture and prayer as "useful resources" implies that there is some end more valuable than communion with God. This is as absurd as saying that sexual intercourse is an "effective resource" for Christian marriage. Couples have sexual intercourse not because it is an important resource enabling them to achieve improved oxygenation of the blood, fewer marital conflicts, or more nuanced nonverbal communication (though it may bring such benefits). Rather, it is one way for them to share in the mutual self-giving that expresses the meaning of marital love. Husbands and wives who cherish each other would not treat their partner as the means to an external good, for they know their partner's intrinsic worth as the unique human being to whom they are gladly yoked. Yet our ways of speaking about God sometimes betray a lack of concern about God for his own sake. We focus on how God might be used for our personal gain. Too many contemporary books, conferences, and meditative practices have as their premise that the meaning of prayer lies in what it is *good for*. And what it is good for is usually some self-appointed end toward which we are striving. If we are to honor God as *God*, as the

---

8. John Calvin, *Commentaries on the First Book of Moses Called Genesis*, vol. 1, trans. Reverend John King (Grand Rapids: Calvin Translation Society, 1965, 1975), p. 400.

Lord with whom we are invited into a relationship of daily intimacy, we will eschew all such understandings. Orthodox theologian Anthony Bloom makes the point when he says, "We want something from Him, not Him at all. Is that a relationship? Do we behave in that way with our friends? Do we aim at what friendship can give us or is it the friend whom we love?"[9]

Having the Word in Our Heart

In the second half of the twentieth century, the memorization of Scripture ceased to be a major objective of the church — at least that's what the recent history of mainline U.S. Protestantism would suggest. But in fact, many churches retain the practice of committing Scripture to memory. In other parts of the world — Africa, Asia, and Latin America — church members regularly learn large portions of Scripture by heart.

Earlier eras also highly prized committing Scripture to memory. Bishops in the Middle Ages were required to memorize "the entire David," that is, all 150 psalms. Certain saints of the church are reputed to have committed whole books of the Bible to memory. By contrast, devout members of the church today know very little by heart. Under the influence of "progressive education," mainline denominations in the United States ceased to encourage memorization, which came to be considered emotionally deadening. Early in the twentieth century, George Albert Coe, father of the modern Religious Education Association, stated that the aim of religious education was to promote growth rather than to impose truth, the latter of which was considered "authoritarian" or "dogmatic." Interpersonal interactions and experiences with the world were the primary subject matters to which the Bible was subservient. Sophia Fahs, one of Coe's followers, considered memorizing Scripture anathema. Children should not even be introduced to the Bible, she argued, until they were old enough to compare Christianity to other religions, recognize Jesus as simply one among many historical figures, and extract the universal religious sentiment from Christianity's particular teachings. Furthermore, religious educators should not be called "teachers," because their function was not "to give instruc-

---

9. Anthony Bloom, *Beginning to Pray* (New York: Paulist Press, 1970), p. 29.

tion, to pass on knowledge, to affirm beliefs, to preach principles or to proclaim a message."[10] Such basic assumptions about pedagogical method and the role of Scripture in the life of faith persist into the present. The progressive ideal was to teach children to become independent thinkers, not mere robots who could spew out chapter and verse without essential comprehension. Commonly referred to as "rote memorization," it is still spoken of in disparaging tones. Real education, according to this view, needs to involve the whole human being and should not be reduced to a mechanical task.

Educators today, however, are calling these assumptions into question. Roger Shattuck, for example, makes this argument:

> The eighty-year monopoly of progressive ideas (for example, the project method: teaching the child, not the subject) has failed to improve American education compared to its own past and to other countries. . . . Based on a Romantic notion of the child learning naturally and discovering things for itself, this set of ideas has deprived American schools of a coherent and demanding curriculum and has sought to produce "independent thinkers" while opposing "rote learning."[11]

American churches most influenced by these ideas have suffered widespread ignorance of Scripture and basic theological illiteracy. While it may be true that "learning by rote" can be deadly, it does not follow that all memorization is of this nature. The noted literary critic Harold Bloom argues persuasively for memorizing poetry as a way to indwell a poem, so as to make it fully a part of oneself:

> Very good short poems are particularly memorable, and with that, I have arrived at a first crux in how to read poems: whenever possible, *memorize them*. Once a staple of good teaching, memorization was abused into repeating by rote, and so was abandoned, wrongly. Silent intensive rereadings of a shorter poem that truly *finds* you

10. Sophia Fahs, *Today's Children and Yesterday's Heritage: A Philosophy of Creative Religious Development* (Boston: Beacon Press, 1952), p. 156. See also George Albert Coe, *A Social Theory of Religious Education* (New York: Scribner, 1927).

11. Roger Shattuck, *Candor and Perversion: Literature, Education, and the Arts* (New York: W. W. Norton, 1999), p. 32.

should be followed by recitations to yourself, until you discover that you are in possession of the poem.[12]

Memorizing Scripture is obviously no substitute for penetrating its inner meaning. But memorizing can help one develop a higher quality of attention. One gets inside the structure of a passage and can trace the exact movement of ideas. A web of associations begins to take shape as one ponders the verses over and over again, enriching one's understanding. Links are made not only with other parts of Scripture but also with one's life experiences. In this way, one's personal history is informed by Scripture such that Scripture actually gives it its form. Scripture is truly embodied when it is learned "by heart."

Memorized Scripture provides comfort and guidance in situations of crisis. One woman I know, interceding for a dying friend, prayed psalms she had learned long ago as she did morning laps in the pool. Another quieted her dread by reciting a psalm as she waited to be wheeled into surgery. A third, recalling the Twenty-Third Psalm from childhood, spoke it within her father's hearing as he lay semiconscious, attached to various life-support machines. American hostages in the Middle East attest to the sustenance provided by the fragments of Scripture, prayers, and hymns of the church that they actively recalled during their long years of captivity. Terry Waite recounts how he kept hope alive during his imprisonment:

> As a boy in church, sitting in the quire [sic] — Sunday by Sunday — I thought often I was bored. . . . Often the sermons meant nothing to me. They seemed to float over my head.
>
> I didn't think I was learning anything but, years later in captivity, the language came back. I had no books, no prayer book, but I could remember the services of the church: they were there. They were stored in my memory, and I could draw on them.
>
> I reverted to the prayers that I had learned through the prayer book, which were simple, straightforward and balanced and, in that way, was able to find some inner peace amidst the conflict raging all around. That was a great and wonderful gift.[13]

12. Harold Bloom, *How to Read and Why* (New York: Scribner, 2000), p. 73.
13. Terry Waite, *Taken on Trust* (New York: Harcourt, Brace, 1993).

Sometimes Scripture is the bridge by which a caregiver can reach another. A student of mine who was working as chaplain in a nursing home was pleased to see an old woman's face light up when she heard a familiar psalm. In earlier visits, the chaplain had felt discouraged by the woman's lack of responsiveness. Suddenly it became possible for a connection rich in meaning to be made, as passages memorized long ago provided a bond between them.

There is real power in pastoral caregivers who have Scripture "in their bones" (Jer. 20:9). A distinguished minister once recounted the story of her visit to a man on the brink of death. After they had talked for some time, the pastor said, "In my Father's house are many rooms." The man surprised her by answering, "If it were not so, would I have told you that I go to prepare a place for you?" The pastor responded, "And when I go and prepare a place for you, I will come again and will take you to myself, that where I am you may be also." The man replied, "And you know the way where I am going." Together they went on, reciting the Word of God as they offered it to one another from memory, fortifying each other with hope. They continued all the way through the passage in John 14, when the pastor spoke these words of Jesus: "I will not leave you desolate; I will come to you. Yet a little while, and the world will see me no more, but you will see me; because I live, you will live also." The dying man ended with the words, "In that day you will know that I am in my Father, and you in me, and I in you."[14]

God Speaks through the Text:
The Inseparability of Word and Spirit

A man once claimed that God spoke to him directly in the words of Scripture. To prove his point, he opened the Bible at random, closed his eyes, and ran a finger down the page. When he opened his eyes, his finger rested on the words "Judas went out and hanged himself." Disconcerted, he shut the Bible and reopened it to another page. Here his finger alighted on "Go, therefore, and do likewise." While it is easy to

14. This story was recounted in a sermon given by the Reverend Ansley Coe Throckmorton in December 1985 at Hammond Street Congregational Church in Bangor, Maine.

poke fun at such simplistic conceptions of how God communicates through Scripture, it is not so easy to state just how Scripture conveys a living word to us. How do Christians conceive of the Word of God as not only the vehicle through which God has revealed himself historically, but also the means through which God continues to speak today? To reject a magical understanding does not mean that we should repudiate the conviction that God speaks through the Bible. Otherwise, how could the church fulfill its task of preaching? Preaching and pastoral interpretation both rest upon the presupposition that God speaks the Word of Life that we each need to hear through the human, fallible words of Scripture.

That God's Word and Spirit are inseparable is at the heart of this Christian conviction. John Calvin writes,

> For as God alone is a fit witness of himself in his Word, so also the Word will not find acceptance in [our] hearts before it is sealed by the inward testimony of the Spirit. . . . Scripture seriously affects us only when it is sealed upon our hearts through the Spirit.[15]

The Spirit brings certain passages to our attention as we ponder God's work in our lives. When the Spirit "seals [Scripture] upon our hearts," we are seriously affected. We are given grace to discern God's intention for our lives. The knowledge we receive is not theoretical but self-involving. It demands our response. We experience ourselves as addressed by God. Karl Barth points to the living quality of this knowledge:

> In the language of the Bible knowledge does not mean the acquisition of neutral information, which can be expressed in statements, principles, and systems. . . . It is the process or history in which man . . . certainly observing and thinking, using his senses, intelligence and imagination, but also his will, action and "heart," and therefore as whole man, becomes aware of another history . . . in such a compelling way that he cannot be neutral . . . but finds himself summoned to disclose and give himself . . . in return.[16]

---

15. John Calvin, *Institutes of the Christian Religion,* Library of Christian Classics, vols. 20-21, ed. John T. McNeill, trans. Ford Lewis Battles (Philadelphia: Westminster Press, 1960), 1.7.4, 1.7.5.

16. Karl Barth, *Church Dogmatics,* IV/3 (Edinburgh: T&T Clark, 1960), pp. 183-84.

There can be no true knowledge of another, whether of another human being or of God, apart from a living encounter. For centuries the church has come to Scripture expecting to be addressed. There will be no renewal of pastoral care if practices of devotional reading and meditation on Scripture cannot be recovered.

Listening, Interpreting, and Hermeneutics

Ordinary Christians today are often daunted when approaching the Bible. As noted, they have lost confidence in their ability to interpret what they read. Daily reading of the Bible has for the most part been abandoned, along with any effort to teach children how to perceive God's work in their lives. In a volume on today's crisis of the Bible in the church, George Lindbeck laments,

> The Bible is increasingly a closed book even for those Protestants and Catholics who make an effort to know it better. To the degree that instruction is guided by historical criticism, as it is for most educated laity, the lesson is that interpretation is a technical enterprise which requires prolonged specialized training. . . . In those circles where the text itself is widely and assiduously studied — conservative Protestant, charismatic, base communities, and groups interested in spirituality, the reading is often so remote from the classic hermeneutics, so divisive and/or individualistic, that the kind of historical reconstructions which stay within the Christian mainstream seem preferable. *It is now the scholarly rather than the hierarchical clerical elite which holds the Bible captive and makes it inaccessible to ordinary folk.*[17]

How can the church avoid the impression that interpreting Scripture is an esoteric art? Or how, on the other hand, can it prevent its members from using Scripture merely as a "resource" for narrowly defined personal issues? Does the tradition have anything to offer here?

According to one classic pattern of interpretation, Scripture, both

---

17. George Lindbeck, "Scripture, Consensus, and Community," in *Biblical Interpretation in Crisis,* ed. Richard John Neuhaus (Grand Rapids: Eerdmans, 1989), p. 90; emphasis added.

in its entirety and in part, needs to be understood as an interrelated whole that interprets itself. Lindbeck points to it:

> Stated compactly and technically, the issue which concerns us is the extent to which the Bible can be profitably read in our day as a canonically and narrationally unified and internally glossed (that is, self-referential and self-interpreting) whole centered on Jesus Christ, and *telling the story of the dealings of the Triune God with his people and his world in ways which are typologically . . . applicable to the present.*[18]

When biblical texts came to be read less as realistic narratives and more as historical documents, as they have in the modern period, the church lost its sense of the text as a "plotted interaction of intention and circumstance"[19] between human beings and God. It became preoccupied with the historical factuality of the events recounted. With the loss of narrative meaning, the Bible ceased to be read *as a whole.* Any overarching meaning of the disparate parts could no longer be sustained. With the surrender of the classic pattern, the church split into two factions. Inerrantists claimed that the Bible was completely true, both in its entirety and in every particular, which meant that each sentence was historically or scientifically verifiable. Historical critics claimed that the Bible could not possibly be true in this sense. They made critical judgments about what could be true according to cultural definitions of historical or scientific truth.

The problem with both positions, as Lindbeck indicates, is that mere facts are not intrinsically self-involving. What relevance would the Bible have for us if it were only about the practices and beliefs of ancient communities? If these stories did not convey something true *about God* and God's work in the world today, only those with serious historical preoccupations could approach the text with interest. If the narrative meaning of Scripture could be recovered for the contemporary era, however, ordinary readers would be personally addressed. God would be seen not only as the primary actor in a covenantal drama grounded in history but as still active today. Antiquarian meanings pale when juxtaposed against a story about a living God, still at work in the world. Scripture, conceived in this way, is understood as a living Word. It depicts the great sweep of God at work through the ages, a

18. Lindbeck, "Scripture, Consensus, and Community," p. 75; emphasis added.
19. Lindbeck, "Scripture, Consensus, and Community," p. 82.

story into which believers seek to fit their lives. It is understood, Lindbeck says, "not simply as a source of precepts and truths, but the interpretive framework for all reality."[20]

Fathers and mothers of the early church, monasteries and convents of the Middle Ages, and Reformers of the sixteenth century all read Scripture in this way. They sought to fit their lives into the biblical story, not the other way around. They did not, as in the modern era, attempt to translate Scripture into other idioms, but rather sought to understand the meaning of their lives from within Scripture's own framework. They studied patterns of meaning found in Scripture and applied them to events in their communal and personal lives. This is a typological reading of the text, which bears further definition here:

> Typology . . . is the study of "types," "figures," or recurrent patterns, such that a person, thing, event, or idea at one time is compared to another on the basis of a single point of comparison and is interpreted to belong to the same genre or to have the same significance as another. [It] is used . . . as a means to relate the Old Testament to the New on the basis of an overarching type, the Old Covenant and the New. Following ancient Jewish principles of exegesis, typology compares on the basis of like to like, external to internal, known to unknown, or lesser to greater.[21]

---

20. Lindbeck, "Scripture, Consensus, and Community," p. 77. It is worth noting that Lindbeck builds in part on the work of Old Testament scholar Brevard Childs, who argues for a theological reading of the entire canon of Scripture, in contrast to historical-critical readings that fragment biblical meaning. (See Brevard S. Childs, *Introduction to the Old Testament as Scripture* [Philadelphia: Fortress Press, 1979].) Though Childs uses historical-critical tools to understand specific texts, he places them within a larger theological framework by setting them within their canonical context. According to Robert M. Wall, "The canonical approach to biblical interpretation is less interested in lining up behind the reconstructed historical or linguistic intentions of a precanonical stage in the formation of a particular composition or collection." See "Reading the New Testament in Canonical Context," in *Hearing the New Testament: Strategies for Interpretation,* ed. Joel B. Green (Grand Rapids: Eerdmans, 1995), p. 75.

21. Paul Scott Wilson, *God Sense: Reading the Bible for Preaching* (Nashville: Abingdon, 2001), p. 122. Frederick Fyvie Bruce offers a more specific explanation: "Typological interpretation . . . involves the tracing of correspondences between the Old Testament and New Testament so as to find the essential meaning of an Old Testament passage in its New Testament counterpart. The New Testament writers, for the most part, resort to typology *(q.v.)* to illustrate points already established by more direct means (cf.

Take, for example, the event of baptism. On the one hand, baptism is presented in the Gospels as an event in the life of Jesus, something he underwent in the Jordan River at the beginning of his public ministry. At the same time, baptism is a sacramental event that occurs in the life of every believer as he or she becomes a member of the Christian community. These are unique and unrepeatable events that occur in history. Baptism is the event by which Christians become members of Christ's body and thus by which they are incorporated into the church.

Typology holds what is unique and unrepeatable together with subsequent recurring patterns. The event of baptism is the original template. The typological pattern is grounded in the unique and derives its meaning from it. Thus our baptism is meaningful because of its connection to Jesus' baptism. Baptism is always a symbolic event, beginning with Jesus' own. Its meanings are multivalent, having to do with the cleansing of sin, the renunciation of evil, the renewal of life, being incorporated into Jesus' death and resurrection, and becoming a member of his body, the church. Jesus alludes to his death as a "baptism" with which he is to be baptized (Mark 10:38). The church eventually came to speak of baptism as a "dying and rising with Christ," a dying to sin and a rising to Christ's righteousness. Baptism thus came to be seen as disclosing a (previously hidden) pattern of Christ's death and resurrection.

In the interpretive practice of the early church, the Old Testament was read Christologically, so that a pattern of dying and rising was discerned there as well. According to Lindbeck, the entirety of the Hebrew scriptures were understood as "a Christ-centered narrationally and typologically unified whole in conformity to a Trinitarian rule of faith."[22] Thus, Joseph's betrayal by his brothers and descent into the waterless pit, as well as Jonah's terror in the belly of the fish, were read typologically as stories that illuminated — and were illuminated by —

Paul's treatment of Adam as a "type" of Christ in Romans 5:12ff.). The most helpful, and permissible, form of typological interpretation is that which, viewing the Bible as a recital of God's saving acts, discerns a recurrent rhythm in this recital. Israel's deliverance from Egypt, e.g., is regarded as foreshadowing the redemptive work of Christ, and the behavior of the redeemed people on the earlier occasion constitutes a solemn lesson for the redeemed people on the later occasion (cf. I Cor. 5:7; 10:1ff.)." See "Interpretation (Biblical)," in *Baker's Dictionary of Theology*, ed. E. F. Harrison (Grand Rapids: Baker Book House, 1960), p. 293.

22. Lindbeck, "Scripture, Consensus, and Community," p. 77.

the saving death and resurrection of Christ. His descent into suffering and death, followed by his vindication in the resurrection, gave new meaning to other stories of betrayal and death, even historically prior ones. The typology of baptism, so central for what it means to be a disciple of Jesus Christ, has shaped entire communities in the history of the church. Whenever a person or community suffered for the sake of obedience to God's command, its essential spiritual significance could be discerned in the light of a baptismal dying and rising with Christ, typologically understood. The biblical drama of baptism became the narrative that provided Christians with their central identity as those who are baptized *into* Christ.

Whenever we interpret our lives in light of the biblical text, we implicitly or explicitly use typology. Instead of "translating" Scripture into a modern idiom "to make the Bible relevant for us today," we seek to place our own lives into the scriptural idiom in order to make ourselves relevant, so to speak, as genuine Christian witnesses. We put extra-biblical categories of thought to Christian use, instead of seeking to translate biblical categories into contemporary thought forms.

We thereby assess the presuppositions of various secular idioms by the Gospel, rather than the reverse. Thus, we judge the ideologies or movements for social change such as feminism and psychotherapy and socialism by the standards of the Gospel, rather than judging the Gospel by the standards of these movements. The criticism that such movements offer the church are deemed valuable insofar as they reflect the underlying patterns, the intrinsic, though perhaps tacit, core affirmations of Scripture itself. Contemporary forms of feminism, for example, have helped the church become aware of its sinful sexist practices, but its insights would have no moral authority if it could not also be shown that *the Gospel itself* understands such patriarchalism and sexism to be contrary to God's purposes for human life. The fundamental criteria for bringing about change in the church, therefore, are finally found by conforming ourselves to the Gospel, even if the impetus for change originates in sources outside — sometimes far outside — the institutional church.[23] Conforming ourselves to Christ is not possible without regular meditation on Scripture.

23. See George Hunsinger's essay entitled "Secular Parables of the Truth" in *How to Read Karl Barth* (New York: Oxford University Press, 1991), pp. 234-80.

The Bible is used in varying circumstances with different needs in mind. Studying the Bible for the sake of preaching is a different exercise than meditating on a passage to discern God's leading. While singing the Scriptures in worship and studying a book of the Bible in a Sunday school class both build faith, they do so in different ways. Analyzing biblical passages for their help in moral guidance is different from using those same passages to witness to God's grace to those outside the church. James Buckley comments on these different uses and the different skills entailed:

> It takes different skills to use the Bible for prayer than for study, to listen to the readings at the Lord's Supper and to sing them, to use the Bible with adults and children, with Catholics and Christians and non-Christians. It takes yet different skills — e.g., the virtues of faith and hope and love — to seek and find in these texts the Word of God.[24]

All of these ways of using Scripture build up the body of Christ. Whether we are studying or praying, alone or in community, we seek to understand our lives according to Christ. We seek an understanding of Jesus Christ in the Bible and of ourselves under his gracious sovereignty. Yet each mode of study, worship, listening, and prayer builds the body in a different way.

How is the Bible to be read for the purpose of revitalizing pastoral care in the church? First, it needs to be read in community. Small groups of Christians who gather with each other on a regular basis to ponder Scripture do so in order to hear God's word, not only for themselves but also for their brothers and sisters in Christ. The purpose of gathering is to glorify God and to build *koinonia*, Christian fellowship centered in Christ. Praying for one another binds Christians together in bonds of mutual need and affection. Christians need one another to hear God's word and interpret their lives on its basis communally. Discernment of God's leading cannot be done in isolation.

Second, the Bible should be read under the guidance of the historic doctrines of the church. Particularly, the Trinitarian and Christological

24. James J. Buckley, "Beyond the Hermeneutical Deadlock," in *Theology after Liberalism: A Reader*, ed. John Webster and George P. Schner (Oxford: Blackwell, 2000), pp. 192-93.

doctrines provide an overarching interpretive framework for reading the Old and New Testaments. Ephraim Radner comments, "Our spirits are formed by the reading of Scripture, more than by anything else, and this reading is the particular discipline of hearing the whole Bible, Old and New Testaments together, speak of Christ Jesus."[25] The Bible addresses us in our inmost need because it tells us about Christ. Knowing him through Scripture, we grow to love him through prayer.

Third, we should read the Bible expecting the Holy Spirit to guide our understanding. Our reading, listening, and discernment all take place in the context of common prayer. We open our lives up to God with the expectation that we will be guided concretely in our next steps. Our life history with God takes shape in the context of daily meditation and prayer, weekly worship, fellowship with other members of the household of faith, and work, witness, and service in the world. Radner stresses the importance of communal Scripture-reading in our lives, describing the pattern that God's people traditionally used: "Under the guidance of their preachers — for their reading was communal, not individualistic — they searched the Bible with close attention both to its details and encompassing patterns in order to shape their lives and thoughts in obedience to God's Word."[26] A commitment to such reading and personal study would return the church to more classic and Reformed understandings, to ways of interpretation that perdured in the church for countless generations.

Lectio Divina

The daily practice of meditating on Scripture that originated in the monasteries of the Middle Ages (and was thus also Luther's own practice) is known as the *lectio divina*. The practice of *lectio divina* has four steps: *lectio, meditatio, oratio,* and *contemplatio:* reading, meditation, prayer, and contemplation. The Carthusian monk Guigo II in the twelfth century was the first to articulate this fourfold pattern of prayer. In his treatise *The Ladder of Monks,* he writes,

25. Ephraim Radner, *Hope among the Fragments: The Broken Church and Its Engagement of Scripture* (Grand Rapids: Brazos Press, 2004), p. 91.
26. Radner, *Hope among the Fragments,* p. 81.

Reading is the careful study of the Scriptures, concentrating all one's powers on it. Meditation is the busy application of the mind to seek with the help of one's own reason for knowledge of hidden truth. Prayer is the heart's devoted turning to God to drive away evil and obtain what is good. Contemplation is when the mind is in some sort lifted up to God and held above itself, so that it tastes the joys of everlasting sweetness.[27]

Lectio divina begins by calling upon the Holy Spirit to make the Word of God come alive through the reading. A passage of Scripture is then read aloud in an unhurried way so that the images or phrases that are especially vivid can be attended to. Is there a specific word or phrase that speaks with particular force? Next the passage is read a second time. Ordinary human words of the text are transfigured by God's Spirit, "sealing them on our hearts" (Calvin) when a single word or phrase comes alive. A contemporary writer who has taught the *lectio divina* for years writes,

> If each day as we do our *lectio* one word, one idea, one insight, of his becomes ours, we will quickly come to have the mind of Christ. "Let this mind be in you which is Christ Jesus" (Phil. 2:5). Some days the Lord will powerfully speak a word to us. It will echo in our being and perhaps be there forever. As I reflect now, I can remember a "word" he spoke thirty years ago.[28]

After we read the passage, our initial meditation should be a simple repetition of the "word" received to allow inner resonances and associations to grow. The church fathers illustrated the process by alluding to the work of the humble cow. First, the cow eats the grass. This is the *lectio*, the taking in of the Word of God as daily nourishment. Then the cow chews the grass; this is the assimilation of the Word into our being. After the cow eats and digests the grass, it produces milk. This is our response to the Word, the nourishment we give others from our

27. Guigo II, *The Ladder of Monks and Twelve Meditations,* trans. Edmund Colledge and James Walsh (Garden City, N.Y.: Doubleday, 1978; reprinted in Kalamazoo, Mich.: Cistercian Publications, 1981), pp. 67-68, as cited by Jonathan W. Linman, "Meditative Reading of Scripture," in *See How They Love One Another,* LWF Studies 2002 (Geneva: Lutheran World Federation, 2002), p. 85.

28. M. Basil Pennington, *"Lectio Divina:* Receiving the Revelation," in *Living with Apocalypse,* ed. Tilden Edwards (San Francisco: Harper & Row, 1984), p. 67.

own substance after we ourselves have been fed by God. Finally, the cow produces cream. This is the richest part of our experience — our joyous contemplation of God's ways in the world, the fruit borne in our life in myriad ways, the fruit of witness, love, and service.[29]

Listening to God through the Word of God requires the same kind of attentive listening we would give a friend we are seeking to understand. The quality of the interaction depends, in large part, upon the quality of our listening. Just as mutual understanding grows in conversation when there is a true heart-to-heart meeting, so we experience fellowship with God in pondering Scripture and responding in prayer. Aware of our longing to be met by God, we find ourselves comforted or challenged, forgiven or questioned, truly met in our most basic need. This event is quintessentially outside of human control, for it depends upon the presence of another — indeed, the Other, the Holy Spirit, who vivifies all genuine encounter. Jonathan Linman explains it this way:

> In the elusive space between reader and text, the Holy Spirit cannot be captured or put in easy categories of conceptual manageability. . . . There is a serendipitous quality to reading in the context of *lectio divina*. Personal meaning is evoked, called forth, not contrived or confected. Practically speaking, when reading the Bible and a word, image, idea, phrase "leap off the page at you," when you are so moved to see connections between your life and the claims of the text, the Holy Spirit may well be speaking and this, then, lays the foundation for meditation.[30]

When we read Scripture with an attitude of faith and expectancy, we are directly addressed: we feel a burden lifted; we hear a word or a phrase that gives guidance; we receive clear knowledge that we have been forgiven a wrong. We are addressed personally in our particular need as Christ speaks through the power of the Spirit. Events such as these become the narrative of our history with God. As Catholic theologian Hans Urs Von Balthasar has written,

> If we want to live in his light, we must listen to his word, which always addresses us personally, which is always new since it is always

29. Pennington, "*Lectio Divina:* Receiving the Revelation," p. 68.
30. Linman, "Meditative Reading of Scripture," p. 86.

free. It is impossible to deduce this word from some prior word that we have already understood and put into store: clear and fresh, it pours forth from the wellspring of absolute, sovereign freedom. The word of God can require something of me today that it did not require yesterday; this means that, if I am to hear this challenge, I must be fundamentally open and listening.[31]

By our own powers we cannot even guess what word God might speak to us at any particular point in time.[32] We always remain dependent upon the Holy Spirit to guide our understanding.

Dietrich Bonhoeffer gives detailed instructions to seminarians about undertaking a practice of daily meditation and prayer. In his book *Meditating on the Word*, Bonhoeffer writes,

> We want to meet Christ in his Word. We turn to the text in our desire to hear what it is that he wants to give us and teach us today through his Word. . . . In the same way that the word of a person who is dear to me follows me throughout the day, so the Word of Scripture should resonate and work within me ceaselessly. Just as you would not dissect and analyze the word spoken by someone dear to you, but would accept it just as it was said, so you should accept the Word of Scripture and ponder it in your heart as Mary did. That is all. That is meditation. . . . Ponder this word in your heart at length, until it is entirely within you and has taken possession of you.[33]

As a preacher and teacher of Scripture, Bonhoeffer was familiar with the temptation to use our contemplation as material for lectures or sermons, to study the passages rather than reading them meditatively. He warned against using *lectio* as surreptitious study time, recognizing "the danger of fleeing once again from meditation to Bible scholarship or the like."[34] He admonished his students, "Do not ask how you should tell it to others, but ask what it tells you!"[35]

31. Hans Urs Von Balthasar, *Prayer* (San Francisco: Ignatius Press, 1986), p. 21.
32. Von Balthaser, *Prayer,* p. 24.
33. Dietrich Bonhoeffer, *Meditating on the Word* (Cambridge: Cowley Publications, 1986), pp. 32-33.
34. Bonhoeffer, *Meditating on the Word,* p. 35.
35. Bonhoeffer, *Meditating on the Word,* p. 33.

A contemporary testimony to the power of this practice can be found in the recent work of Dale Aukerman. Aukerman, perhaps best known for his profound biblical reflection on peacemaking in a nuclear age,[36] contracted lung cancer and was given a sobering prognosis of a few weeks to four months to live. He writes movingly about his experience:

> When we found out that I might have only a few weeks to live, there came the urgent question of priorities. What was important enough to give time to? My pattern of reading shifted. As for the daily newspaper, I would look at the headlines and check the weather. Time seemed too precious for more than that. We didn't have the television on for maybe three months. I read the cards and letters from friends, but very little else that came in the mail. Reading in the Bible was what seemed so crucially important.
>
> God speaks to us in many ways. For me the most personal and vital way is through the words of scripture. It is sometimes said that a verse in one's devotional reading can jump out at a person to be God's "marching orders for the day." Continually during the past months I've been given such verses. . . .
>
> I have kept returning to verses having to do with fear. It has many ways of getting a hold on us, even through lesser threats. . . . Jesus, walking on the water, said to his trembling disciples in the boat (and to me): "Take heart, it is I; have no fear" (Mt. 14:27). . . . Even if death comes close to stalk us or a loved one, we don't have to be afraid. . . .
>
> We are given these years of life on earth as testing and preparation within God's scrutinizing view. Each day is precious. . . . Feed on God's Word and take with you each day words that spring out at you as God's special promise or command. In times that aren't so hard, give God your deepest attention, and when the hardest times come, God will be right there with you.[37]

Aukerman testifies to God's provision through his Word even as he was called to walk through the valley of the shadow of death.

---

36. See Dale Aukerman, *Darkening Valley* (New York: Seabury Press, 1981).

37. Dale Aukerman, "Living with Dying," *Messenger* (Elgin, Ill.: Church of the Brethren), April 1998, pp. 18-19.

When we receive the Word from God each day, at some point it will take root, sprout up, and, like the proverbial mustard seed, bring forth a harvest, though sometimes not until days, months, or even years later. To be attuned to God's Spirit, we need to listen for God's Word. We do this for ourselves first, but also for the sake of those we serve in ministry. For we cannot fully grasp the significance of the stories we hear apart from the *basso continuo* of Scripture. We may hear stories of depression or alcoholism or anorexia but fail to hear the spiritual hunger buried in an inventory of psychological symptoms. We may diagnose psychological or emotional dilemmas but fail to hear the spiritual word of consolation or judgment or mercy that another may need. To be pastoral caregivers, we must not only see through the lens of Scripture, but also have a living faith that trusts in the concrete word that God gives us in our — and our congregation's — moment of need.

Conclusion

Just as God uses the human words of Scripture to bring persons to faith through the power of the Spirit, so God also uses the community's stumbling efforts to pray to provide ongoing care and nurture. If the Lord is our Shepherd, he nevertheless uses human shepherds to watch over, guide, and feed his flock. The church needs to trust that God will use its members' spiritual gifts, whether splendid or paltry, as they offer them in service to others. As they listen with compassion to those in need, they will also listen for the Spirit of God. God's Word is in them whenever they take it as their daily bread; when it nourishes them, it is also there to nourish those who come hungry for hope.

Three Listening to Others

Christian caregivers seek to orient persons toward God as the One who will provide for them. All ministry is Christ's ministry, in which the church is privileged to participate. As Andrew Purves explains, "Pastoral theology is understood properly first of all as a theology of the care of God for us in, through, and as Jesus Christ. . . . Only secondarily, derivatively, and above all, participatively . . . is pastoral theology an account of the pastoral work of the church."[1]

In his book *Life Together,* Bonhoeffer theologically grounds the practice of listening in God's love for humanity. God demonstrates his love for us by listening to us when we pray. By analogy, we are to show our love for our brothers and sisters by listening to them:

> The first service that one owes to others in the community involves listening to them. Just as our love for God begins with listening to God's Word, the beginning of love for other Christians is learning to listen to them. God's love for us is shown by the fact that God not only gives us God's Word but also lends us God's ear. We do God's work for our brothers and sisters when we learn to listen to them.[2]

We show our love for God by imitating his love for us. Our work of listening to another attests and mediates the love of the listening God.

1. Andrew Purves, *Reconstructing Pastoral Theology: A Christological Foundation* (Louisville: Westminster/John Knox Press, 2004), p. xviii.

2. Bonhoeffer, *Life Together* (Minneapolis: Augsburg/Fortress Press, 1996), p. 98.

In listening to others, pastoral caregivers need to have an empathetic imagination and set aside their own preoccupations. They must seek to empty themselves in order to be fully present to the other. By attending to the other's story, they aim to create a bridge of understanding. What needs emerge in the narrative being told? What concerns might be brought before God in prayer? Since they aim to intercede on the other's behalf, caregivers strain to hear the inarticulate longings beneath the needs or feelings that are expressed. They endeavor to deepen the other's connection with himself so that he might bring all of himself — his joys and sorrows, his fears and doubts, his gratitude, regret, and lament — before God.

At the same time, caregivers listen to everything that is said in the light of God's purpose and calling. There is a divine drama hidden in each person's story that cries out to be heard. Trusting that Jesus Christ is already at work in this situation, they will seek guidance from God. Because the Gospel addresses fundamental human needs — for forgiveness and reconciliation, for love and hope, for justice and mercy, in short, for salvation — caregivers listen to God as well as to the other. They wait for a divine word. How might God be calling this person forth in and through this challenging situation? What word might offer comfort or hope in a day of trouble?

As caregivers listen on behalf of the other, they also monitor their own emotional reactions. How does this story touch them? Where are they moved or not moved by it? How do they enter it intelligently? Knowing how to listen to themselves gives them tools for distinguishing between the issues of the person they are seeking to serve and their own. (The question of how we can listen productively to ourselves will be addressed in the next chapter. Here we will focus on listening to the other.)

Listening to another requires one to be fully present, undistracted by the background static of one's own concerns. As Robert and Kathy Eddy point out, "Every person has a priceless treasure to offer others: full attentiveness. Your whole undivided attention, given to another, is of inestimable value, a luminous gift."[3] These words evoke the scene of Mary sitting at Jesus' feet (Luke 10:38-41), so attentive to him as to be

---

3. Robert M. and Kathy W. Eddy, *Writing with Light* (Cleveland: United Church Press, 1997), p. 84.

oblivious to her sister's need in the kitchen. Although Martha is aggrieved, "the better part" chosen by Mary is her spiritual communion *(koinonia)* with Jesus. Her undivided attention exemplifies the clarity of focus striven for in pastoral care. Yet many caregivers, like Martha, find themselves preoccupied with other things and unable to learn Mary's simple attentiveness.

The key to pastoral listening lies in keeping one's clear intention on being present for the other. When one pays more attention to oneself than to the real needs of the other, one fails to hear the significance of what is being shared. Martin Buber tells of a time when he was distracted by his own inner life. He writes,

> What happened was no more than that one forenoon, after a morning of "religious" enthusiasm, I had a visit from an unknown young man, without being there in spirit. I certainly did not fail to let the meeting be friendly, I did not treat him any more remissly than all his contemporaries who were in the habit of seeking me out about this time of day. . . . I conversed attentively and openly with him — only I omitted to guess the questions which he did not put. Later, not long after, I learned from one of his friends — he himself was no longer alive — the essential content of these questions; I learned that he had not come to me casually, but borne by destiny, not for a chat but for a decision. He had come to me, he had come in this hour. What do we expect when we are in despair and yet go to a man? Surely a presence by means of which we are told that nevertheless there is meaning.[4]

The young man died "not long after" this meeting. The unstated intimation is that he took his own life. He had come "not for a chat but for a decision"; he was in despair and yet sought something from Buber. Elsewhere Buber acknowledges that the meeting was "an event of judgment" for him.[5] Thereafter, he understood faith not as the pursuit of ecstatic experiences but as a life of attentiveness to others, the life of "I and thou" in encounter. This incident marked a major turning point in Buber's theological understanding, a turning away from

---

4. Martin Buber, *Between Man and Man* (New York: Macmillan, 1948), quoted by Frank Lake in *Clinical Theology* (London: Darton, Longman & Todd, 1966), p. 6.

5. Buber, quoted by Lake in *Clinical Theology,* p. 6.

otherworldly ecstasy and a turning toward the concrete human being whom God has sent.

Buber suggests that the young man needed a human presence that would convey a sense of purpose. He needed a trusted other to embody faith in the meaningfulness of life. A Christian appropriation of Buber's insight might suggest a person who embodies the hope of Christ in full knowledge of the shadow of the Cross. Like all Christians, pastoral caregivers are called to live by the grace of God, by forgiveness through the Cross of Christ. As they participate in Christ's ministry, they come to know that their justification lies not in themselves but in Christ alone. As they are united with Christ, they recognize that their anxious striving cannot sustain their lives, and they seek to rely on a power not their own. As they depend on Christ's promise of intercession, they can openly listen for the needs of others, no matter how desperate. As they trust in Christ's work of forgiveness, they are able to face the worst about themselves, and hence will not be shocked by the misdeeds of others. As they struggle with their own doubts and fears, they learn to depend on Christ's faithfulness when their own fails. If they know the power of God in their own encounters with temptation, they can provide a calm presence when others face their demons.

The presence that Christian pastoral caregivers are called to offer, therefore, cannot be learned simply as a technique. There is an offering of oneself in Christ that cannot be created simply by learning skills. Pastoral caregivers cannot convey "a presence by means of which [others are] told that nevertheless there is meaning" unless they understand themselves as participating in a ministry not their own but Christ's. They cannot manufacture meaning out of their own resources. The seventeenth-century French priest St. Vincent de Paul said, "If God is the center of your life, no words are necessary. Your mere presence will touch hearts." Yet no mere creatures can make God the center of their lives simply by willing it. Christ alone lived a life of obedience that truly had God at its center. Not by their own power but by virtue of their union with Christ, caregivers may witness to a compassionate presence that their own only dimly reflects.

Each caregiver is given a *charism* or gift of the Spirit that points beyond itself to the Giver of all good gifts, the One who sustains people in times of trouble. The psychiatrist Karl Stern once described Jacques Maritain as embodying a unique combination of these gifts:

He asked me the most personal questions about my spiritual life, but there was not for a moment the feeling of obtrusiveness or indiscretion. I had from the first moment the deep impression of a strange and pleasant form of personal directness which was the result of a great charity and humility.[6]

Whether they speak or remain silent, interpret or pray, or even give direct advice is less important than the quality of presence that Christian caregivers offer. Each way of offering that presence will be unique, for each person's relationship with God is unique. Yet, in each case the caregiver seeks to offer herself with an open heart, which will foster a quality of connection that builds trust and deepens relationship.

Is such presence a matter of nature or nurture? If one's character type is more like Martha's than Mary's, can one nevertheless learn to listen in a life-giving way? Certainly there are skills to be learned. While they cannot manufacture faith, presence, or humility, they can help us listen with empathy.

Listening with Empathy

What, then, is empathic listening? Is it a skill that can be learned, or is it a God-given gift? Nearly fifty years ago, Carl Rogers described empathy in this way:

To sense the client's private world as if it were your own, but without ever losing the "as if" quality — this is empathy, and this seems essential to therapy. To sense the client's anger, fear, or confusion as if it were your own, yet without your own anger, fear, or confusion getting bound up with it, is the condition we are endeavoring to describe.[7]

Heinz Kohut, who took empathy as the central conceptual category in his approach to psychotherapy, considered it the single most essential

---

6. Karl Stern, *The Pillar of Fire* (London: Michael Joseph, 1951), quoted by Lake in *Clinical Theology,* p. 14.

7. Carl Rogers, "The Necessary and Sufficient Conditions of Therapeutic Personality Change," in *The Carl Rogers Reader,* ed. H. Kirschenbaum and V. Land Henderson (London: Constable, 1990), p. 226.

quality that enabled emotional well-being. He considered it a nutrient as essential to psychological life as oxygen is to the body: "[The human being] can no more survive in a psychological milieu that does not respond empathically to him than he can survive physically in an atmosphere that contains no oxygen."[8] Practical theologians, feminist thinkers, psychoanalysts, and philosophers have all developed the concept with different emphases according to the purposes of their particular field. Pastoral theologian A. J. van den Blink makes six observations about empathy that have important implications for pastoral care.

First, according to van den Blink, empathy is "inherently relational," which makes it the "preferred method of cross cultural engagement." Empathy enables connection between people who are different from each other and who may have quite different cultural assumptions. Second, empathy involves "constant reciprocal feedback" between the persons involved. It is a mutual undertaking, not something that one person actively does to another who passively receives it. The presence of empathy is felt when there is a sense of rapport between persons, a mutual responsiveness. Third, empathy is a "way of knowing." One who empathizes with another attunes herself to the other's inner and outer world in such a way that the other feels himself to be understood and valued in his uniqueness. Fourth, empathy enhances the sense of self of both persons, heightening each person's uniqueness even as it creates a bond between them. Fifth, empathy "does not imply approval or agreement." Understanding another from within her own frame of reference does not mean that one agrees with her. Conflicts can and do arise even when empathic skill is highly developed. Sixth, empathy is affected by the total context in which it occurs. "There is no such thing as disembodied empathy," van den Blink asserts, and goes on to explain,

> I have found it helpful to think of context as the total environment *in which we are and which is in us.* These dynamic internal and external environments, then, constitute the context in which we find ourselves at all times. [They are] incredibly complex, inextricably interrelated, and mostly out of our conscious awareness.

8. Heinz Kohut, *The Restoration of the Self* (New York: International Universities Press, Inc., 1977), p. 253.

Empathy, says van den Blink, is a "respectful and caring exploration" of another's life, attempting "to discern the shape of [one's] experience."[9] In all empathic relating, self-disclosure and feedback are essential.

The feminist thinkers of the Stone Center at Wellesley College have analyzed concrete conversations that demonstrate empathic connection. Though many studies of empathy involve the close observation of parents and infants, Jean Baker Miller and her colleagues at the Stone Center emphasize the importance of certain qualities for fostering growth in human beings of all ages. They have identified the features that characterize the presence of empathy as zest, action, knowledge, a sense of worth, and a greater sense of connection that leads to a desire for more connection. The feeling of "zest" is the increased energy and vitality that occur when a real emotional connection is made. The "zest" or aliveness "is noticeably there when people make emotional connections and it is notably absent when they do not."[10] As one person experiences being heard by the other, each is empowered to act, first in the immediate conversation as the other's impact is fully felt, and then in other relationships outside the immediate one. In addition, both one's self-knowledge and one's knowledge of the other increase. One develops a deeper connection with oneself that enables a more accurate personal picture. At the same time, one's knowledge of the other also increases. One's sense of self-worth also increases because one experiences oneself as worthy of the other's attention and recognition. Finally, empathy deepens mutual caring, which generally gives rise to a desire for more encounters where connection may occur:

> This feeling is different from being the recipient of another's concern, or being loved, and very different from feeling "approved of." It is much more valuable. It is the active, outgoing feeling of caring about another person because that person means so much to us or is so valued in our eyes. It leads to both the desire for fuller connection with that person and a concern for that person's well-being. . . . And it leads to wanting more connection with others as well.[11]

9. A. J. van den Blink, "Empathy amid Diversity: Problems and Possibilities," *Journal of Pastoral Theology* 3 (Summer 1993): 7-8.

10. Jean Baker Miller and Irene Pierce Stiver, *The Healing Connection: How Women Form Relationships in Therapy and in Life* (Boston: Beacon Press, 1997), p. 30.

11. Miller and Stiver, *The Healing Connection,* pp. 33-34.

The theological significance of mutual empathy lies in its commitment to know and be known. One cannot be known apart from one's willingness to make oneself known, apart from revealing oneself through speech. Karl Barth says, "As [the other] speaks with me, his aim is to be known by me, i.e., to seek me out in his own new and strange and different being, and therefore to be seen and grasped from within."[12] Mutual self-disclosure lies at the heart of mutual empathic relationship, as each person opens up her world of meaning for the other to know. In the church, such mutual willingness depends upon the trust that each member of the body of Christ is indispensable to the whole. Each member needs the others as hand, ear, eye, or foot so that the whole body might function together as one organic whole.

While volumes have been written on the importance of developing empathic skill, little attention (apart from the world of psychotherapeutic training) has been given to teaching it. Feminist therapist Janet L. Surrey comments, "The ability to be in relationship appears to rest on the development of the capacity for empathy in both or all persons involved . . . but almost no attention has been devoted to the topic of *teaching* and *learning* empathy."[13]

An exception is the work of Marshall Rosenberg. For more than forty years, Rosenberg has devoted himself to the task of teaching the skill of empathy to ordinary people. Originally trained as a psychologist, Rosenberg became convinced that these skills were too valuable to be restricted to a professional guild. Given the vast social upheaval, conflict, and violence on every continent, Rosenberg wanted to develop a mode of communication that would contribute to peace — in the home, in the workplace, in schools, in prisons, and in countries at war. He has served as a mediator among warring parties in Israel and Palestine, Bosnia and Croatia, as well as Nigeria, Rwanda, and Sierra Leone. Workshops in Nonviolent Communication (NVC) are now offered in more than twenty-five countries for "families, educators, healthcare workers, mediators, business managers, prison inmates and guards and many other groups."[14]

12. Karl Barth, *Church Dogmatics*, III/2 (Edinburgh: T&T Clark, 1960), p. 258.

13. Janet L. Surrey, "The Self-in-Relation: A Theory of Women's Development," in *Women's Growth in Connection* (New York: Guilford Press, 1991), p. 53.

14. Marshall Rosenberg, *A Model for Nonviolent Communication*, 2d rev. ed. (La Crescenta, Calif.: Center for Nonviolent Communication, 1999), p. ii. See also www.cnvc.org.

Learning Empathy through Nonviolent Communication

Marshall Rosenberg's four-step approach to empathic communication has been shown to entail a set of teachable skills. Its economy and memorability commend it as a model. The purpose of nonviolent communication, called NVC, is to develop a quality of connection between persons. Honesty and empathy are the basic building blocks for fostering connection. When one is open about what is going on in oneself and endeavors to offer empathy to another, one creates a bridge, a living connection, with another. This interpersonal bridge provides the basis for mutual understanding and respect.

Rosenberg's model proposes four steps for sending and receiving empathic messages:

1. Developing the capacity to differentiate between what one is *observing* (hearing, seeing, remembering) and evaluating the action one has observed;
2. Developing the capacity to describe what one is *feeling* in relation to what one observes;
3. Developing the capacity to notice the connection between those feelings and the underlying *needs* (values, desires, longings) that are creating them;
4. Developing the capacity to make a *request* based on the needs one hopes to meet.

In NVC shorthand, these steps — Observation, Feeling, Need, and Request — are referred to as OFNR. When one develops facility in each of these four capacities, he will be adept at offering empathy not only to another but also to himself. Because the inner world mirrors the outer world and the outer mirrors the inner, as one grows in compassion for others, one develops the ability to be compassionate with oneself as well. Similarly, if one is judgmental toward others, one is generally harsh toward oneself as well.

Step One: Differentiating Observation from Evaluation

When one wants to foster a quality of emotional connection with another, it is important to have the capacity to describe what the other is

doing without also judging or evaluating it. When one mixes evaluation with the observation, one is liable to evoke defensiveness in the
other. For example, if one were to state that another left his dirty dishes
on the dining room table, this is an observable fact. By contrast, if one
were to characterize the other as slovenly in his habits, one would likely
provoke a defensive reaction. "Brian, you're such a slob" might well
provoke a counterattack: "Sally, you think that's bad; I saw the state
you left the kitchen in last night. Who are you to call me a slob?" Similarly, observe the contrast between saying, "There you are again, late for
no good reason," and saying, "When you come later than the time we
agreed to meet. . . ." The first sentence contains assumptions and evalu-
ations that are not purely observation. In the second, the speaker aims
to distinguish between the observation and any possible evaluation or
interpretation of it.

Step Two: Identifying and Expressing One's Feelings

The second step in NVC is developing the capacity to identify and express what one is feeling. Feelings communicate whether one is comfortable or uncomfortable, satisfied or dissatisfied in relation to one's
basic needs. One speaks of hunger when one's need for nutrition is not
met, boredom when one's need for intellectual stimulation or social
connection is not met, sorrow when one has lost someone or something of value. As Rosenberg explains it,

> Our feelings serve as a gauge telling us whether or not what is hap-
> pening is in harmony with our well-being. If what is happening is
> in harmony with our needs and values, our body fills with varia-
> tions of pleasurable feelings. If what is happening is not in har-
> mony with our needs and values, our body fills with unpleasant
> sensations and screams for us to do what is necessary to take care
> of ourselves.[15]

Sometimes one confuses a thought or a judgment with a feeling.
One might think that one is sharing a feeling, for example, by saying, "I
feel manipulated." Technically such a statement reflects how one is in-

---

15. Rosenberg, *A Model for Nonviolent Communication*, p. 19.

terpreting another's behavior, not what one is feeling. It could be translated as "I think that you are manipulating me" without essential loss of meaning. In such a situation, one might be annoyed or infuriated, sad or afraid, but it is important to identify the feeling as it connects with the underlying need. If one is "feeling manipulated," the underlying need is probably for one's own power of choice to be respected. If one were to express this in NVC, one might say, "When you tell me what you think I should do in this situation, I feel irritated because I need respect for my ability to make my own choices." First this sentence makes an observation ("You tell me what you think I should do"), then it identifies the feeling (irritation), and finally it connects the feeling with the underlying need (needing respect for one's ability to make one's own decisions). This leads to the third step.

Step Three: Connecting Feelings to One's Needs

This is the crucial step in learning to offer empathy — whether to another or to oneself. It is a basic premise of NVC that one's motivation for action is related to meeting basic needs. According to this framework, human needs are universal. All human beings need food, water, shelter, and warmth. When these needs are not met, one suffers, sometimes acutely. But human beings also have interpersonal needs: a need to give and receive love, a need for acceptance, trust, support, companionship, and understanding. Human beings also have a need to contribute to the well-being of others. Such contributions to another's thriving undergird much of one's sense of purpose in life.

When one's needs are being fulfilled by what is happening, one may feel jubilant, enthusiastic, satisfied, glad, or happy. When one's needs are not being met, one may feel disappointed, confused, hurt, angry, or afraid. Whenever one is upset in some way, it is helpful to ask what need is not being met in the present moment. Only when one has identified the unmet need can one do something about it. If the need remains unidentified, one can remain stuck in the uncomfortable feeling indefinitely. The key to shifting feelings is in connecting them with underlying needs.

Sometimes one has the mistaken impression that one's feelings are *caused* by another's action, whereas in fact the cause of the feeling lies in whether or not one's own need is being met. The child's running into the street may be what *triggers* the mother's fear, but the *cause* of her fear is connected to her need for the child's safety. In NVC, it is important to take responsibility for one's feelings by noticing how they are connected with one's own needs. When one has an intense negative reaction to something another does, the other person's actions may be the detonator, but one's unmet needs are the dynamite.[16] If the need has been frustrated for years and the longing for it is huge, the triggering action may be very small and the reaction may be enormous. The intensity of the response is related to the depth of the longing.

Let's return to the initial example of the dirty dishes on the dining room table. Using the first three steps, one might say, "Brian, when I see your dirty dishes on the table, I feel annoyed because I have a need for order in our common living space." The dirty dishes may have been the trigger for the annoyance, but its cause lies in the unmet need for order. Someone who didn't have a similar need would not likely be annoyed by the presence of the dishes.

Step Four: Making a Request

Once one has made the observation and then expressed one's feelings and needs, one can then make a clear request of the other based on the identified need. To follow up on the example, one might ask, "Would you be willing to wash the dishes before lunch?" or "Would you mind if I put them into the dishwasher?" The request needs to be do-able; that is, it needs to be stated in positive action language, expressed as something that can be said or done by another. If, for example, I'm feeling lonely and need companionship, I might ask a friend, "Would you be willing to come over for tea at four o'clock tomorrow?" If I state my request in vague, general terms — for example, "Would you be willing to spend more time with me?" — the request is not do-able. Similarly, if I am seeking understanding and ask a friend, "Do you know what I mean?" little is accomplished if my friend replies "Yes" or "No." However, if I ask, "Would you be willing to say back to me what you hear me

---

16. This is a paraphrase of a comment by Kelly Bryson, quoted by Jane Connor and Dian Killian in *Connecting across Differences: An Introduction to Compassionate, Nonviolent Communication* (New York: Hungry Duck Press, 2004), p. 76.

saying?" then I would get a clear picture of whether or not she heard what I intended to communicate.

There are three kinds of clear, specific, concrete, do-able requests: (1) an action request ("Would you be willing to wash your dishes before lunch?"); (2) a connecting request ("Would you tell me what you just heard me say?" or "Would you tell me how you feel about what I said?"); and (3) a request for help in discovering a strategy that will meet the needs of both the one asking and the one being asked ("Would you be willing to help me find a strategy that will meet your need for relaxation and my need for order?"). In making a request, it is important that it be a genuine request and not a demand. When one makes a demand of another, the other's needs for active choice are not acknowledged. They will likely either submit to the demand or rebel against it. In neither case will there be a glad willingness to contribute to the other's quality of life.

Like Barth, Rosenberg emphasizes this glad willingness to contribute to another as the secret of human flourishing. A person is to fulfill another's request only if he is giving joyfully from his heart, if he is doing it from a need to contribute, or if it meets some other value or need of his.[17] Rosenberg often quips in workshops that one should respond positively to another's request only if one can do so "with all the gladness with which a young child feeds a hungry duck."

Learning to Listen More Deeply

Hearing Another's Needs

A person's needs are embedded in her feelings. Learning how to connect feelings with underlying needs is the key skill in learning to relate empathically. If one becomes aware of feeling lonely, for example, the underlying need might be for connection with others, companionship or community. Depending on the context, if one is feeling worried, one might be needing peace or reassurance. If one is embarrassed, one might be needing acceptance or perhaps self-acceptance. When one focuses only on one's feelings and fails to identify the underlying needs,

---

17. See the Oregon Network of Compassionate Communication: www.orncc.net.

one can get ensnared in simply rehearsing how bad one feels. By contrast, once the need is clearly identified, one is empowered to act. One can ask others for help, pray for what is needed, or undertake any number of strategies that might address the identified need.

When a pastoral caregiver seeks to listen empathically to another, he should make an effort to listen to how this person's feelings connect with underlying needs, values, and desires. This kind of listening deepens self-connection and helps the other articulate what she is longing for. Consider the following example, in which a nurse connects a wife's feelings with her underlying needs as she struggles with the pain of losing her husband:

> **Wife** *(referring to a physical therapist):* She's a bad therapist.
>
> **Nurse** *(listening empathically to what the wife is feeling and wanting):* Are you feeling annoyed and wanting to see a different quality of care?
>
> **Wife:** She doesn't do anything. She made him stop walking when his pulse got high.
>
> **Nurse** *(continuing to hear the wife's feelings and wants):* Is it because you want your husband to get better that you're scared if the physical therapist doesn't push him, he won't get stronger?
>
> **Wife** *(starts to cry):* Yes, I'm so scared!
>
> **Nurse:** Are you scared of losing him?
>
> **Wife:** Yes, we've been together so long.
>
> **Nurse** *(listening for other feelings behind the fear):* Are you worrying about how you would feel if he dies?
>
> **Wife:** I just can't imagine how I am going to live without him. He's always been there for me. Always.
>
> *And later:*
>
> **Wife:** . . . I don't know how I am going to get through this alone. I haven't anyone . . . not even to talk to, except with you here . . . now. Even he won't talk about it. . . . Look at him! *(Husband remains silent and impassive.)* He doesn't say anything!
>
> **Nurse:** Are you sad, wishing the two of you could support each other and feel more connected?
>
> **Wife:** Yes. *(She pauses, then makes a request):* Talk to him the way you talk to me.
>
> **Nurse** *(wishing to clearly understand the need that is being addressed be-*

hind the wife's request): Are you wanting him to be listened to in a way that helps him express what he's feeling inside?
Wife: Yes, yes, that's exactly it![18]

In this example the nurse focuses her attention on the wife's feelings and needs. She is doing more than simply reflecting back the woman's feelings; she is focusing her attention on how those feelings are connected to what the wife wants and needs. This woman is desperate to connect with her husband before he dies. Yet, when she begins the conversation, she seems relatively unaware of this longing. Instead, she criticizes the physical therapist. The nurse hears the criticism and translates it into what she guesses the woman might be feeling and wanting. She refuses to take the criticism at face value and hears it instead as an expression of the woman's underlying pain and unfulfilled longings. Similarly, when the wife criticizes her husband, the nurse hears her unexpressed longing for meaningful connection. As the conversation unfolds, the nurse is able to help the couple talk to each other about the loss they are facing. They are able to share their love and sorrow rather than remain isolated in their pain.

Listening and Reading

The skills involved in listening to another with empathy are remarkably similar to those required in carefully reading a text, though they are seldom considered in relation to each other. Students who have been taught to exegete biblical texts for sermon preparation, for example, typically are not taught to reflect on the parallels between understanding a text and understanding a person. Yet several can be drawn. In studying a biblical passage, students first learn to pay attention to the historical context. For whom was this text written? In Paul's letters, for instance, what is known about the communities to whom he wrote? What were their values, practices, and conflicts? What was the nature of their relationship to Paul? What was Paul's purpose in writing to them at this particular point in time?

In pastoral care, questions of context are also important. John

---

18. Marshall Rosenberg, *Nonviolent Communication: A Language of Life* (Encinitas, Calif.: PuddleDancer Press, 2003), pp. 105-6.

Patton highlights three "magic" questions that help orient any pastoral conversation: "What are you looking for? Why now? Why me?" Each question helps draw out the significance of what is being said. All three are essentially questions of context. They focus not so much on the *content* of the story as on its interpersonal *context*. Patton argues that when a conversation seems to lose its focus, these "magic" questions will help the narrative to get back on track. When the caregiver loses the narrative thread, he or she needs to ask how what has just been said relates to the purpose that brought caregiver and seeker together. What is the person looking for? Further, how is he shaping the story for this particular caregiver? And why now? What events have occurred most recently that prompted him to take action? Narratives unfold in particular interpersonal contexts for particular purposes, and a great part of their meaning can be discerned by paying attention to these specificities.[19]

Another parallel between reading and listening is the attention that one gives to key words that emerge in the course of the narrative. For example, students of Scripture have pondered what Paul means when he uses the difficult term *law* in Romans. What is its range of meaning? Does the word appear in his other letters? Does its appearance or nonappearance elsewhere shed light on how it is used in Romans? Attentiveness to such a key word can not only illumine the meaning of a particular passage but also increase one's understanding of Paul's theology as a whole.

While key words are important to ponder, one also attends to recurring themes or larger patterns of meaning. One cannot understand a unit apart from its context in the chapter, nor the chapter apart from the book, nor the book apart from the Bible as a whole. One works in two directions: inward, focusing on particular details in the passage, and outward, toward more comprehensive wholes. Roger Shattuck refers to this procedure as a circular method:

> My "circular method" is, in fact, nothing but an expansion of the common practice of "reading books"; reading at its best requires a strange cohabitation in the human mind of two opposite capaci-

19. John Patton, *Pastoral Counseling: A Ministry of the Church* (Nashville: Abingdon Press, 1983), pp. 83-105.

ties: contemplativity on the one hand and, on the other, a Protean mimeticism. That is to say: an undeflected patience that "stays with" a book until the forces latent in it unleash in us the recreative process.[20]

One contemplates the sense of the whole as well as of each individual part. One meditates on the relation between the whole and the part. One reads and re-reads, gaining understanding as one meditates on the layers of meaning that begin to emerge. At the same time, one develops the capacity to attend to the significance of each detail, internalizing the text as one ponders it.

Trained listeners develop similar skills. They listen for particular details, for the possible meanings of key words at the same time that they seek to discern larger patterns or recurring themes. What the person may regard as an inconsequential slip of the tongue, for example, might emerge in time as the interpretive key that unlocks the door to an unconsidered aspect of the meaning of his suffering. Freud investigated these so-called parapraxes carefully until they yielded meanings that were not at first apparent (the so-called Freudian slips). Finding each person's metaphorical universe to be utterly unique, he urged his students to consider nothing inconsequential. Freud also taught them to strive for a sense of the whole by listening with "free-floating attentiveness." Such a relaxed and leisurely mode of listening corresponds to the "free association" he requested of his patients. In free-floating attentiveness, associations, images, thoughts, and feelings are noted but not grasped tightly. Listeners gain insight into another's story as they allow it to mingle with their own associations. Meanings emerge as they meditate on the overall shape of the unfolding story.

Of course, differences do exist between reading and pastoral listening. One may read and re-read a passage in order to ponder its significance, whereas in conversation one hears another's words only once. On the other hand, in conversation one can ask the speaker directly about the possible significance of a word or an expression that seems noteworthy, something one cannot do with a text. Additionally, in the interpersonal context one can note changes in vocal inflection,

---

20. Roger Shattuck, *Candor and Perversion: Literature, Education, and the Arts* (New York: W. W. Norton, 1999), p. 38.

facial expression, and body posture, all of which provide clues about the significance of what is being said.

It is important to remember that listening, like reading, is a creative endeavor. In both situations one synthesizes complex material, attends to salient details, and contemplates the whole. There are no recipes or techniques which offer assurance that meanings will come to light, so careful attentiveness is necessary. Linguist Leo Spitzer comments,

> Why do I insist that it is impossible to offer the reader a step-by step rationale to be applied to a work of art? For one reason, that the first step, on which all may hinge, can never be planned: it must already have taken place. This first step is the awareness of having been struck by a detail, followed by a conviction that this detail is connected basically with the work of art; it means that one has made an "observation" . . . that one has been prompted to raise a question — which must find an answer. To begin by omitting this first step must doom any attempt at interpretation.[21]

As someone gives her full attention to another, whether person or literary text, something in particular may strike her. By making an observation, by meditating on the whole, by following up her hunches, she begins to uncover hidden layers of significance.

Finally, careful readers, like careful listeners, seek to convey the ideas of others as accurately as possible. Faithful interpreters of Scripture do not gloss over thorny issues; instead, they bring them fully into the light. They have an acute sense of the *otherness* of the text, knowing that it does not necessarily share their presuppositions. Seeking to understand the author on his own terms, good readers are vigilant about not importing themselves into the text. Nevertheless, they stay with a passage until it yields a question or some point of connection. Similarly, careful listeners seek to hear the particularity of another's expression along with its emotional significance. They seek to understand the *otherness* of the other within the framework of his or her own metaphorical universe. Good listening, like close reading, is a disciplined activity. In both instances, space needs to be made so that

---

21. Leo Spitzer, *Linguistics and Literary History: Essays in Stylistics* (Princeton: Princeton University Press, 1948), p. 27.

the other, whether text or person, can truly be present in their particularity.

Mastering the Three Skills of Good Listening

Good listening involves three essential skills. The first is accurate paraphrase — to receive with accuracy the concrete content of what is being said. One learns to demonstrate one's understanding by means of paraphrase, to recognize key words, and to reflect back content in a concise manner. One gathers up several layers of the story by accurately summarizing what has been said, both its content and its associated feeling tones. One focuses especially on feelings and needs, both expressed and implied.

The second skill of good listening is productive questioning. It involves the ability to ask both questions that are open-ended, which serve to elicit further sharing, and questions that are essentially closed, which serve to clarify meaning.

The third skill of good listening is what's called perception check. One needs to be able to distinguish one's observations from the inferences one makes on the basis of those observations and to inquire about what one perceives.

Accurate Paraphrase

Accurate paraphrase shows the speaker that the listener has heard her accurately. He merely restates what she has said in his own words, letting her know what he understands her to mean. In some cases the paraphrase in effect shows the speaker that the listener has misheard or misunderstood her. Even this is useful, however, because it helps her focus her comments on the misunderstood part.

Consider the need for a more skillful use of accurate paraphrase in the following example. In this interview, a pastor recounts a visit with a parishioner, "Grandma," who lives with her daughter and son-in-law and is completely dependent upon them. In introducing the case, the pastor states that "the son-in-law deeply resents the restrictions her presence places upon him and his wife."

Pastor 1: Well, how are things going today?

Grandma 1: Oh, I don't know, pastor. *(She wiped a few tears. Sensing that something was on her mind, I waited. But she didn't speak. So I prompted her.)*

Pastor 2: You have lots of time to think while you lie up here by yourself all day.

Grandma 2: Yes. *(Long silence.)*

Pastor 3: Perhaps you would like to talk about it.

Grandma 3: Well, I just lie here and think about everything.

Pastor 4: And something worries you?

Grandma 4: No — except I just wonder if I'll be missed.

Pastor 5: You're not sure of what some of the children think, or how they feel about you?

Grandma 5: That's right. All my life I slaved for my family. I would take in washings all day and then at night go down and get down on my hands and knees in one of the office buildings and scrub floors until after midnight. I would have to come home alone on the streetcar at one o'clock in the morning. It wasn't easy. My life was terribly hard. *(Tears and silence.)* But what thanks do I get? None!

Pastor 6: In other words, you worked hard to rear your family, but now they don't seem to appreciate it. They don't seem to care that you have done so much for them.

Grandma 6: Is it my fault that I am no longer as strong as I once was? I can't help it that I can't take care of myself. Believe me, I don't want to be here in bed any more than they want me to be here. All my life I have taken care of myself, and it isn't a bed of roses to have to lie here like a baby and be waited on by people who grumble at you all the time they are doing it. I'd almost rather die — much as I dread that — than have to lie here much longer! *(And again she wiped her eyes.)*

Pastor 7: I'm sorry, very sorry that you feel this way. I would like to feel that I understand. But I'm sure that behind all the family might say, they love you very much and are pleased they are able to take care of you now that you need help. *(I'm afraid I said this halfheartedly, not quite sure that I believed it myself.)*

Grandma 7: Well, I hope so. I don't know. *(She didn't say anything for a while, and then abruptly changed the subject by saying, "By the way, how's the new president in the Women's Society doing?" We then talked about many superficial things, but little by way of deeper feeling was revealed. I later wondered if I were too hasty in trying to give her reassurance about her family's love for her.)*[22]

Let's look at what happens in this exchange. With the pastor's encouragement, Grandma begins to disclose her feelings (Grandma 4). In the pastor's responses labeled "Pastor 5" and "Pastor 6," he paraphrases what he understands her to be saying, which has the effect of eliciting some of the depth of her anguish. She expresses her resentment over what she sees as her children's lack of gratitude for all her hard work and sacrifice (Grandma 6). The pastor's neutral paraphrase has the salutary effect of drawing out her bitterness: Grandma confesses how unbearable it is to be dependent on those who resent her presence.

The conversation shifts precisely when the pastor ceases to paraphrase. Instead, he offers reassurance. He says something he believes to be untrue, that Grandma's family is pleased to care for her. Notice how this response affects her. After that, she ceases to share anything of emotional significance. The pastor is bewildered and wonders whether he has offered premature reassurance. He is on the right track here. His reassurance effectively silences her and isolates her by implying that her feelings are regrettable and her perceptions distorted. He is unable to stay empathically connected with her.

If the pastor had continued to paraphrase, how might the conversation have been different? How might the pastor have stayed attuned to Grandma through paraphrase when she worried about being a burden? If he had focused on her needs, he might have said, "You want your presence to be a blessing, not a burden." He would thus identify her need to retain her human dignity in a time of helplessness. He would recognize her unstated longing for her family to give to her without resentment. In order to hear Grandma's unexpressed needs, the pastor would guess at the desires underlying the expressed frustration. Hearing what is bad or uncomfortable or anxiety-provoking, he would translate it into the good that is wanted, the comfort that is

22. *Casebook in Pastoral Counseling,* ed. Newman S. Cryer Jr. and John Monroe Vayhinger (Nashville: Abingdon Press, 1962), pp. 240-41.

sought, the peace that is desired. Once her longings were identified and Grandma felt fully heard, the pastor might offer to mediate between Grandma and her family so that their feelings and needs could also be heard.

Productive Questions

As I mentioned earlier, there are two kinds of productive questions: open-ended and clarifying. Open-ended questions elicit the person's story, and clarifying questions focus on its essential aspects. The pastor's first question to Grandma, for example, is open-ended: "How are things going today?" A closed question, by contrast, can be answered with a "yes" or a "no" (e.g., "Are you having a good day today?"). With an open-ended question, it is helpful to notice when a person offers free information — that is, information beyond what was specifically requested. In the conversation cited, Grandma offers free information in her fifth and sixth responses by elaborating on her problems. In doing so, she conveys trust in her pastor. Had the pastor received what she shared with empathy, she might have become aware of her bitterness and of her need for acceptance.

Given her initial reluctance, it is remarkable that Grandma shares as much as she does. Yet as long as the pastor communicates his acceptance through simple paraphrasing, she reveals her distress. It is a sign that the pastor has lost rapport with her when she abruptly shifts the focus of the conversation, as she does after the pastor offers reassurance. She then avoids further disclosure and relates to him more superficially.

By following freely offered information with sensitive questions or empathic listening, the caregiver allows the speaker to set the agenda, so that she may decide how much to share. While it is unethical to urge someone to disclose more than she wishes, exploration usually moves toward some sort of resolution when good rapport exists between listener and speaker. Experienced caregivers take their cue from the speaker without forging headlong into unexplored territory. They seek to walk *alongside* the other, not twenty steps ahead on the path. Trust is built step by step, by staying focused on the person's present feelings and needs.

Inappropriate or nonproductive questions are not attuned to the speaker's needs. Either they are too intimate for the level of trust established, or they have more to do with the listener's anxiety than with the speaker's need. If a daughter is reflecting on her day in response to her mother's query, for example, and her mother interrupts with a question about a dental appointment, it would likely sever the empathic connection between them. If the mother needs factual information, it would be better not to ask an open-ended question in the first place.

Productive questions can also help to clarify what the person is saying. Sometimes a person will assume he is being clear, yet the listener finds his words vague or confusing. It is better to ask for clarification than to fill in the blanks with assumptions of one's own. If a colleague says, for example, "I didn't like the way everyone was talking about changing the curriculum at the meeting the other night," several things might need clarification. Which meeting is he referring to? Whom does he mean by his reference to "everyone"? To which specific comments did he object? What was it about those suggestions that he didn't like? Is he saying that he likes the curriculum as it is and doesn't welcome any change at all, or only that the specific suggestions were not appealing to him? Focused (or closed) questions would help elicit the specific, concrete information needed for understanding. They would elicit the particulars of the story in terms of place, time, persons involved, and his concrete reactions to what occurred.

Perception Check

The third skill that good listeners need to develop is perception check. It involves not only grasping another's verbal content but also noticing his nonverbal and behavioral cues (e.g., tone and rhythm of voice, rate of breathing, facial expression, body position) in order to infer his emotional state. Perception check is more complicated than simply reflecting back the content or the meaning of a speaker's statement. One might listen to a man speak, for instance, noticing his clenched fists, narrowed eyes, tight jaw, raised voice, and rapid breathing. As a way of summarizing what one perceives, one might say, "You seem angry about the way your friend has been treating you." The man may not have said in so many words that he was angry, but his behavioral cues suggest it. Indeed, as much as 93 percent of interpersonal communication may consist of the interpretation of nonverbal cues. In a noted article in *Psychology Today,* Albert Mehrabian claimed that only 7 percent of communication depends upon words, whereas 38 percent depends upon tone of voice, and 55 percent depends on facial expression, posture, eye contact, and gestures.[23] Even those who don't understand a culture's language are sometimes able to grasp the emotional significance of human interactions by careful attention to nonverbal cues.

Inferring another person's feelings conveys interest and caring. Even very young children benefit from a sensitive perception check. If a child hangs his head and cries, caring parents will notice and ask whether he is sad about something. Some parents make the mistake of trying to cheer up a sad child. They might say something like, "It's not really so bad" or "You'll get over it soon," not realizing that they thereby communicate a lack of acceptance of the child's feeling. It is much more empathic to guess at the child's feeling: "You seem sad about Katy's moving away." Such understanding does not dispel the sadness, but it does acknowledge the loss. The child will likely feel his parents' support and caring through their acknowledgment of his sorrow.

When assessing one's perceptions of another's feelings, it is important to guess in a tentative manner, basically asking whether one's perception is accurate. If one's tone of voice communicates that one already knows how another feels, it might be heard as an accusation or an imposition. For example, if someone feels ashamed of being sad, she will be likely to deny her sorrow in order to avoid the shame linked to it. In such a scenario, it is important to allow the denial to remain unchallenged. Even if one is convinced that one has guessed accurately, it serves no good purpose to insist on it. The whole point of guessing is to deepen the emotional connection. If the other denies her feelings, it is likely due to fear and defensiveness. Insisting that she feels something she is not ready to acknowledge will only exacerbate her defensiveness.

Good listeners know how to hear the specificity of the other's response, not only in terms of its content but also in terms of its feeling tones. Even when the emotional nuances of an issue are generally familiar, one listens for what it means *to this person.* One ought not to assume that one already knows. One needs to match the tone and the in-

23. Albert Mehrabian, as cited in John Savage, *Listening and Caring Skills in Ministry* (Nashville: Abingdon Press, 1996), pp. 40-42.

tensity of the other as one listens. If the speaker is subdued, an accurate paraphrase would not only get the words right but also get the feeling tones right. An enthusiastic and upbeat paraphrase of a downcast speaker's words would be inaccurate, even if the content were otherwise correct.

Care in listening is especially important when one reaches across boundaries of race, culture, gender, or class. With each new variable the potential for misunderstanding grows. People interpret gestures, tone of voice, and facial expressions differently in diverse cultures. In situations of cross-cultural communication, finely honed skills of perception check are crucial. Even with expert skills, it is still possible for communication to break down due to differences in interpreting nonverbal cues. For instance, a Korean businessman was puzzled by what he understood as the defiant response of a West African taxi driver. As he chastised the driver, the businessman was annoyed by the driver's direct eye contact with him. Irritated by what he interpreted as a lack of respect, the Korean man rebuked the driver further. Though silent, the taxi driver continued to look directly at the businessman. Later, the businessman learned from his West African host that in his culture it was a sign of disrespect to look *away* from the other, whereas to look someone in the eye indicated attentive listening. It was just the opposite in Korea.

The key to understanding came only when the businessman consciously chose to check out his perception with his West African host. As he related the story, he was able to distinguish between what he had observed of the other's behavior and the inferences that he had drawn from it. This differentiation is the key skill in learning to do a perception check. Listeners do not need to study the emotional nuances of every culture of the world (an impossible feat); instead, they need to observe nonverbal communication carefully and be conscious of how they are interpreting it. When they know how to distinguish their observations from the inferences they draw from those observations, they can interpret others with greater accuracy and ease. They will also notice when others are drawing inferences about them on the basis of *their* observations. Because each person's feelings are integrally connected to the inferences he draws and the interpretations he makes of his environment, such close questioning has the potential to shed light on the emotional significance of the conversation.

While human feelings are universal, not all cultures deal with them in the same way. How to interpret another person's smile or silence or tone of voice can be challenging even in a common culture. But if listeners know how to distinguish between observed behavior and the inferences they draw from it, they can inquire into the possible meaning. Miscommunication occurs when they assume that they understand the other's behavior without checking out their perception.

Skill in perception check is needed when asking about perceived incongruities between someone's words and their tone of voice or body language. For example, if a smiling woman were to say, "My best friend died last week," one might be confused. If one gently draws attention to the incongruity — "I noticed that you were smiling when you told me about your friend's death" — it may possibly tap directly into a well of grief. By commenting sensitively on the incongruity, one gives the other space to express her underlying feelings. One communicates an acceptance of her grief and implicitly invites her to share it.

Other aspects of perception check might include the following. When does the other seek eye contact, and when does she avoid it? What is the emotional effect of sustained eye contact or an averted gaze? How does the other's tone of voice affect one? Is the speaker's voice lively, or does it sound monotonous, dull, or depressed? Does the breath seem constricted and the voice thin and breathy? Or is it full-bodied and resonant? By paying attention to such things, one gets a wealth of information about possible underlying feelings.

One might also notice when and how the speaker changes the focus of the conversation. Did the change of focus deepen the emotional connection, or did it bring the conversation to a more superficial level? How might one track the various levels of the conversation? When is the sharing more superficial, and when is more significant emotional communication taking place? How well does one follow the lead of the speaker, facilitating significant sharing but also allowing the speaker to set his own pace?

Other dynamics can be observed as well. When and how is humor used? What function does it serve? Is it used to ease tension in such a way that the emotional connection is sustained? Is it used to shift the focus away from something painful? What happens after the catharsis of shared laughter? Does the speaker return to renewed exploration, or does the humor divert the conversation? What is the quality of silence?

Is it tense and anxious, or is it a restful pause, enabling a fuller connection? Beginning listeners are sometimes uncomfortable with long stretches of silence. Experienced listeners are usually able to rest in the silence while the speaker gets more fully connected to what he is expressing.

*   *   *

Mastering these three skills of good listening — accurate paraphrase, productive questions, and perception check — fosters the emotional connection between persons. While they presuppose a certain level of basic trust, they also function to further that trust. If a person begins to speak hesitantly and the listener conveys his respect by empathically focusing on her feelings and needs, she has the space to consider sharing further. The more that one receives with care, the more trust will be engendered. As the speaker tells her story, she will gain a deeper emotional connection with herself. She will also gain a new and wider perspective. The listener offers this wider perspective to her not by presenting it to her in the form of advice or information but rather by eliciting it from her in the form of empathy and understanding.

Conclusion

Koinonia means empathy at the interpersonal level and prayer at the spiritual level. When caregivers empty themselves of their own preoccupations in order to be fully present to another, they are, in their own small way, following the example of Christ, who emptied himself of his equality with God in order to participate fully in our human plight (Philippians 2). By showing attentive concern to others, pastoral listeners point beyond themselves to the listening God. Such conversations take place not for their own sake, but as a "sign and witness"[24] to the God who takes human need to heart. As members of Christ's body, pastoral listeners participate in Christ's attentiveness. When those in the church serve others through listening, they strengthen faith that God is the One who hears every anguished cry.

24. Barth, *Church Dogmatics*, IV/3.2, p. 885.

Caring listening made possible by finely honed empathic skill engenders mutual understanding and trust. Deepened emotional connection paves the way for richer spiritual conversation. Pastoral caregivers seek to listen to those in need so that they may intercede on their behalf, trusting in Christ's power of intercession with the Father. The prayer offered on behalf of their sister or brother asks God to use this struggle for the upbuilding of faith, the deepening of love, and the quickening of hope. As caregivers come to those they serve in and through Jesus Christ, they endeavor to see the other in the light of Christ's sacrificial self-giving. They seek to listen with the same love with which Christ listens to them in prayer. As they pray together, they trust that Christ will deepen the bonds of fellowship between them even as he draws them to himself in love.

Four   Listening to Ourselves

Pastoral caregivers need to be anchored in their relationship with God through their own active life of prayer. This alone will give them the ease they need to pray aloud in another's presence. If God is their regular conversation partner, they will have little trouble including another in the conversation. Like all conversation, prayer includes both listening and speaking, as well as pauses for silence and self-reflection. Pastoral caregivers need to be aware of their own feelings and needs not only as they pray but also as they listen to others. They need a secure sense of self in order to give freely of that self. Clinical Pastoral Education, or CPE, an international network of education and training, has developed a number of tools for raising the self-awareness of ministers in pastoral encounters. Through role plays, verbatim reports, interpersonal groups, and various kinds of self-reflection, CPE has afforded pastoral caregivers the opportunity to learn about their strengths, motivations, and growing edges in offering care.

In the eighty years of CPE's existence, the analysis of pastoral interviews has been a major tool of training. Just as we analyzed the conversation between "Grandma" and her pastor in the previous chapter, so small groups of CPE students examine not only the parishioners' particular circumstances but also, more importantly, the ministers' active responses to those circumstances.

It is axiomatic in pastoral care that people cease to listen well when they are anxious. A student training in chaplaincy work in a hospital once asked me, "What would you do if you were pastor to a dying man who has lost his faith and doesn't want you to speak about God?" A question like this cannot be answered without understanding what meaning it has for the student, on the one hand, and for the man himself on the other. The student's question may be related to his anxiety about learning new pastoral skills, while the man's request has a meaning that arises out of his own life narrative. For the student to be helpful to the man, he needs to distinguish his own concerns from those of the man he seeks to understand.

More important than the actual request itself (i.e., that the student not talk about God) is the need to understand the underlying *reason* for the request. The request is a clue that can lead the student to a deeper connection with the man only if the student is able temporarily to set aside whatever anxiety the request might raise for him and to focus on what it means to the man himself. There are two sets of interrelated issues, in other words, that require two sets of interrelated skills. The first set has to do with hearing what any specific request means to the person one seeks to serve. The second has to do with what it means to oneself as the listener. The first requires skill in offering empathy, while the second requires skill in working with oneself empathically. As a pastoral caregiver develops skill in listening to others, she simultaneously needs to listen to herself. The key is to notice when her anxiety is triggered so that she can reflect on it later. When a caregiver learns the skills entailed in self-empathy, she has an invaluable tool not only for pastoral care but also for self-care.

CPE supervisors are frequently able to guess the exact moment that a pastor's anxiety is triggered by examining his verbal responses in pastoral interviews. When anxiety enters the picture, the pastor typically stops focusing on understanding the other and begins to offer advice or reassurance. Frank Lake identifies the presence of anxiety as the single most important factor that prevents genuine listening from occurring:

> Let us admit . . . that our disinclination to spend time listening to troubled people tells us more about our own unsolved anxieties than it does about their avowedly insoluble ones. . . . Much of what passes for counseling of the parishioner is actually the pastor's treatment of his own anxieties. . . . Before he has heard the story out he begins to give the sort of reassurance which the [person] recog-

nizes cannot be meant for himself, since he has not yet come to the end of his story. The half is not yet known. Therefore, it must be that the [pastor] is reassuring himself.[1]

In light of Lake's comment, we can recall the pastor's interaction with Grandma examined in the last chapter. Though the pastor assumed that she needed reassurance, it actually did nothing to deepen the connection between them. On the contrary, it effectively severed it. Lake might suggest that the pastor was reassuring himself. Further, he might suggest that if the pastor were to examine the exact moment he began reassuring Grandma, he would likely gain some insight into his own anxiety. Such an effort would help him not only in future encounters with Grandma but also in encounters with any of his other parishioners. He would have a reliable tool for listening to himself that would enable him in turn to listen more effectively to others.

By studying their pastoral conversations, caregivers can learn to pinpoint the unresolved issues in their own lives that prevent them from listening empathically.

Analyzing a Pastoral Conversation

What was it about Grandma's bitterness that was intolerable for the pastor? What made her lament so unacceptable? What did her resentment evoke in him? Any number of hypotheses might be explored. Perhaps he identified with her son-in-law, feeling that this old lady was impossible to please. Or maybe he wished that the son-in-law would take a kindlier attitude toward the old woman. Or perhaps it was painful for him to listen because he remembered his own aging mother's loneliness. As an outsider to the pastor's emotional history, one can only speculate. Only the pastor can answer these questions.

That he failed to do this indispensable work becomes obvious in the subsequent pastoral interview. Once again Grandma tries to share what is troubling her. Her need to to be heard is evidently urgent

1. Frank Lake, *Clinical Theology* (London: Darton, Longman & Todd, 1966), p. 62.

enough for her to risk sharing her concerns despite the earlier failure. She seems to be struggling with something of importance:

> **Grandma 1:** . . . There are so many things I ought to do that I haven't done. I sometimes wish I could live my life over. I wonder if I'm ready to go. Do you think God punishes us for the things we do that are wrong?
>
> **Pastor 1:** Yes, the Bible teaches that there is a judgment. Men are rewarded for the good they do; they are punished for their evil. I do not know the nature of the punishment. Perhaps it is separation from God. But I know we are not to be concerned with the details of all this. We can trust God. But naturally, it concerns us, doesn't it?
>
> **Grandma 2:** I do think about it a lot. You know —
>
> **Pastor 2:** Just a moment. There is something else I want to say in response to your question. You are a charter member of our church and have faithfully served God through the years. You are safe in his love and care. You have been a good woman and have nothing to worry about. Will you remember that when you think about these things?
>
> **Grandma 3:** I will try. Still, I can't help but think about some things.
>
> **Pastor 3:** These we cast into the sea of God's forgetfulness to be remembered against us no more. God is full of mercy and forgiveness. You can trust him.
>
> **Grandma 4** *(after long silence):* I know. I have tried to do the things that are right. But sometimes I wonder —
>
> **Pastor 4:** We need not wonder. We can know we have passed from death unto life. *(I waited, but she didn't seem to have anything more to say, and so I felt I had satisfactorily answered her question.)*
>
> **Pastor 5:** Before I go, I would like to have a prayer with you, committing your life into the love and care of your heavenly Father, sure in the knowledge that with him we are safe. And he will reward you for the good you have done in life.
>
> **Prayer:** O Lord, we thank thee for all thy saints. We particularly thank thee for this good woman, who through the years has served thee and loved thee. Bless her now with the comforting assurance that in thy care all things are well. We also pray for

her family. Bless them and bind them together with cords of love and affection. Through Jesus Christ our Lord. Amen.[2]

If we analyze this interview from the point of view of its content rather than its process — that is, *what* was communicated rather than *how* it was communicated — we might note that the pastor's understanding of God's judgment and righteousness on the one hand and of God's mercy and forgiveness on the other are so split off from each other that there seems to be little coherence in his understanding of God. We might further ask what role Jesus Christ plays, if any, in his understanding of God's judgment and mercy. Perhaps because of Christ's conspicuous absence, the pastor has little to offer Grandma apart from "works-righteousness." He tries to convince her that her good works will guarantee God's mercy. He implies that *her* faithfulness to God will elicit *God's* faithfulness to her. Not only is such a view contrary to biblical teaching; it also has the potential to deepen the despair of one with unconfessed sins on her heart.

There is, however, another way to analyze the interview. If the pastor were to consider the *emotional process* rather than the *theological content* of what he said, different issues would emerge. From a "process" point of view, the minister seems emotionally disconnected from what he is saying. He spouts doctrine as if it were something he has read about that has little relevance for people's lives. He seems to be giving a lecture rather than listening to an attempted confession. He seems unaware that he is answering the question of a human being who might be harboring unconfessed sins. Though he advises Grandma "not to be concerned with the details of God's judgment," he fails to hear that her present anguish may well be caused precisely by such "details." In short, he fails to consider the context: What might be prompting her question at this point in her life?

"Naturally, it concerns us," he hastens to say, as if suddenly remembering the woman before him. But he fails to wonder about her need. It seems that his lecture on God's judgment has terrified *him*, for he is determined at all costs to assure her of God's forgiveness. His assurances sound hollow, however, because he refuses to hear her confes-

---

2. *Casebook in Pastoral Counseling*, ed. Newman S. Cryer Jr. and John Monroe Vayhinger (Nashville: Abingdon Press, 1962), pp. 241-42.

sion. Yet what is preventing him from hearing her remorse? Is he so frightened of God's judgment that he needs his own reassurance? Grandma is not easily dissuaded and persists three times in voicing her concern (Grandma 2, 3, and 4). Unfortunately, the pastor also persists. He finally succeeds in silencing her, assuming that he has effectively answered her question. In seeking to comfort and reassure her, he ironically does exactly the opposite. Not only does he himself refuse to hear her, but in effect he conveys that God will not listen either.

What is one to make of the pastor's prayer? It doesn't seem to be directed toward God at all; rather, as one commentator notes, it appears to "ram reassurance down her throat."[3] Karl Barth's insight is pertinent here: "Prayer as a demonstration of faith, as disguised preaching, as an instrument of edification, is obviously not prayer at all. Prayer is not prayer if it is addressed to anyone else but God."[4] The pastor's prayer seems less like a prayer to God on the woman's behalf than a wishful fantasy addressed to the woman.

One later learns that Grandma has refused to speak with her son for seventeen years, ever since he married without her permission. The daughter informs the pastor that her brother tried to visit, but their mother had refused to see him. Finally some light is shed on the possible source of Grandma's qualms of conscience. Unfortunately, her misgivings are never expressed because her pastor is too anxious to hear them.

Facing Anxiety

Frank Lake writes that the "primary task which will fit the physician for the life of therapeutic dialogue is to have faced and dealt with his own anxieties."[5] If this is true for the physician, how much more for the pastor! Yet facing one's anxieties is seldom easy. Whenever one listens to another's challenging life issues, one's own unresolved questions are stirred up. Much of the self-discipline required in listening to others without interjecting one's own reactions develops as one learns to pay

3. *Casebook in Pastoral Counseling*, p. 245.
4. Karl Barth, *Church Dogmatics*, III/4 (Edinburgh: T&T Clark, 1960), p. 88.
5. Lake, *Clinical Theology*, p. 63.

attention to one's anxiety. In order to focus on another, one must know, paradoxically, how to pay attention to oneself. This is the dual awareness that every listener needs. Frieda Fromm-Reichmann, a psychotherapist trained by Freud, understood the magnitude of the difficulty:

> To be able to listen and to gather information from another person in the other person's own right, without reacting along the lines of one's own problems or experiences, of which one may be reminded, perhaps in a disturbing way, is an art of interpersonal exchange which few people are able to practice without special training.[6]

The special training that has evolved in the field of pastoral care is the disciplined examination of pastoral conversations. Nothing can replace such reflection, which typically repays one with a measure of valuable insight. Exchanging feedback in small groups provides an opportunity to learn how one's anxiety can impair even one's best-intentioned efforts to minister.

Is there a way to face one's own anxiety so that one might avoid sabotaging one's pastoral care of others?

The Skill of Focusing

Focusing is a complex skill developed by psychologist Eugene Gendlin at the University of Chicago in the 1970s. Though designed with other purposes in mind, it is well-suited for teaching caregivers how to face their anxiety. Wondering why psychotherapy didn't succeed more often, Gendlin and his associates studied thousands of taped sessions to identify the factors that made for emotional growth. They discovered that successful psychotherapy had less to do with the therapist's theoretical framework, training, or technique, and more to do with how counselees talked about their problems.[7] Gendlin developed a vocabulary for describing what occurred in these salutary exchanges and then developed a method that could be taught to ordinary people. Since the 1970s, focusing workshops and institutes have sprung up around the

---

6. Fromm-Reichmann, quoted by Lake in *Clinical Theology*, pp. 7-8.
7. Eugene Gendlin, *Focusing* (New York: Bantam Books, 1981), p. 3.

world. More than thirty studies have concluded that the ability to focus correlates with a positive outcome in psychotherapy.[8]

Gendlin eventually wrote a book about focusing. Building on the
concept of biological intelligence developed by Ward Halstead at the
University of Chicago, Gendlin argues that the body is a kind of "biological computer" that knows far more than the mind: "The equivalent
of hundreds of thousands of cognitive operations are done in a split
second by the body."[9] When we pay attention to our physical bodies, we
are able to examine responses that usually lie outside our mental
awareness. For example, imagine meeting an old friend, someone you
haven't seen for years. You recognize him not by his receding hairline or
his expanding waistline, but by processing myriad observations that
take place outside awareness. You may consciously note a familiar inflection in his voice or something unique about his gait, but the experience of recognition transcends conscious awareness of any single trait.
It involves the whole gestalt, hundreds of details that your body notes
in a single instant simply by being in your friend's presence. Curiously,
if you trusted your friend decades earlier, that trust rarely needs to be
laboriously re-established. You might pick up the conversation you began years earlier, as if no time at all had intervened. It is as if the friend
were already a part of you. You know how to be with this friend, for
what Gendlin calls the "felt sense" of him is in your body. You have a
level of comfort with him *in your body* because of the trust established
years earlier. Gendlin says this "felt sense" is the key to focusing. Once
you're able to find words that match the felt sense, you can work
through any emotion. This is the essential tool that can provide the
help pastoral caregivers need to face their anxiety.

Another example may shed further light. Imagine speaking with a
trusted friend about something of emotional significance. Halfway
through the conversation, a not-so-well-trusted colleague joins you.
Notice how something shifts inside your body when this person arrives. Since there is unresolved tension between you and him, you

---

8. Cf. http://www.focusing.org/fot/friedman_other_body_interventions.html;
Internet; accessed 29 May 2006. See also Marion Hendricks, "Research Basis of
Focusing-Oriented/Experiential Therapy," in *Handbook of Research and Practice in Human-
istic Psychotherapies,* ed. D. Cain and J. Seeman (Washington, D.C.: American Psychological Association, 2002).

9. Gendlin, *Focusing,* p. 34.

might notice actual physical discomfort as he approaches. The felt sense is a *bodily* occurrence, not a mere thought; that's why Gendlin underscores the importance of paying close attention to how your body feels in the whole context. Another example might elucidate this. Imagine trying to recall something that you were about to say but have momentarily forgotten. Your body experiences this "mental event" as a kind of felt tension. When you finally remember the word or sentence, you feel a palpable sense of relief.

In his book Gendlin sets forth a step-by-step process that can be learned through active practice. There's no substitute for reading the book, but the discussion here can serve as a useful introduction to the process.

In order to focus, you first relax, close your eyes, and direct your attention down into the core of your body — toward your belly. You focus on feelings that are at first inchoate, perhaps difficult to put into words. You ask yourself how you are and to wait for a "felt sense" to emerge. If something is bothering you, wait until a sense of "the whole thing" begins to form. You need to ask yourself, "What is the sense of all that, the sense of the whole thing, the murky discomfort or the unclear body-sense of it?"[10] Then wait for a word or image to filter into awareness. An intuition of your anxiety or concern will arise in what Gendlin calls a "handle." Go back and forth between the felt sense and the "handle" that best describes it to see if they fit together. Perhaps the word will change slightly to match the felt sense, or perhaps the felt sense will shift slightly to match the word. When you find the right "handle," you'll know it, because something will shift in your body.

The bodily shift is distinctly physical, similar to the palpable relaxation that occurs when you remember the name of a person you've been trying to recall. When the "felt sense" and the word match, a similar letting go is experienced, sometimes accompanied by a literal sigh of relief. "Ah yes, that's it! That word captures the felt sense exactly." At this point, Gendlin suggests probing further in order to elicit more information from the felt sense. Previously unconscious feelings and needs may begin to emerge. You might ask, "What is it about this whole issue that makes it so . . . ? What is the worst thing about this problem? How would I feel inside if it were solved? What do I need to

10. Gendlin, *Focusing*, p. 173.

keep from feeling so anxious [or "jumpy" or "frightened" — whatever word seems to fit the felt sense]?" After asking the question, wait for your body to answer with its inner wisdom; do not fill in the blanks with conscious ideas or thoughts.

If we now return to the first interview in the previous chapter (page 70), we see that the pastor's seventh response indicates that Grandma's immediately previous words were what probably activated his anxiety. She had just expressed intense anger and resentment, saying that she'd almost rather die than be subject to the kind of treatment that she faced each day. At that particular moment the pastor may have found it hard to focus any attention on himself. Nevertheless, with proper training, he could have noted that his anxiety had been activated and recognized that he needed to be especially intentional about listening. His anxiety would have set off a kind of inner alarm, alerting him to the danger of missing the significance of what was coming next.

He could return to this moment later and focus on the *exact sentence* that activated his anxiety. "What was it that Grandma said that made me feel so . . . 'what'?" Perhaps "anxious" is the word that would best describe his feeling, but perhaps not. Instead of a word, perhaps an image would arise of himself as a small child hiding from an angry mother. Focusing on that image might bring up the word "frightened" or "terrified." He could then ask himself, "What's the worst thing about this feeling? How would I feel if it were resolved? What do I need to feel less terrified?" And then he would wait to see what might shift in his body. Through focusing, he might see how he ceased to hear Grandma the moment his anxiety was activated, becoming intent instead on relieving his own anxiety. The point is this: In order to attend fully to Grandma's feelings and needs, he must also learn to attend to his own.

Those experienced in focusing would not fear another person's feelings, no matter how powerfully expressed, because they would have the tools to deal with their own. They would be able to work with intense feelings like grief, sorrow, and rage. They would know how chronic anxiety can erode a sense of self. They would have the skills to differentiate among anger, annoyance, frustration, resentment, indignation, and rage on the one hand, and among love, tenderness, affection, admiration, fondness, and adoration on the other. Such differentiation skills would be the result of their learning to identify and accept a full range of feelings in themselves. At home with their own feelings, they could stay connected with others who wished to explore theirs. They would be able to stay present without needing others "to get over" their feelings; they could help others work through their difficulties at their own pace.

Gendlin acknowledges that some feelings are painful to admit. However, he notes that suppressing them doesn't make them go away. Whenever you try to eliminate your feelings, you merely give them more power. If you're afraid of your anger and deny its existence, you become unconscious of it and are consequently in greater danger of acting it out. For example, you may make sarcastic comments to someone you love. If she responds with hurt, you may protest that you were only joking. But this type of joking isn't amusing, as the root meaning of "sarcasm" discloses: "the tearing of flesh." Alternatively, unacknowledged anger might contribute to depression if you turn the anger inward against yourself. Whatever the unacknowledged feeling, it typically presses for acknowledgment. Because people develop a variety of tactics — most of them negative — to stay unaware of painful feelings (eating compulsively, drinking too much, working incessantly), it is much healthier to deal with them directly. In his book Gendlin shows that one doesn't need to remain "stuck" with any particular feeling, that it can be worked through.

Reviewing the Steps of Focusing

In the previous section I briefly described Gendlin's step-by-step focusing process. In this section I'm outlining the sequence of steps a bit more more fully, with the suggestion that leaders first learn the focusing skill themselves in order to teach it to members of their caregiving team. This practice can assist anyone, but I'm recommending it here for those who want to face their anxiety in order to minister more effectively.

Relaxation is the first step. Consciously tightening and releasing various muscle groups and deepening one's breathing are widely known relaxation techniques. Any kind of body awareness training — particularly yoga, Feldenkrais, t'ai chi, and qigong — can provide understanding of the connection between breathing and relaxation.

Knowing how to breathe deeply as a way of centering oneself and calming the mind is crucial. Focusing, like other creative endeavors, entails physical relaxation, focused concentration, and directed imagination.

After relaxing one's body and calming the nervous system, one directs one's attention inward. Gendlin's steps, which appear below, should be spoken aloud in a gentle, inviting tone of voice when one is leading a group through a focusing exercise.

1. Clear a Space
How are you? What's between you and feeling fine? Don't answer; let what comes in your body do the answering. Don't go into anything. Greet each concern that comes. Put each aside for a while, next to you. Except for that, are you fine?

2. Felt Sense
Pick one problem to focus on. Don't go into the problem. What do you sense in your body when you recall the whole of that problem? Sense all of that, the sense of the whole thing, the murky discomfort or the unclear body-sense of it.

3. Get a Handle
What is the quality of the felt sense? What one word, phrase, or image comes out of this felt sense? What quality-word would fit it best?

4. Resonate
Go back and forth between the word (or image) and the felt sense. Is that right? If they match, have the sensation of matching several times. If the felt sense changes, follow it with your attention. When you get a perfect match, the words (images) being just right for this feeling, let yourself feel that for a minute.

5. Ask
"What is it about the whole problem that makes me so . . . ? What is the worst of this feeling? What's really so bad about this? What does it need? What should happen?" Don't answer; wait for the feeling to stir and give you an answer. What would it feel like if it was all OK? Let the body answer. What is in the way of that?

6. Receive

Welcome what came. Be glad it spoke. It is only one step on this problem, not the last. Now that you know where it is, you can leave it and come back to it later. Protect it from critical voices that interrupt. Does your body want another round of focusing, or is this a good stopping place?[11]

Imagine yourself clearing a room crowded with cardboard boxes, stacking them and setting them to one side. Each box contains a specific concern. When you acknowledge each concern, greet it, and then set it aside, you get an overview of your emotional landscape without becoming immersed in your problems. Clearing an inner space gives perspective. It helps you to see that you are more than (and other than) the problems plaguing you.

Gendlin acknowledges that sometimes you may be afraid to focus. Perhaps you've neglected your feelings and needs for a long time. Imagine the trepidation of cleaning out an attic you haven't entered for years. Cobwebs, spiders, mice, outgrown clothing, and piles of old letters may litter the space. Memories lie dormant. Layers of personal history — including some things you have left undone that you ought to have done, and things you have done that you ought not to have done — might spring into awareness. Gendlin provides this helpful reminder:

> What is true is already so. Owning up to it doesn't make it worse. Not being open about it doesn't make it go away. And because it's true, it is what is there to be interacted with. Anything untrue isn't there to be lived. People can stand what is true, for they are already enduring it.[12]

Focusing gives you access to what you are already enduring.

It is important to acknowledge that everyone has a choice about how far to venture in focusing. One should only take on this practice voluntarily, and not with a sense of obligation but with a desire to learn about oneself. In teaching focusing to groups, therefore, it is helpful to give people permission to use the time simply to relax if they

11. Gendlin, *Focusing*, pp. 173-74.
12. Gendlin, *Focusing*, p. 140.

wish. If they so choose, they may close their eyes and take an imaginary trip to the beach. Since they alone are in charge of their inner world, they can use the time to imagine clouds floating through the sky. They might dive into turquoise waters and behold multicolored fish. They might let the leader's words float above their heads, like white foam on gentle waves. It should also be made clear that the participants will not be expected to share what they discover. However, if there is a level of established trust in the group, individuals may choose to share their discoveries with others later.

If the pastor in our example had gone through a process of focusing, he could not have sustained the rationalization that he had satisfactorily answered Grandma's questions when all he had done was silence her by his refusal to listen. Nor would he have been so anxious about letting Grandma speak her mind, because he would have faced within himself whatever he feared to hear. In other words, the pastor would have had a tool for listening to himself so that he could continue to listen to Grandma. Without such a tool, he would risk losing the confidence of any parishioner that activated his anxiety.

The Value of Focusing: An Example

In an article entitled "Transference and Religious Practices," James O. Laughrun, a trained and certified pastoral counselor, describes his work with a young man who came to him for counseling.[13] At the end of their first session, the young man asked Laughrun to pray for him. The counselor suggested that they forgo prayer until he understood him better. The young man was at first surprised, then angry, and finally indignant, complaining that "a real minister" would not have refused so simple a request. He agreed to a second session only if it would focus on the request for prayer and its refusal.

Such an extreme reaction gave the counselor a clue that more was going on than met the eye. For this person, prayer was clearly a topic with intense feelings surrounding it, feelings that were perhaps "transferred" from elsewhere. Though he had been verbally attacked,

---

13. See James O. Laughrun, "Transference and Religious Practices," *Journal of Pastoral Care* 33, no. 3 (September 1979): 185-89.

Laughrun remained nonreactive and calm, maintaining his focus on the young man and the significance of prayer *for him*. He didn't get sidetracked into defending his status as a "real" minister. Instead, he attended to what it meant to the young man that his new counselor had refused to pray for him.

During the course of the next year, Laughrun eventually discovered what was at stake in his counselee's apparently innocent request. The man had been raised by an emotionally absent, alcoholic father and an emotionally invasive, pious mother, who repeatedly prayed aloud for her son in his presence. Her prayers essentially instructed God what to do so that her son would not grow up to be like his father. Laughrun came to understand that the man had expected his counselor to continue in his mother's role — that is, to actively pray for him so that he himself could remain in a passive, dependent role. When Laughrun had refused to play the part of the transference figure (the man's mother), the man's anxiety had been (unconsciously) activated, which accounted for his indignation. On a level outside his awareness, the young man experienced his counselor's refusal to pray as a dismissal of his unacknowledged need for motherly care.

Further exploration disclosed that the man himself was not a person of prayer. As he worked through various issues, the man eventually decided that he wanted to learn to pray for himself. His initial elation over his newfound freedom to pray eventually gave way to the feeling that God didn't listen to him anyway. So what difference did his prayers make? Laughrun comments,

> Rather than enter into a theological discussion of his questions, [I] suggested that it was possible that, just as his unconscious relationship with his mother had disturbed his attitude toward prayer, perhaps now his difficulties had to do with feelings toward his passive-alcoholic father.[14]

As matters progressed, it became apparent that the man's unexamined feelings about his father were indeed the source of his despair over ever being heard by God.

In technical terms, the man had unconsciously transferred first

14. Laughrun, "Transference and Religious Practices," p. 188.

his mother and then his father onto the counselor. If the counselor had in either case responded anxiously to the content of what the man was saying, he would have thwarted the man's healing process. Happily, because the counselor had the conceptual tools for understanding transference reactions, he was able to investigate the man's emotional process rather than react to it. The eventual results were heartening:

> With the working-through of the transference obstacles this man was free to perceive the reality of God as it was communicated through the spoken and written word within the worshipping community. In addition, he was able to participate in this reality as a "man of prayer" himself.[15]

The counselor had a means of assessing how his initial refusal to pray for the young man had affected him, as well as a way of dealing with any possible anxiety that the counselee's accusations may have triggered for him. He had the consummate skill, in other words, of dual awareness: being able to listen to himself while keeping his primary focus on his counselee.

The story that Laughrun tells demonstrates a basic psychotherapeutic principle — that one's emotional reactions in the present can be traced back to early formative events. In this situation, Laughrun employed conceptual tools that generally lie beyond the scope of what most caregivers have at their disposal. Nevertheless, it demonstrates two basic points that pertain to any caregiver. First, it shows the value of keeping one's focus on what any particular utterance might mean to the person saying it. The pastoral counselor was single-minded in his focus on uncovering the meaning of the man's "overreaction" to his refusal to pray in their first session. Though it took a year to uncover all of the layers involved, the counselor's efforts to stay empathically connected to the man were essential to the success of the counseling relationship. Second, the story shows that the counselor clearly had the necessary tools for working with himself. Though not the focus of the article, it is clear that the minister was secure enough in his own identity to remain unthreatened by the man's accusation that he was not a "real" minister when he refused to pray for

15. Laughrun, "Transference and Religious Practices," p. 189.

him. If the minister's anxiety was triggered by the accusation, he was able to work through it so that it did not threaten the quality of his connection with his counselee. These interrelated skills are essential for anyone seeking to offer empathic listening.

Important Connections between Self-Empathy and Focusing

In the previous chapter we discussed Marshall Rosenberg's ideas about self-empathy, which converge in remarkable ways with Gendlin's ideas about focusing. The key step in self-empathy lies in being able to identify what one needs. Focusing concentrates on identifying one's feelings, and Nonviolent Communication focuses on connecting the feelings with underlying needs. Interestingly, the shift that one gets in focusing occurs when one connects with the underlying need. Although Gendlin does not draw the reader's attention to the importance of identifying the need, that is implicit throughout. For example, he suggests that one ask oneself what it would feel like physically if things were all better. Then he asks, "What is standing in the way of that?" What, in other words, is needed?

In Rosenberg's model, identifying the needs explicitly is the conceptual linchpin of the whole. It is the fulcrum between one's feelings, on the one hand, and any action that one might take on the other. If one feels lonely, for example, one can express that many times over without actually connecting it to the underlying need. One's loneliness might point to a need for companionship, or for community, or for a more satisfying quality of connection in one's friendships or one's marriage. Simply identifying the feeling of loneliness doesn't give one enough information to be able to take action. Compassionate exploration of the loneliness would identify the precise need underlying the loneliness. Being lonely in a crowd is different from being lonely in a marriage, for example. Being lonely after the death of a life-long friend is different from being lonely because one spends hours in frenetic activity, never fully connecting with one's colleagues or oneself. Being able to identify the specific longing is crucial if one is going to take action to change one's life for the better. Helping to create a lively community of scholars might help alleviate one person's loneliness, while reading to four-year-olds at the public library might be just the thing for someone else. Clarifying the need is paramount. Is it companionship in valued tasks that one needs? Is it a need to make a contribution to the world in a way that will connect one with others? Does one long for intimacy in one's marriage or one's friendships? Loneliness is just the tip of the iceberg that leads one down into the soul's longings.

In self-empathy, one attends to oneself with the same quality of gentle openness that one seeks to give another in pastoral care. One refrains from judging or criticizing oneself as diligently as one would refrain from judging others. One approaches oneself with patience, seeking self-understanding and self-acceptance. Let us consider one of the pastor's comments in his interaction with Grandma and imagine how he might use tools of self-empathy for connecting with himself in a life-giving way. After he offered reassurance to Grandma, he added parenthetically — *"I'm afraid I said this halfheartedly, not quite sure that I believed it myself."* Here we have an indication that the pastor senses that something has gone wrong. He feels somewhat uncomfortable with his own words. If he were to notice his discomfort, he might work with himself in the following way: "I'm feeling a little uncomfortable with what I just said because it doesn't fully meet my need for honesty. I guess I want to reassure Grandma of her family's love because I'm really longing for family harmony. It's so painful to hear how her family is treating her. I'm longing for a way to contribute to the well-being of the whole family, but I don't really know how to do it. I need more skill and competence in this situation than I currently have."

In this scenario, the pastor's feelings connect with his basic needs — for honesty, for harmony, for contribution, and for competence. If he were fully able to connect with each of these needs, he could then address how he might take action to get them met. He might begin by calling a colleague to ask for some empathy about his perceived lack of skill. In doing so, he might discover some regret and a need for self-acceptance about the choices he has already made. He did the best he could with what he had. In reassuring Grandma, he was trying to meet certain needs of his own. He longed for Grandma to be loved and accepted by her family, and so he reassured her that this was the case. In self-empathy, it would be essential for the pastor to uncover which needs he was trying to meet when he offered reassurance. In seeking collegial empathy and feedback, the pastor could take the opportunity to explore all the aspects of the situation that triggered his anxiety. In attending to each need with care, the pastor would open a path for his own healing and growth. When fully connected to his needs, the pastor might be able to conclude with gentle compassion for himself: "I regret that I reassured her in the way that I did because I didn't fully believe what I was saying, and I value honesty and integrity."

If the pastor could offer himself empathy regarding his own feelings and needs, he would be in a better position to hear Grandma's pain. His need for family harmony will not be met simply by his wishing it or denying its absence. It can emerge only when he acknowledges the pain of its absence right now and becomes aware of how powerful this need is, not only for Grandma but also for him. Self-empathy would not only enable him to be present to Grandma; it would also offer him a tool for self-care in dealing with other painful situations. As he became aware of the urgency of his own needs, he could bring them to God in prayer. (See Chapter Five.)

Conclusion

Caregivers seek to pay attention to the concrete needs of the other. What they must remember is that listening to themselves helps them to better hear those they serve. The skills of focusing and self-empathy have been suggested as ways to become aware of unresolved issues that interfere with the ability to listen. As caregivers work actively with their anxiety, they may become clear about the underlying needs that prompt it. Are they insecure about their identity as ministers — do they need greater confidence? Do they become anxious when their parishioners are angry with them because they need acceptance? Are they worried when the connection seems to break down because they want to make a contribution to the other? As caregivers learn to focus on their feelings, they will get deeper insight if they seek to connect these feelings with underlying needs. It is not enough to simply identify feelings of anxiety: one must go on to uncover the needs that are causing the anxiety in a particular situation. What does one want to contribute? What seems to be preventing that from happening? These are the essential skills of self-empathy, which are just as important as the skills of empathy described in the last chapter. Having compassion for one-self when confronted with one's limitations and mistakes is indispens-able if one is to continue learning to hone one's skills as a pastoral care-giver.

In these first four chapters, I have presented the essential compo-nents of the caregiving relationship. Pastoral care that arises from prayer and leads back to prayer is pastoral care with God at its center. "Unless the LORD builds the house, those who build it labor in vain" (Ps. 127:1). God grants his gift of *koinonia* to all those who turn to him in prayer. As we learn to rely on God for our basic needs, we will turn to him for daily guidance. Listening to God is the first essential step for those who want to offer pastoral care. After listening to God in prayer, pastoral caregivers will also listen to those they seek to serve, hearing them with compassion and empathy. Finally, they will seek tools to help them discover when their own anxiety might impede their ability to be present to another. This final step leads inevitably back to the first, that of listening once again to God. "Cast all your anxieties on him, for he cares about you" (1 Peter 5:7). As caregivers listen in these three ways — to God, to the other, and to their inmost selves — they will learn to entrust themselves and all their work to God.

Five Prayers of Petition

The work of pastoral care is rooted in petitionary prayer. Prayer is our daily bread: it not only sustains our efforts to provide care for others; it is also our own basic sustenance. Before we can learn to intercede for others, we need to know how to pray for ourselves. We never grow beyond this need. As pastoral caregivers, we cannot give what we do not have, and all that we have depends upon our daily petition to God. We cannot credibly witness to God's love unless we ourselves are sustained by it. We cannot speak convincingly of God's grace in times of trial unless we have known it by the power of the Holy Spirit. Living by faith *means* living by prayer.

Prayers of petition focus on our needs. They are requests to God for healing or for reconciliation with one estranged from us. They seek the restoration of our families, where emotional wounds inflicted decades ago may still be felt. They express a yearning for an understanding of one who has harmed us, or perhaps an understanding of ourselves when we have hurt another. They are pleas to be granted a child, a job, a friend, a life partner. They implore that a depression will lift, that help will be found, that a slender thread of hope will not be taken away. They cry for peace, for safety, for deliverance from grinding poverty, for release from daily anxiety or from dread that makes the heart leaden. They are supplications for grace, for courage, or simply for the grit to get through the day at hand.

Prayer, according to Karl Barth, expresses our true freedom before God. Since God himself wills that we pray, prayer is obedience to God's command. Though we might think of petitionary prayer as arising solely from human need, Barth reminds us that our needs can lead us to stumble as often as they do to pray. They can lead us into futile attempts at self-help, to weak resignation, or to defiance of God. They do not necessarily lead to petition. The basis of prayer, therefore, lies not in ourselves but rather in God, whose freedom enables our own. We are given the freedom simply to ask for what we need. We pray because we are permitted, commanded, and enabled to do so by a power not our own. As Barth explains,

> The real basis of prayer is man's freedom before God, the God-given permission to pray which, because it is given by God, becomes a command and order and therefore a necessity. As he is created free before God, man is simply placed under the superior, majestic, and clear will of God. He is not, therefore, asked about his power or impotence, worthiness or unworthiness, disposition or indisposition, desire or lack of desire for prayer, but only whether it can be otherwise than that God's will shall be done by him and in him, and therefore whether he has not to pray irrespective of all possible objections and considerations. What God wills of him is simply that he shall pray to Him.[1]

This insight frees prayer from self-doubt on the one hand and perfectionism on the other. Anxiety about whether prayer will be effective or whether we are qualified has no place. If it is God's will that we pray, then we may and must do so. Our freedom to pray is God's gracious provision for our lives. It is the means by which we enter into communion with God so that our lives are grounded in divine love.

Prayers of petition inspire an attitude of watchfulness. We wait with eager longing for God to fulfill his promises (Luke 11:9-13), and we watch for the moment when we ourselves are called to act. Petitionary prayer is a kind of spiritual training. It equips us to discern the signals of God. A deepening takes place in us so that we cannot ask for peace without also working for peace. We cannot pray for reconciliation without striving for justice. We cannot pray for forgiveness without trying to address the breach between us and an estranged friend. We cannot pray for a neighbor in need without reaching out to her as the opportunity arises. We cannot pray for the poor while ignoring the conditions that make them poor. Prayer leads to action, not because it gives up on

---

1. Karl Barth, *Church Dogmatics*, III/4 (Edinburgh: T&T Clark, 1960), pp. 92-93.

God but because God does not give up on us. Through our prayer, God impels us in certain directions. As Anthony Bloom puts it, "A prayer makes sense only if it is lived."[2]

The Lord's Prayer

The Lord's Prayer, which Jesus taught his disciples, is essentially a prayer of petition. According to Calvin, it sets forth "all that [God] allows us to seek of him, all that is of benefit to us, all that we need ask."[3] Barth regards it in a similar way, saying, "We have good cause to remind ourselves again that the Lord's Prayer, apart from the address and the doxology, consists exclusively of pure petitions."[4] As *The Study Catechism* of the Presbyterian Church USA notes, the six petitions of the prayer are structured in two groups of three; the first group focuses on the glory of God and the second group on our salvation: "The first part involves our love for God; the second part, God's love for us."[5] *Lex orandi, lex credendi:* As we pray, so we believe. Praying shapes our faith, even as faith informs our prayer. The petitions of the Lord's Prayer guide us in what to ask for.

Since prayer is the wellspring of all pastoral care, we will have called upon God before initiating any pastoral conversation. As we prepare ourselves to listen to another, we become aware of our neediness, our anxiety, and our limitations. When God frees us to place all this before him, we await what we need from God's hand. As the Lord's Prayer determines both the form and the content of our petitions, each petition may be pondered in relation to pastoral care.

"Our Father, who art in heaven"

With the first petition, we align ourselves with Jesus Christ. Apart from him, we would have no access to God as our Father. Calvin explains it this way:

2. Anthony Bloom, *Beginning to Pray* (New York: Paulist Press, 1970), p. 59.

3. John Calvin, *Institutes of the Christian Religion,* Library of Christian Classics, vols. 20-21, ed. John T. McNeill, trans. Ford Lewis Battles (Philadelphia: Westminster Press, 1960), 3.20.36, p. 897.

4. Barth, *Church Dogmatics,* III/4, p. 97.

5. *The Study Catechism: Full Version* (Louisville: Witherspoon Press, Office of the General Assembly, PCUSA, 1998), p. 73.

For in calling God "Father" we assuredly put forth Christ's name. If we had not been adopted to Christ as children of grace, with what assurance would anyone have addressed God as Father? Who would have broken forth into such rashness as to appropriate to himself the honor of a child of God?[6]

Only through Jesus Christ as God's Son are we adopted as sons and daughters of God. While the Psalms call upon God with many names ("governor," "stronghold," "crag," "haven," "rock," "shield," "horn of salvation," "refuge," "shepherd," "king," "Lord," "God"), only three of them describe God as a father: "Father of the fatherless and protector of widows" (Ps. 68:5); "He shall cry to me, 'Thou art my Father, my God, and the Rock of my salvation'" (Ps. 89:26); and "As a father pities his children, so the LORD pities those who fear him" (103:13).[7] When Jesus teaches his disciples to call upon God as Father, he is inviting them into the intimacy of his own relationship with God. Those who have seen Jesus have seen the Father (John 14:8-9), for Jesus is the Beloved Son of God (Matt. 3:17; Mark 9:7; John 5:26).[8] Because we have seen Jesus' faithfulness on earth, we can trust his Father in heaven. The Father of our Lord Jesus Christ is the God of Israel, who "is merciful and gracious, slow to anger and abounding in steadfast love" (Ps. 103:8). The essential point for pastoral care is that we can trust this God with all of our needs. As *The Study Catechism* (PCUSA) explains, "Our opening address expresses our confidence that we rest securely in God's intimate care and that nothing on earth lies beyond the reach of God's grace."[9]

As we prepare for a pastoral conversation, we call upon the Father through the Son in the Spirit. Just as Christ mediates our prayers to the Father, so also Christ is the One through whom I will hear the needs of the other. I do not have to meet the other as if I were his Savior. I am not superior to him in any way. He is not the problem to which I am the solution. I should expect to receive a blessing from him even as he hopes for a blessing from me. We both stand in a position of

---

6. Calvin, *Institutes of the Christian Religion*, 3.20.36, p. 899.

7. C. Clifton Black, "The Education of Human Wanting," in *Character and Scripture: Moral Formation, Community, and Biblical Interpretation*, ed. William P. Brown (Grand Rapids: Eerdmans, 2002), p. 250.

8. Black, "The Education of Human Wanting," p. 250.

9. *The Study Catechism*, p. 73.

neediness, as children asking for the blessing of our Father. We are on the same plane. Even ordained priests who may be addressed as "Father" or "Mother" are given this title only as a sign of reverence for the office they hold. When the first petition is prayed, each person is simply a brother or sister addressing God as Father. Humanly created hierarchies fall away. We are all as little children. Barth comments,

> In prayer — and this is why it is commanded — all masks and camouflages may and must fall away. There are necessary and legitimate masks and camouflages. We all wear them. We all have definite roles to play in life, definite functions to exercise, definite services to render, in which we have in some way to "give" ourselves with more or less energy. But in prayer we must and may step out of our role. In prayer man does not perform a function or service. . . . All that remains is his need in relation to God.[10]

No matter what our role, we never grow beyond childlike reliance on the Father of our Lord Jesus Christ.

In addressing God as our Father, we also recall the communion of saints, all who ever have called upon this God or ever will. Even when we pray in our solitary room, the word "our" reminds us that we join our voice to the prayer of the generations. This awareness can be comforting when we feel burdened by the pastoral confidences we must carry. It ameliorates any sense of isolation we may feel. Why should our time and place be exempt from the anxieties of life? We share the same fear of death, remorse over sin, and care about our daily needs with Christians throughout the ages. In praying to "our Father," we are reminded that God has been sufficient for them and will be for us as well. And, as Martin Luther points out, we are reminded that God sustains all:

> It is not we who can sustain the Church, nor was it our forefathers, nor will it be our descendants. It was and is and will be the One who says: "I am with you alway, even unto the end of the world." . . . The Church would perish before our very eyes, and we with it (as we daily prove), were it not for that other Man who manifestly upholds the

---

10. Barth, *Church Dogmatics,* III/4, p. 98.

Church and us. This we can lay hold of and feel, even though we are loth to believe it, and we must needs give ourselves to the One. . . .[11]

Moreover, as Barth observes, the "we" of "our" Father is not limited to Christians alone, but expresses our solidarity with all peoples of the earth:

"We" do not form an exclusive circle. On the contrary, "we" are most intimately bound to the human world around us. "We" are united and made brethren among ourselves in order that we may be responsible for the world around us, representing our Lord among them and them before our Lord. The only advantage "we" have over the world around us is that we know that He is our Lord and theirs too, and that we may use the access to God which He has opened for both us and them.[12]

We petition God in solidarity with all who need God; therefore, our asking is never private or egotistical. Our prayers are inclusive, not exclusive, of the needs of others, even those who do not pray. We need not be ashamed of asking for what we need, for we ask on behalf of all creatures who look to God for help.

"Hallowed be thy name"

This petition lifts our hearts up to a holy God. It is placed at the beginning of the prayer because "it comprehends the goal and purpose of the whole prayer. The glory of God's name is the highest concern in all that we pray and do."[13] The hallowing of God's name acknowledges the infinite qualitative difference between God and sinful humankind. The name of Israel's God is considered so holy that it cannot be uttered. The four letters — YHWH — signify a sacred name, one that should not be spoken. When reading Scripture, a pious Jew will see the name "YHWH" on the page but will say the word "Lord." The name of God evokes awe because it is equivalent to God's essence and signifies his power and

---

11. Martin Luther (W.A. 54, 470, and 474f.), quoted in Barth, *Church Dogmatics,* I/2 (Edinburgh: T&T Clark, 1956), p. xi.

12. Barth, *Church Dogmatics,* III/4, p. 102.

13. *The Study Catechism,* p. 74.

majesty. Human beings are to approach God with this reverence. In the Lord's Prayer, we pray that God's name (and therefore God) will be held in reverence by all. Yet God alone guards the holiness of his name:

> Thus says the Lord God: It is not for your sake, O house of Israel, that I am about to act, but for the sake of my holy name, which you have profaned among the nations to which you came. And I will vindicate the holiness of my great name, which has been profaned among the nations. . . . (Ezek. 36:22-23)

God acts in history to vindicate the holiness of his name. This petition asks that we might participate in God's cause on earth by attesting to that holiness. It is a plea that all creation will hallow God's name, that God will be blessed, honored, and worshiped for who he is. God "in heaven" means a God beyond our powers of conception, one whose strength, beauty, and wisdom are not of this world. God transcends all creation, far beyond what we can know or imagine. When we contemplate the divine holiness, we perceive that God is not a power at our disposal, not a talisman carried about in our pockets or our "chum." In pastoral care, prayer without reverence is no prayer at all. It takes God's name in vain. Though God has given us access to himself through Jesus Christ, and though we are instructed to come to him as little children, we can never lose our sense of awe without losing the holiness, and therefore the reality, of God.

"Thy kingdom come"

The petition for God's kingdom to come is filled with longing and hope. It knows the heart's restlessness that finds refuge in God alone. Our hearts are restless — not only *until* they rest in God (Augustine), but also *because* they rest in God (Jürgen Moltmann). This petition expresses a longing for God to be all in all. It cries out for the fulfillment of what began in the resurrection of Jesus. In this petition, *The Study Catechism* (PCUSA) explains, "we are asking God to come and rule among us through faith, love and justice — and not through any one of them without the others."[14] The petition not only bids us to suffer with those who

---

14. *The Study Catechism*, p. 74.

suffer but also to yearn for an end to death and sin. Those who live by this prayer will not be complacent about the evils of this world. They will actively work for an end to injustice, cruelty, and greed, both in themselves and in the institutions that shape them. They are called to attest to the myriad dimensions of the one great salvation: God's works of mercy, healing, reconciliation, and peace. For it is finally God himself who will bring about his kingdom at the end of time, when God will be all in all. Until then, we with all of creation groan in travail like a woman in labor (Rom. 8:22-23), beseeching God for the fulfillment of our hope. This petition keeps our hearts open in even the most depressing circumstances. If God is the bringer of his kingdom, we may hope for it in every situation. We may trust that every state of affairs, no matter how grave, can be transformed by God's gracious action.

"Thy will be done on earth as it is in heaven"

This petition commits us to seek God's will in every circumstance of life. We know that God wills our good, but seldom do we know what is in fact good for us. As we are faced with crucial decisions, we seek to align our will with God's. We ask God to reorient our desires so that they will match his perfect will. For of course not all desires are good: "The heart is deceitful above all things, and desperately corrupt; who can understand it?" (Jer. 17:9). Just as we are incapable of creating, redeeming, or sustaining ourselves, so also are we incapable of purifying our own hearts. Nor can we simply will ourselves into new desires. Yet it is not required that our desires be pure before we pray. We approach God in prayer, as in all things, *simul justus et peccator,* sinful and yet justified by grace. Our impure desires, we may trust, are purified by the intercession of Christ.

Rather than judging our desires, we pour them out before God, knowing that he will sanctify them: "We ask for the grace to do God's will on earth in the way that it is done in heaven — gladly and from the heart."[15] With a deadly cancer growing in his body, Dale Aukerman opened a Chinese fortune cookie and read that his "deepest wish would be fulfilled." His immediate thought was, "Yes, the wish that I would continue to live much longer with my loved ones." Yet anguished

---

15. *The Study Catechism,* p. 75.

prayer had already taught him that this was not his deepest wish. Deeper even than his desire to live was his desire to live for God's glory and the coming of God's kingdom. He writes, "With that as my deepest desire I can look confidently to God to help me toward its fulfillment, whether my remaining time on earth is very short or very long."[16] His desires had been sanctified in a crucible of suffering. His heart had aligned with God's will. A heart sanctified by the love of Christ is a heart that seeks first God's kingdom.

Pastoral care thus seeks to embody a nonanxious acceptance of whatever comes from God's hand. It seeks trust in God in situations of dire need. This trust is not a matter of weak resignation but rather one of confidence in God's good will for our lives. We learn the sufficiency of God's grace even as we walk through the valley of the shadow of death. This is the wisdom of the sanctified heart.

As we can see, the first three petitions of the Lord's Prayer situate life in its proper context. God's holy name, God's kingdom, and God's will determine all that we have and are. We ask for what only God can give, and we strive to live in accord with what we ask. We seek to accept what we receive from God's hand. As we do so, we adopt God's cause of attesting to and mediating his goodness into the fullness of life on earth. Barth elaborates:

> If we pray, "Hallowed be thy name. Thy kingdom come, thy will be done," we place ourselves at God's side, nothing less than that. God invites us to join his designs and his action. . . . All our entreaties presuppose that we ask to participate in God's cause.[17]

Only after we have aligned ourselves with God's purpose on earth are we to bring our particular needs before God in prayer.

"Give us this day our daily bread"

The next three petitions ask for what we need to sustain our lives. Daily sustenance, forgiveness, preservation from temptation, and deliverance

---

16. Dale Aukerman, "Living with Dying," *Messenger* (Elgin, Ill.: Church of the Brethren), April 1998, p. 16.

17. Karl Barth, *Prayer,* 2d ed., ed. Don E. Saliers (Louisville: Westminster/John Knox Press, 1985), p. 48.

from evil are the staples of our life before God. The imperative form of these petitions is not importunate, for it captures the trust of children toward a loving father. Children secure in their parents' love do not worry about being demanding; they simply ask for what they need. They experience neither shame nor fear in approaching their parents with their desires. Through Jesus Christ we are given the childlike freedom to ask for what we need. Because Christ in his office as Mediator joins our prayers to his own, the prayers coming to God's ear are quite literally from Christ himself. Moreover, because God draws us through Christ into the communion of the Holy Trinity, our freedom to ask is grounded in God's own desire to include us in his life and work.

Like all creatures, Christians need their daily bread — that is, they need their lives to be sustained by God: "The eyes of all look to thee, and thou givest them their food in due season. Thou openest thy hand, thou satisfiest the desire of every living thing" (Ps. 145:15-16). Just as we pray to *our* Father, so also we ask for *our* bread, not for *my* bread alone. The petition presupposes that we ask as a community, on behalf of all. While there is no shame in asking for what we need, we are cautioned against asking for the frivolous. The petition joins our prayer with the prayers of the wretched of the earth. The cavernous abyss of desire, to which we are predisposed by our avaricious hearts, and which is magnified by our North American consumer-oriented context, is implicitly judged by this word "our" and thereby held in check.

What does the petition mean by "daily bread"? In Luther's *Small Catechism*, as Barth reminds us, the reformer lists the following: "food, drink, clothes, shoes, houses, farms, fields, lands, money, property, a good marriage, good children, honest and faithful public servants, a just government, favorable weather (neither too hot nor too cold!), health, honors, good friends, loyal neighbors."[18] Barth comments,

> That is no small order! This list contains the necessities and requirements for the life of a German "bourgeois" farmer in the sixteenth century. And nothing hinders us from interpreting and expanding it according to the needs of our time and of our individual situations. We are certainly permitted to think of our daily bread in the wide sense of the term. Nevertheless, I wish to emphasize that it

18. Barth, *Prayer,* p. 69.

is advisable for us not to lose sight of the original word "bread" in all its simplicity.[19]

Naturally we desire shoes and clothing, property and children, even favorable weather. But Barth's comment reminds us not to take our basic physical sustenance for granted. It is God who sustains our life at its most fundamental level: "God commands us to pray each day for all that we need and no more, so that we will learn to rely completely on God."[20]

Jesus assures us that our basic needs will be met and that we are not to be anxious about them: "Therefore I tell you, do not be anxious about your life, what you shall eat or what you shall drink, nor about your body, what you shall put on. Is not life more than food, and the body more than clothing?" (Matt. 6:25). What is the "more" that Jesus refers to if not himself, the "bread of heaven"? When we pray for our daily bread, we ask not only for physical sustenance but also for spiritual sustenance. We can have material abundance and yet live in misery if we lack a living relationship with God. Jesus Christ is the manna that comes down from heaven, the Bread of Life that gives us the strength we need each day. Here is an obvious allusion to the Eucharist, whereby Christ nourishes our souls as bread nourishes our bodies. As we take Christ into ourselves, he becomes the animating center of our lives. We abide "in him" even as he abides "in us." In asking for this bread, we acknowledge our need for faith and hope as well as for food and drink.

The "daily bread" that sustains pastoral caregivers is the freedom from anxiety that trusts God's providence to give what is truly needed. If the day's own trouble is sufficient, pastoral caregivers need to ask for the courage to face that, and for the faith not to worry about tomorrow. When they pray this petition, they are reminded that God is sufficient for guiding, caring, and providing sustenance for them and for those they serve. They do not internalize the distress of those in need, but rather entrust each person to God.

---

19. Barth, *Prayer,* p. 69.
20. *The Study Catechism,* p. 76.

"Forgive us our debts, as we forgive our debtors"

This petition presupposes that we are sinners who stand in need of daily forgiveness. Since we owe everything to God, our indebtedness is incalculable. But this debt grows exponentially when we add the weight of sin. We fail to use rightly the inestimable gift of life. We sin against God by squandering our time, ignoring a neighbor's need, and telling lies. We are greedy for gain, envy our sister's good fortune, and foolishly act as if we need no one, least of all God. We anxiously hoard what we've been given. We stand in judgment of others as if we were their Creator and Judge. We fail to love and honor God as we ought. We cannot justify ourselves, for each of us fails to fulfill God's law. "For whoever keeps the whole law but fails in one point has become guilty of all of it" (James 2:10).

Our need for forgiveness becomes obvious when we attend to the evil hidden in our hearts. When we are honest with ourselves, we know that even when we keep one commandment, we fail to keep another. Moreover, none of us can cleanse ourselves of evil thoughts and desires. Jesus says, "You have heard that it was said, 'You shall not commit adultery.' But I say to you that every one who looks at a woman lustfully has already committed adultery with her in his heart" (Matt. 5:27-28). It does no good to try to justify ourselves before a God "to whom all hearts are open, all desires known, and from whom no secrets are hid."[21] Moreover, "if we say that we have no sin, we deceive ourselves, and the truth is not in us. If we confess our sins, he [God] is faithful and just, and will forgive our sins and cleanse us from all unrighteousness" (1 John 1:8-9). Thus a plea for forgiveness of our sins is a daily need.

However, the plea for forgiveness as Jesus taught it involves us in a difficult obligation. When we ask God to forgive us our debts, we also pledge to forgive the debts of those who have harmed us. While we cannot forgive their guilt as God does, we acknowledge our willingness not to hold any anger, vindictiveness, or resentment against them. Listen to what Calvin says:

> This, rather, is our forgiveness: willingly to cast from the mind wrath, hatred, desire for revenge, and voluntarily to banish to obliv-

21. *The Book of Common Prayer* (New York: Oxford University Press, 1979), p. 323.

ion the remembrance of injustice. . . . If we retain feelings of hatred in our hearts, if we plot revenge and ponder any occasion to cause harm, and even if we do not try to get back into our enemy's good graces, by every sort of good office deserve well of them, and commend ourselves to them, by this prayer we entreat God not to forgive our sins.[22]

Here the vertical and the horizontal axes — the connection between ourselves and God, and the connection between ourselves and our neighbors — intersect. Our forgiveness of each other is placed within the larger context of God's forgiveness of us. When we focus on all that God has done and continues to do to forgive our sin, then any sin committed against us is greatly relativized. Rather than fueling our resentment and nursing our grievances toward someone who has injured us, we are to gaze upon God's mercy regarding our own sins. Thereby we are given power to do what otherwise would be impossible — namely, to forgive the injustice done to us.[23] *The Study Catechism* (PCUSA) expresses it this way: "We ask that we will not delight in doing evil, nor in avenging any wrong, but that we will survive all cruelty without bitterness and overcome evil with good, so that our hearts will be knit together with the mercy and forgiveness of God."[24]

If we do not immediately receive the power to forgive, at least we can pray for the willingness to forgive. The daily prayer for forgiveness opens our hearts a crack toward those who have wronged us. In the last year of his life, C. S. Lewis wrote, "Last week, while at prayer, I suddenly discovered — or felt as I did — that I had really forgiven someone I have been trying to forgive for over thirty years. Trying, and praying that I might."[25] Because God's forgiveness of us is linked to our forgiveness of others, we are left to ponder our solidarity in sin with those who have harmed us. Lewis went on to say, "It also seemed to me that forgiving (that man's cruelty) and being forgiven (my resentment) were the very

22. Calvin, *Institutes of the Christian Religion*, 3.20.45, p. 912.

23. Cf. Deborah van Deusen Hunsinger, "Forgiving Abusive Parents," in *Forgiveness and Truth*, ed. Alistair McFadyen and Marcel Sarot (New York: T&T Clark, 2001), pp. 71-98.

24. *The Study Catechism*, p. 77.

25. C. S. Lewis, *Letters to Malcolm: Chiefly on Prayer* (New York: Harcourt, Brace & World, 1963), pp. 106-7.

same thing."[26] Barth captures the relative weight of these two factors in relation to each other:

> For those who know that they are cast upon the mercy of God, that they cannot exist without the divine forgiveness . . . cannot do otherwise than to forgive . . . those who have offended against them (we are all offenders, debtors one to another, and we are so daily). Even if the debts of our offenders appear to us to be very heavy, they are always infinitely lighter than ours with God. How could we, who ourselves are such great debtors, hope to have the divine forgiveness if we did not of ourselves wish to do this small thing, namely, to forgive those who have offended us? The hope one entertains for oneself necessarily opens the heart, the feeling, and the judgment, in respect to others.[27]

Those who live by this prayer know that peace comes by contemplating the mercy received from God's hand. Resentment is hard to keep alive when the heart is filled with gratitude.

"And lead us not into temptation, but deliver us from evil"

This petition reminds us of our limits apart from God. We need God's help in every trial and challenge of our lives. When tempted by the enticements of evil, we are to entrust ourselves to God and rely on his strength. Since our fallen wills tend toward evil, we must pray daily to be delivered: "We ask God to protect us from our own worst impulses and from all external powers of destruction in the world."[28] Much of the time we have scant awareness of the powers that hold us captive. Often we are only semiconscious of our sins, both personal and corporate. One of the chief marks of sin is that it obscures our perception of it, like a fox that covers its tracks.

What are the temptations from which pastoral caregivers in particular need deliverance? Pastoral caregivers may pray for deliverance from despair when they accompany those who suffer, from hardness of heart as a way to protect themselves from pain, and from using the

26. Lewis, *Letters to Malcolm*, p. 107.
27. Barth, *Prayer*, p. 76.
28. *The Study Catechism*, p. 77.

caregiving relationship as a way to gain power over others. How do the hospice volunteer, the hospital chaplain, the church deacon, and the local pastor retain a wellspring of hope in the midst of sorrow and death? As pastoral caregivers accompany others through the valley of the shadow of death, there is no conceivable way that they can be delivered from evil by their own power. Those who attempt to uproot evil by their own strength are vulnerable either to hubris or to despair. Medieval theologians warned against looking the devil in the eye. One should never look at the devil directly, they counseled, but over his shoulder toward Christ.

Those who voluntarily enter into the suffering of others on a daily basis need spiritual fortification. Feelings of helplessness grow easily in soil that is not nourished with reminders of God's sovereignty. Pastoral caregivers cannot dispense with daily meditation on God's grace to sustain them in hope. Saint Paul's exhortation to the church at Philippi is very much to the point: "Finally, brethren, whatever is true, whatever is honorable, whatever is just, whatever is pure, whatever is lovely, whatever is gracious, if there is any excellence, if there is anything worthy of praise, think about these things" (Phil. 4:8). While these characteristics might be found among the saints of God, they are quintessentially present in God himself. God alone is true, honorable, and just. God alone is pure, lovely, full of grace, and worthy of praise. Pondering the excellences of God renews the human spirit. Those whose work plunges them daily into suffering need to be refreshed with reminders of God's grace in its manifold forms. They will not be blind to the presence of evil, nor foolishly deny it. Instead they will learn to fight evil by building up the good, by focusing on those things worthy of praise.

Focusing on God's goodness is the antidote not only to despair but also to hardness of heart. While some may succumb to feelings of helplessness, others may refuse to admit another's pain into their heart. If *koinonia* is the aim of pastoral care, the caregiver needs to be fully present. Yet how does one keep one's heart open when another's suffering is excruciating? When a pastoral caregiver accompanies a dying woman the age of his own wife or witnesses the affliction of a small child who resembles his own, how is it possible to keep anxiety at bay? One can develop a spiritual version of what is called "medical student's disease": every malady is fearfully anticipated to strike close to home.

Hardening one's heart toward the other seems to promise a way of avoiding one's own vulnerability.

When we pray for God's deliverance from evil, we are reminded of God's goodness and power to save. The key to such deliverance is found in the doxology that follows the petition: "for thine is the kingdom, the power, and the glory forever." We cannot contemplate evil — whether that of the world or of our own hearts — apart from faith in the kingdom, power, and glory of God. As mere mortals, we cannot look the devil in the face and survive. But as we ponder the goodness of God's kingdom, the extent of God's power, and the majesty of God's glory, we may be sustained with hope and courage. "We give God thanks and praise for the kingdom more powerful than all enemies, for the power perfected in the weakness of love, and for the glory that includes our well-being and that of the whole creation, both now and to all eternity."[29]

A third temptation from which pastoral caregivers might pray for deliverance is of a different sort. It is the temptation to use their position of trust as a platform for gaining power over others. In its most damaging form, they take advantage of another's vulnerability through sexual exploitation.[30] Perhaps they seek a caregiving role in order to enjoy the pseudo-intimacy of hearing another's secrets. Rather than respecting the inviolability of another's soul, they voyeuristically pry into the other's history. Or perhaps the caregiver might enjoy being seen as the "giving" one or the one who "knows better," who can offer guidance to the less enlightened.

In his study of such phenomena, Adolf Guggenbuehl-Craig examines the "shadow" of those who seek to work in the "helping" professions. The Jungian concept of the shadow refers to all those characteristics that we would rather disavow, those attributes that conflict with our ideals and aspirations. "The most difficult thing for everyone," says Guggenbuehl-Craig, "is to become conscious of the workings of the archetypal shadow, of one's own destructive and self-destructive tendencies, and to experience them in oneself rather than only in projections."[31]

29. *The Study Catechism*, p. 78.
30. Cf. Marie Fortune, *Is Nothing Sacred?* (San Francisco: Harper, 1989).
31. Adolf Guggenbuehl-Craig, *Power in the Helping Professions* (New York: Spring Publications, 1971), p. 124.

When we see our own destructive tendencies "only in projections," we perceive others to be struggling with issues that we refuse to acknowledge in ourselves. Thus *others* might exploit someone's vulnerability, but we never would. *Others* might enjoy the gratification of having power over others, but we are dedicated to equality and mutuality. What is required to prevent this kind of thinking and behavior is a kind of rigorous honesty. Not only do we need to take time for self-reflection, but we also need relationships with friends and colleagues who will be honest with us. Moreover, ongoing supervision of our work is essential, especially in the early years, and regular collegial consultation is needed throughout our lives. Sometimes we may learn the most from our enemies. They may perceive some denied aspect of our character that it is essential for us to know about. Similarly, those who annoy us may be expressing openly something we wish to disavow in ourselves. The key is to notice those situations in which we are particularly agitated. An agitated response often indicates that a raw nerve has been struck. Something has hit close to home. Small groups where these kinds of situations can be explored in trust are indispensable for those engaging in pastoral care.

Christians attest to a divine power that shines forth in human weakness. Pastoral caregivers are able to acknowledge their brokenness because they have access to a God who gives them strength when they are stretched beyond their limits. They can acknowledge their fallenness because they know God's mercy, forgiveness, and grace. They don't need to deny their "shadow" side because they know God's radical acceptance of them as both sinful and redeemed children of God.

Only as we are given God's daily provision — food, strength, hope, guidance, forgiveness, and deliverance — are we equipped for the task of providing care for others. For those whom we serve need what we ourselves need — to be directed to God in the midst of life's temptations and hardships. As pastoral caregivers, we not only call upon God each day ourselves but also direct others toward God and teach them how to pray on their own behalf. While the primary work of pastoral care is arguably that of intercessory prayer, it is also important to teach others to petition God for their most basic needs.

Teaching People to Pray

When we cease to pray, we lose our living connection to God. We may speak *about* God, but if we no longer speak *to* God, our conversation becomes meaningless. Real knowledge of God involves the whole person. In his book *The Tragic Sense of Life*, Miguel De Unamuno writes,

> Those who say that they believe in God and yet neither love nor fear Him do not in fact believe in Him but in those who have taught them that God exists. . . . Those who believe that they believe in God, but without any passion in their heart, without anguish of mind, without uncertainty, without doubt, without an element of despair even in their consolation, believe only in the God-Idea, not in God.[32]

God cannot be known without being loved, and love for God grows only in the context of relationship. When we come before God, we bring with us all our longings and fears. We submit them to God in confidence and hope. We entrust them to God's greater wisdom and power.

Prayer begins by giving voice to the desires of our hearts. Though they may be impure, God will take them as they are. Who can transform them but God alone? It is better to start with what we want than to be overly scrupulous about our prayers. God is the One to whom all desires are known. Knowing our desires better than we do, God is not deceived by pretense or dishonesty. How do we know our true desire? How can we see ourselves as God sees us? To know ourselves truly is reserved for the kingdom of heaven. Only then shall we see "face to face." In this life we are often self-deceived. And yet we must begin somewhere.

In his book entitled *Into the Light: A Simple Way to Pray with the Sick and the Dying*, Ron DelBene develops a way to identify the desires of the heart. In three steps he introduces a contemporary version of the ancient practice known as the breath prayer. A form of "praying without ceasing," the breath prayer is so called because it can be uttered in a single breath. Perhaps best known is the "Jesus Prayer," a petition that has

---

32. Miguel Unamuno, *The Tragic Sense of Life*, trans. J. E. Crawford Flitch (New York: Dover Publications, 1954), p. 193, quoted by Don Saliers in *The Soul in Paraphrase* (New York: Seabury Press, 1988), p. 21.

been prayed daily by Christians for hundreds of years: "Lord Jesus Christ, Son of God, have mercy on me, a sinner." DelBene has taken the basic concept of the breath prayer and applied it to his work with the sick and dying.

People who are sick need a way to pray during their last weeks of life, and families need a way to pray with and for them. After learning about the particular struggles of the dying person to whom he was sent, DelBene explains, he would initiate a conversation like this:

> "Carl, before I leave, I'd like to share something with you that I've found helpful, and so have a lot of other people. It's a simple little thing known as the breath prayer. Tell me, what do you usually call God? Do you say 'Father'? 'Creator'? 'Jesus'? 'Shepherd' . . . ?"
>
> "Just 'Lord,' I guess."
>
> "Fine. If the Lord were standing in front of you right now and asking, 'Carl, what do you want' — what would you say?"
>
> He closed his eyes for a time.
>
> I repeated, "If the Lord were standing in front of you right now and asking, 'Carl, what do you want' — what would you say?"
>
> His eyes blinked open and without hesitation he said, "Lead me to the light."
>
> "Okay, now let's put that together with what you normally call God and make a little prayer out of it. 'Lead me to the light, O Lord.'"[33]

This kind of conversation helps people identify what they need and form it into a breath prayer. Those who are afraid of death might find themselves praying for trust — "Let me trust you in all things, O God" — while those who are worried about their children might entrust them to God: "Surround my children with your love, O Lord." The breath prayer helps people focus on God. It allows them to address the unfinished business of their lives as they prepare for the gift of eternal life with God.

DelBene likens preparing for death to preparing for childbirth. A mother-to-be can be helped by a coach as she labors to bring forth her

---

33. Ron DelBene, *Into the Light: A Simple Way to Pray with the Sick and the Dying* (Nashville: The Upper Room, 1988), p. 30.

child from the womb into the world. Similarly, a dying person can be helped in leaving this world and entering the next. Though DelBene's primary work has been with the dying, he has also worked with their families. Here he has also developed a simple but effective way of proceeding. He asks family members to envision what it means to say good-bye to their loved one and then assists them in doing so. He coaches them through four basic steps. First, they take the hand of their loved one and call to mind a favorite memory, some moment of shared joy. Next, they ask forgiveness for any hurt they have caused their loved one during their life together. Then they release the other by forgiving him from their heart. Finally, they say good-bye.[34]

At all times DelBene points the reader toward the person's life and being in God. He tells the story of one encounter with a comatose man who had suffered a serious head injury. Knowing how taxing it can be to concentrate on anything at all when one is so sick, DelBene told the man it was all right if he couldn't remember the whole Lord's Prayer. It would be sufficient, he said, if the man remembered the first two words: "Our Father." Months later, after he had come out of his coma, this man told DelBene that it had been enough just to remember these two words. He emphasized how much this had helped him.[35] These two words had given him what he needed in an otherwise terrifying experience. DelBene elaborates on this kind of comfort: "To pray is to raise the mind and heart to God, to reach out to a God who promises: 'I am with you always' (Matt. 28:20). The promise for those who are ill is this: they will never be alone with their anxiety or fear or suffering. God will be with them."[36]

The utter simplicity of the breath prayer means that even those who are very ill, impaired, or easily distracted can pray. The homebound are interconnected through a hidden web of prayer as they pray with and for one another. DelBene also teaches young children their parents' breath prayer and encourages them to pray it throughout the day. He also gives nurses and chaplains their patients' breath prayer so that it can be prayed during times of trauma or crisis. One nurse thanked DelBene for giving her something concrete to offer when a pa-

34. DelBene, *Into the Light,* p. 108.
35. DelBene, *Into the Light,* pp. 53-54.
36. DelBene, *Into the Light,* p. 32.

tient was disconnected from life support. Usually overcome with feelings of helplessness and grief, she found strength and comfort by offering the patient's breath prayer as he or she passed from this life. Through his attentiveness to a variety of concrete situations like these, DelBene helps readers to imagine ways of building up the life of a congregation who pray for themselves and for each other.

Conclusion

Those who offer pastoral care will soon burn out emotionally and spiritually if their own lives are not undergirded by prayer. The difficult work of being present to others is not possible apart from dependence upon God's own presence. Those who drink from the well of prayer will have a reliable spring of refreshment from which to draw. Praying the Lord's Prayer reconnects them with a yearning for God's name to be glorified in all that they do. Such a yearning fuels their work not only by offering inspiration but also by giving direction to daily decisions. It reminds them that God alone sustains their life. They turn to God not only for today's bread but also for forgiveness of yesterday's sins and deliverance from tomorrow's harm. Simone Weil observes that as a template for prayer, "the Our Father contains all possible petitions; we cannot conceive of any prayer not already contained in it. It is to prayer what Christ is to humanity."[37]

While the Lord's Prayer joins us with all the people of God in a common voice, we also need ways to express the unique prayer of our hearts. Essentially this is a matter of giving voice to whatever troubles us and whatever gives us joy. We take our celebration and our mourning to God, our most urgent requests and our most persistent yearnings. In times of crisis and loss, calling out to God in a single breath prayer may grant courage and hope. Pastoral caregivers who use the breath prayer themselves can offer it as a form that may help others in times of great need. The essential point is not providing the form itself, but rather finding a way to support others in identifying their core needs, so that they may speak in their own voice out of the fullness of their hearts.

37. Simone Weil, *Waiting for God,* trans. Emma Craufurd (New York: G. P. Putnam's Sons, 1951), pp. 226-27.

Six Prayers of Intercession

Pastoral caregivers seek to discern the longings of the people they serve and to bring them to God in prayer. They listen to stories of struggle and hope in a particular way. In the midst of the other's emotional turmoil, they strive to hear the soul's basic need. Bonds are forged when the pastoral caregiver accurately perceives the other's feelings and needs. Spiritual communion occurs when those longings are taken to God in prayer. "No matter what objections there may be, it simply could not be any other way," Dietrich Bonhoeffer says. "Christians may and should pray together to God in their own words when they desire to live together under the Word of God."[1] God alone is sufficient for all human need. Yet strength and courage are granted in and through the spiritual fellowship of the church. Life-giving *koinonia* with God and one another occurs when the community's needs are taken to God in prayer.

For the pastoral caregiver, prayer is not an afterthought or a convenient exit strategy when meeting with a person in need. Prayer is integral to the interaction. The pastoral caregiver's listening is aimed toward prayer. What is at stake for this person in light of the Gospel? What does she need in order to face the challenges before her? Where does Scripture offer guidance, hope, inspiration, or wisdom? Moralistic instruction is eschewed as the caregiver listens for how the other is actually addressed by God. Trusting that there is a word that will speak directly to the person's heart, the caregiver will be drawn to prayer as a deer seeks streams of fresh water (Ps. 42:1).

1. Bonhoeffer, *Life Together* (Minneapolis: Augsburg/Fortress, 1996), p. 69.

In prayer the church learns to give voice to its needs. In prayer the church takes delight in the Lord and receives the desires of its heart (Ps. 37:4). Accordingly, Christ cannot use the church if it does not spend time with him in prayer. Jesus Christ challenges, comforts, and guides his people through ministers who offer care in his name. They find themselves included in an ongoing history between the other and God. A story is unfolding in their lives whose central character is God and whose plot is salvation. Caregivers are woven into that narrative. Every pastoral conversation has a sacramental quality, even when what takes place seems on one level to be ordinary and uneventful. Christ's hidden presence transfigures the encounter, though its full significance may not be grasped.[2]

Every pastoral visit instantiates the "communion of saints," confessed by the Creed. The one who gives care and the one who receives it are bound together in the Spirit. They share a common baptism and a common calling. Both are sinners in need of grace. There is no superiority of one over the other. A Christian who bears witness to Christ is one beggar telling another where to find bread. Trust grows as struggles are shared. The "communion of saints" grows to be deeper than any other bond. *The Study Catechism* of the Presbyterian Church (USA) makes this plain:

> All those who live in union with Christ, whether on earth or with God in heaven, are "saints." Our communion with Christ makes us members one of another. As by his death he removed our separation from God, so by his Spirit he removes all that divides us from each other. Breaking down every wall of hostility, he makes us, who are many, one body in himself. The ties that bind us in Christ are deeper than any other human relationship.[3]

This communion may not always be apparent. Like other mysteries of faith, it is in some sense still hidden with Christ in God (Col. 3:3). Yet it is attested to by the Creed and imparted by the Spirit.

The caregiver's intercessions for the other can be the pivot on

---

2. Robert Jenson, "Story and Promise in Pastoral Care," *Pastoral Psychology* 26, no. 2 (Winter 1977): 119.

3. *The Study Catechism: Full Version* (Louisville: Witherspoon Press, Office of the General Assembly, PCUSA, 1998), p. 42.

which the whole interchange between them turns. Here the real drama takes place, as human hearts open up to God. Yet the caregiver's prayers need not be especially moving, beautiful, or dramatic. They need only be sincere requests based on the caregiver's discernment of the other's need. Karl Barth expresses this powerfully:

> It [prayer] does not have to be beautiful or edifying, logically coherent or theologically correct. Neither formally, materially, nor methodically does it have to display any kind of art. Its formation can be determined only by its own inner law. Where man is concerned only with God, he knows that he needs no alien art but must capitulate with all his arts.[4]

Intercession focuses on *God*. Intercession does not worry about saying the right thing or about being eloquent or wise. It merely brings a request to God. It is not a conversation with the other about God but a conversation with God in the other's hearing. Intercession knows that "prayer is not prayer if it is addressed to anyone but God."[5] It does not try to affect its human listeners. The prayer itself is not an attempt to help, edify, or instruct the other. Still less is it an opportunity for camouflaged preaching. It is a request for grace, not a tool of manipulation. Barth makes this point powerfully:

> Prayer as a demonstration of faith, as disguised preaching, as an instrument of edification, is obviously not prayer at all. . . . Even as common prayer, it cannot take place at all . . . on a human front or with thought of a human opposite, but only as orientated toward God. . . . The only thing that counts is that he [the pray-er] shall really be concerned with God and with a request addressed to Him. It may well be that he can only sigh, stammer, and mutter. But so long as it is a request brought before God, God will hear it and understand it, and He will accept it . . . as right, as the prayer demanded by Him, as an act of obedience, infinitely preferring it to the sublimest liturgy which does not fulfill this condition.[6]

4. Barth, *Church Dogmatics*, III/4 (Edinburgh: T&T Clark, 1960), p. 88.
5. Barth, *Church Dogmatics*, III/4, p. 88.
6. Barth, *Church Dogmatics*, III/4, p. 88.

Intercession remains a mystery, like the Spirit, which blows where it will. It may be that one can only sigh, stammer, and mutter. No matter. What counts is being present to others, entering their situations, listening for their needs, and bringing them to God.

Intercessory Prayer and Emotional Connectedness

Shared prayer is often experienced as a moment of intimacy. That may be one reason why it is sometimes avoided. It may seem too threatening. When persons join together in prayer, they are emotionally vulnerable. Experienced pastors can attest to a depth of personal engagement in praying with individuals and families. They are not detached; they take the emotional risks involved. When pastoral caregivers pray with complete strangers (as they do in hospice and hospital chaplaincy), they too open themselves up to an unusual degree of emotional intimacy.

Pastoral care requires a measure of authenticity. It needs to be comfortable with feelings, both their expression and their reception. Sentimentality and emotional distance, twin but opposing dangers, are as deadly in pastoral care as they are in preaching.

In *The Need for Words*, Patsy Rodenburg points out how damaging sentimentality can be:

> The danger of sentimentality is that it is a barrier to genuine feeling. It blocks the need to speak because it is so inauthentic. We carry with us a host of caring words and phrases that coat and dull real expressions of pain, rage, joy, and delight. . . . It is as though we can talk with some feeling, feign instant familiarity without looking at the true intentions and beliefs behind the word.[7]

Such a "host of caring words" is immediately felt as disingenuous. People know instinctively not to open up to someone who speaks in this way. Flannery O'Connor observed, "Sentimentality is to religion what pornography is to love." Pornography violates love as sentimentality discredits faith.

---

7. Patsy Rodenburg, *The Need for Words* (New York: Routledge, 1993), pp. 70-71.

Being emotionally inaccessible can produce the same result as being sentimental. People are loath to share their pain with someone whose interest is detached or whose questions seem stereotypical. Only genuine interest will elicit sharing from the heart. When a caregiver risks sharing his true response with the other, a connection is often made. When he speaks from felt conviction, he is likely to elicit those things that matter most to the other person. In his book *Beginning to Pray*, Anthony Bloom writes, "Whenever I speak, I speak with all the conviction and belief which is in me. . . . It's not the words themselves that are important but reaching down to the level of people's convictions. This is the basis of communication, this is where we really meet one another."[8] If a caregiver is cut off from this level of personal conviction, his words are likely to be superficial and his prayers lifeless. Those in need will sense this and tacitly agree not to expose their souls.

John Patton is a pastoral theologian who has written extensively about pastoral counseling. In one of his books he describes an experience of unusual emotional connectedness that arose from personal authenticity. A thirty-year-old woman, "Joanne," was seeing him for pastoral counseling. She was discouraged and tired, and suffering from a virus she had been unable to shake. She described her loneliness, her grief over the loss of a colleague through a slow, painful illness, and her fear of her own death and the eventual death of her parents. Patton wanted Joanne to become emotionally more connected to what she was saying. So he asked her to sit back in her chair and allow herself simply to feel what she was feeling. She began to sob. Eventually she gave words to her feelings. In response, Patton writes,

> I became aware of my own sadness. I don't think at this point I knew what the sadness was about. It was clear to me that as she began to feel better, my own pain got worse. . . . I shared with her a fantasy that had come to me as she had moved up out of her despair. . . . In my fantasy I went to a wise therapist/friend for supervision. Instead of presenting "a case," I put down my tape recorder and cried for forty-five minutes. . . . The session ended with Joanne coming over, hugging me, and hoping I would feel better.[9]

8. Anthony Bloom, *Beginning to Pray* (New York: Paulist Press, 1970), p. 14.

9. John Patton, *Pastoral Counseling: A Ministry of the Church* (Nashville: Abingdon Press, 1983), pp. 30-32.

This story strikes a note of unusual empathy and emotional attunement. From a psychological point of view, Patton and Joanne were separate beings with their own unique histories. Yet, from a spiritual point of view, they were members of a common body. As Patton empathized with Joanne, he entered into an experience of loneliness, sorrow, and fear. Together they shared a common grief over the brevity of human life and the painful reality of loss. As Joanne began to feel better, Patton began to feel worse. She had the experience of another human being taking her pain to heart, entering into it palpably, even to the point of tears. She received the healing that comes when one is connected to another human being who sees and shares one's pain. In the midst of these psychodynamics, the two of them glimpsed a significant spiritual reality: "When one member suffers, all suffer together" (1 Cor. 12:26).

The Christ who mediates intercessory prayer to God and mediates God's grace in return is also the power of spiritual connection or *koinonia* among those who pray. "Where two or three are gathered in my name," Jesus promises, "there am I in the midst of them" (Matt. 18:20). This promise enables caregivers to intercede for others with confidence. As Bonhoeffer notes, "All our fear of one another, all our inhibitions about praying freely in our own words in the presence of others, can diminish where the common prayer of the community is brought before God by one of its members with dignity and simplicity."[10]

Intercessory Prayer and Political Struggle

It is important to remember that the scope of pastoral care is much wider than the interpersonal relationships that are developed one-on-one in the congregation. The call to intercessory prayer is not simply confined to those whom one knows and loves. Indeed, Christians are called to intercede for churches around the world, for leaders and those in authority, for the sick and the persecuted, even for their enemies. The *koinonia* that they experience in the church enables them to reach out to others in service, prayer, and mission. Alastair Campbell emphasizes this point: "Pastoral care must produce people who are *more* in-

10. Bonhoeffer, *Life Together,* 69.

volved in the world and *more* concerned with justice than they would be without the experience of *koinonia*."[11]

Ruby Bridges is the six-year-old girl who made history in 1960 by desegregating a school in New Orleans. Ruby and her family were undergirded by a church who prayed with and for them. Her story shows not only the power of Christ's presence but also the need for a community of support in times of trial.

The psychiatrist Robert Coles studied Ruby and her family for more than a year, seeking to learn what had enabled Ruby to pass through menacing crowds with equanimity each day. For weeks Ruby had walked past mobs of angry white people on her way to and from school, protected only by a handful of National Guardsmen. How did she remain so composed? When Ruby's teacher reported that she had seen Ruby talking to the crowds one morning, Coles asked her about it. Ruby replied that she hadn't been talking to them; she had been praying for them. Coles asked her why. She replied, "Because they need praying for." Her prayer was the prayer of Jesus from the Cross — that they be forgiven, for they knew not what they were doing.[12]

Unable to grasp how this was possible for a child, Coles again asked Ruby why she prayed for them. "Because I should," she replied. Though he spent hours observing Ruby and her family, Coles's presuppositions prevented him from understanding them. At least his explanations made no sense to Ruby's parents. One day, after more than a year's acquaintance, Mrs. Bridges tentatively approached Coles with a concern. "You're the doctor, I know," she said. "I shouldn't be asking you questions. You know what to ask children. But my husband and I were talking the other night, and we decided that you ask our daughter about everything except God."[13] Finding himself at a loss, Coles asked, "Would you explain what you mean?" Mrs. Bridges replied, "God is helping Ruby, and we thought you'd want to know that."[14]

Mr. and Mrs. Bridges and their daughter believed that Christ was

11. Alastair Campbell, "The Politics of Pastoral Care," in *Spiritual Dimensions of Pastoral Care*, ed. David Willows and John Swinton (Philadelphia: Jessica Kingsley, 2000), p. 62.

12. Robert Coles, "The Inexplicable Prayers of Ruby Bridges," *Christianity Today*, 9 August 1985, pp. 17-20.

13. Robert Coles, *Harvard Diary: Reflections on the Sacred and the Secular* (New York: Crossroad Publishing Co., 1990), p. 135.

14. Coles, *Harvard Diary*, pp. 136-37.

present in the midst of their trial, protecting Ruby from harm. Through her simple prayer, Christ protected her from an angry mob — protected her not only from their hurt but also from any desire to retaliate. Instead of returning their hatred, Ruby interceded for them in obedience to Christ's teaching. Ruby and her family aligned themselves with Christ even as Christ upheld them throughout their ordeal. They were also upheld by the community that surrounded them. Coles writes, "Mrs. Bridges told me Ruby had been told in Sunday school to pray for the people. I later found that the minister in their Baptist church also prayed for the people. Publicly. Every Sunday."[15] Union with Christ and each other kept them open to those who hated them. *Koinonia* was not disrupted but was extended even to enemies.

Loving one's enemies has always been a powerful witness to Christ. Apart from him, it is difficult to account for desiring the good of those who would do one harm. The prayer from the Cross that was echoed in Ruby's prayer for her tormentors reveals the hidden majesty of Christ's power. In this troubled situation, Ruby became not the originator of this prayer but a conduit for it. From a theological point of view, her prayer was a participation in Christ's prayer and a witness to his love. Yet her intercession had belonged to the community before it was hers. Though she prayed it as an individual, it came to her lips because she had been instructed in Sunday school as well as by her pastor and her parents. Her prayer, though it came from her own heart at a specific time, was first the prayer of Christ and then of the community before it was her own.

Intercessory prayer thus clearly extends beyond the hospital room or the pastor's study, beyond what is normally thought of as the scope of pastoral care. Pastoral caregivers, as they intercede for others, belong to a larger community. Members of a common body, all believers are called to instruct and sustain one another, to uphold each other in times of trial, and to encourage one another to pray, by God's grace, for their enemies. Intercessory prayer intersects with political struggle. In and through its intercessions, the church extends its circle of concern. All God's creatures — especially the poor, the hungry, the sick, those in prison, and those who work for justice — claim the church's attention. Ruby's prayer, along with those of her church, gives witness to this real-

15. Coles, "The Inexplicable Prayers of Ruby Bridges," p. 19.

ity. In an article entitled "Torture and Prayer," Georges Casalis widens the scope even further:

> Intercession is not an alibi for some kind of passivity; it is the continuation of the struggle with other means; it is the indispensable prolongation of political action and of participation in the class struggle on the side of the victims of exploitation and domination. It is an act of modesty, not of demobilization, the expression of lucid realism, not of discouragement, even less of any sort of resignation. What matters is that I am always conscious of both the indispensable character and the relativity of the work in which I am engaged with others; waiting for that great final liberation, there are small steps, limited advances, towards more justice and respect for man in this world in which we live. As long as I breathe, I will not rest nor be indifferent toward these brothers, comrades, companions and those I do not know, who are reduced to the last moral and physical extremity. . . .[16]

Though there may be limits to what Christians can do in any particular situation of injustice, their intercessory prayers extend to boundaries beyond their immediate grasp. Intercession strengthens their connection with those whom they cannot help in more direct ways. Though not a substitute for working on their behalf, prayer sustains the church in patience and hope. How could it persevere in a violent world if it could not continually cry to God for the deliverance of all who suffer?

Pastoral caregivers are vulnerable to psychic numbing whenever they are overwhelmed by the evil of the world, when they can no longer contemplate the suffering of others. This can be a challenge in today's world, where every night on the news they see African children with AIDS, Iraqi orphans, and the poor and destitute of our cities. According to Iain Torrance, contemporary imaginations are overloaded and lacking "stable footholds or reference points." In today's world, Christians "get famine fatigue or atrocity fatigue, which is to do with an inability to cope rather than moral dullness."[17] How do caregivers keep

---

16. Georges Casalis, "Torture and Prayer," *International Review of Mission* 66, no. 263 (July 1977): 240.

17. Iain Torrance, "More than Regent's Park," available at www.ptsem.edu/Publications/psb/vxxvn3/v25n3p240.htm; Internet; accessed 29 May 2006.

from becoming overloaded by the vast extent of the evil they witness? How do they keep their humanity intact in the midst of inhumanity?

When the ethicist Philip Hallie was studying the inhumanity of the Nazi era, he pored over documents that described human cruelty and found himself profoundly affected:

> For years, I had been studying the slow crushing and grinding of a human being by other human beings. . . . Across all these studies, the pattern of the strong crushing the weak kept repeating itself and repeating itself, so that when I was not bitterly angry, I was bored at the repetition of the patterns of persecution. When I was not desiring to be cruel with the cruel, I was a monster — like, perhaps, many others around me — who could look upon torture and death without a shudder.[18]

Hallie found it impossible to remain unscathed in his study of human depravity. "Reading about the damned," he says, "I was damned myself, as damned as the murderers, and as damned as their victims. Somehow over the years I had dug myself into Hell, and I had forgotten redemption."[19] He was delivered from this hell by his discovery of a little-known story about the people of a mountain village in France, Le Chambon-sur-Lignon. By refusing to cooperate with the Vichy government, these villagers, putting their own lives at risk, saved about five thousand Jewish children from death. The subtitle of Hallie's book, *Lest Innocent Blood Be Shed,* offers a clue to how to avoid hardening one's heart in the face of overwhelming evil: *The Story of the Village of Le Chambon and How Goodness Happened There.*[20]

Hallie had stumbled upon the lived goodness of ordinary men and women who had committed themselves to resisting the evil of their time through watchfulness, noncompliance, and fidelity and witness.[21] They watched for the needy in their midst, refused to comply with unjust laws, and lived out a commitment to nonviolence. In doing so, they witnessed to God's passionate care for the poor, God's righ-

---

18. Philip Hallie, *Lest Innocent Blood Be Shed* (New York: Harper & Row, 1979), p. 2.

19. Hallie, *Lest Innocent Blood Be Shed,* p. 2.

20. See George Hunsinger, *Disruptive Grace: Studies in the Theology of Karl Barth* (Grand Rapids: Eerdmans, 2000), pp. 108-13.

21. Hunsinger, *Disruptive Grace,* pp. 108-13.

teousness in the midst of injustice, and an atoning love that is willing to suffer and die rather than inflict violence on others. Though each family made its own decision whether to offer refuge to a Jewish child or family, it was the strength of the community as a whole that enabled them to act.

This village serves as a powerful example. The church can remain open and compassionate as it intercedes for those unknown to it but known to God only as it joins together with other members of the body of Christ. Isolated and alone, caregivers are vulnerable to hopelessness, but as they join together in prayer and action, they find the courage they need. As they allow their sorrow to pass *through* them to God, they may find that prayer becomes a means for God's comfort to flow in the other direction — *through* them but also *to* them and *among* them (2 Corinthians 1). As they pray for tortured prisoners and terrified orphans, for family circles broken by death, and for those who wreak destruction, they may find themselves comforted by a God who alone can bear the depth of human pain. God shares in human misery and bears its full weight through the Cross of Jesus Christ. Christians are upheld and encouraged by bonds of love as they are knit together as members of a single body.

A Literary Example

Simone Weil makes the point that literature, unlike a case study, can "give us, in the guise of fiction, something equivalent to the actual density of the real, that density which life offers us every day but which we are unable to grasp."[22] In his short story "Pray Without Ceasing," Wendell Berry captures the "actual density of the real" in the mystery of spiritual kinship that grows in a community shaped by prayer.[23] Berry presents generations of experience through the literary device of

---

22. Simone Weil, "Morality and Literature," in *On Science, Necessity, and the Love of God*, ed. and trans. Richard Rees (Oxford: Oxford University Press, 1968), p. 162. See also Carrie Doehring, *Taking Care: Monitoring Power Dynamics and Relational Boundaries in Pastoral Care and Counseling* (Nashville: Abingdon Press, 1995); and Caroline Simon, *The Disciplined Heart: Love, Destiny and Imagination* (Grand Rapids: Eerdmans, 1997).

23. Wendell Berry, "Pray Without Ceasing," in *Fidelity* (New York: Pantheon, 1992), pp. 3-60.

placing a story within a story. Through a tale told by the narrator's grandmother, he shuttles back and forth through time — into the past, before the narrator was born, and into the future, long after the central drama. He hints at a *communio sanctorum* streaming through time as the intercessory prayers of one generation profoundly impact generations yet unborn.

The narrator, Andy Catlett, is himself an old man when he begins his tale. He remembers a day long past when his grandmother told him how his great-grandfather, Ben Feltner, was murdered. Grandmother had been a young woman then, married to Mat Feltner, Ben's son. At the outset of the story, Andy reflects on the strangeness of the tenses of reality:

> Mat Feltner was my grandfather on my mother's side. Saying it thus, I force myself to reckon again with the strangeness of that verb *was*. The man of whom I once was pleased to say, "He is my grandfather," has become the dead man who was my grandfather. He was, and is no more. And this is a part of the great mystery we call time.
>
> But the past is present also. And this, I think, is a part of the greater mystery we call eternity. . . . This man who was my grandfather is present in me, as I felt always his father to be present in him. His father was Ben. The known history of the Feltners in Port William begins with Ben.[24]

As this beginning suggests, Andy's narrative deals with spiritual reality, with the mystery of the past in the present, with the presence of the dead among the living, and with time framed by eternity.

Grandmother recounts the day Thad Coulter murdered Ben Feltner, his best friend. Thad had received a stunning blow, losing at age sixty everything he had ever worked for. Having put up his farm as bond against his son's business, it was about to be repossessed by the bank to pay off his son's debts. Thad guzzled whiskey for the better part of two days and slept in the filth of the barn. Though his wife, Rachel, and daughter, Martha Elizabeth, implored him to come into the house, he refused. Eventually he found himself at Ben's doorstep "hoping that somehow, by some means that he could not imagine, Ben

---

24. Berry, "Pray Without Ceasing," pp. 3-4.

could release him from the solitary cage of his self-condemnation."[25] Seeing that Thad was in no condition to speak rationally, Ben kindly told him to come back again once he was sober and then they'd see what might be done.

In his drunken state, Thad chose to take offense at Ben, interpreting his words as rejection and humiliation. Later that day, Thad rode a donkey into town, shot Ben point-blank in the forehead, and watched him fall dead to the ground. He then made his way into the neighboring town, where he confessed that he had just killed his best friend and handed himself over to the sheriff. For two nights he languished in the county jail. Unable to bear himself and what he had done, he died by his own hand before his day in court.

Those who loved Ben Feltner and Thad Coulter are also woven into the narrative. In recounting how some of them responded to this event, Berry offers a story of intercessory prayer and the communion of saints. When Ben's son, Mat, learned that his father had been shot by Thad Coulter, he began to run. "He was a man new-created by rage. All that he had been and thought and done gave way to his one desire to kill the man who had killed his father. He ached, mind and body, with the elation of that one thought." He was stopped by his uncle, his mother's brother, Jack Beechum. Jack, having just heard the news himself, had stepped out of Chatham's store to see Mat running toward him.

> Without breaking his own stride, he caught Mat and held him. . . . As soon as Jack had taken hold of Mat, he understood that he *had* to hold him. . . . Something went out of him that day, and he was not the same again.
>
> And what went out of Jack came into Mat. Or so it seemed, for in that desperate embrace he [Mat] became a stronger man than he had been. A strength came into him that held his grief and his anger as Jack had held him. And Jack knew of the coming of this strength, not because it enabled Mat to break free but because it enabled Jack to turn him loose. . . . To Jack, it was as though he had caught one man and let another go.

Later that night, after Mat had laid his father to rest in a coffin in the living room, and neighbors had filled the house with their mourn-

25. Berry, "Pray Without Ceasing," pp. 34, 36-37.

ful whispers, a group of his father's friends arrived at the front door, ready with noose in hand. All they needed was a word from Mat. In the twilight "the people standing on the porch were as still as everything else, except for Jack Beechum, who quietly made his way forward until he stood behind and a little to the left of Mat, who was standing at the top of the steps." With Jack standing behind him on the one side and his mother on the other, Mat stepped forward and declined their offer of revenge, inviting them instead to supper. As he reflected on this scene years later, Andy felt that he could almost see his grandfather "standing without prop in the deepening twilight, asking his father's friends to renounce the vengeance that a few hours before he himself had been furious to exact."[26]

What had enabled him not only to renounce that vengeance, but also to stand firm against the collective grief and mounting rage of the whole town? What had happened in those few short hours that enabled him to forgive his father's murderer, or at least to take steps that would one day lead to such forgiveness? In the scene on the porch, Berry portrays Mat as upheld by the communion of saints, by Jack on his left and his mother on his right. The silent presence of his father is perhaps also evident as his mother implores the men to forswear revenge: "I know you are my husband's friends. I thank you. I, too, must ask you not to do as you propose. Mat has asked you; I have asked you; if Ben could, he would ask you. Let us make what peace is left for us to make."[27] Knowing Ben as they did, the men found her convincing. They knew the truth of her words, that even Ben would want peace.

As a solitary individual, Mat Feltner felt a sorrow that would doubtless have overtaken him. Left to himself, he could not have borne so terrible a grief. But he was not alone, and that is the whole point. His life was interwoven with the lives of those around him, his mother's and his uncle's, his wife's and also his father's. He couldn't have borne the anguish alone, but he could and did bear it as he was upheld by those others, by the community surrounding and sustaining him.

Yet another story intersects with the story of the Feltners, and that is the story of Thad Coulter and those who loved him, most especially his youngest daughter, Martha Elizabeth.

26. Berry, "Pray Without Ceasing," pp. 34, 36-37, 55, 57-58.
27. Berry, "Pray Without Ceasing," p. 57.

"You see," my grandmother said, "there are two deaths in this — Mr. Feltner's and Thad Coulter's. We know Mr. Feltner's because we had to know it. It was ours. That we know Thad's is because of Martha Elizabeth. The Martha Elizabeth you know."

Andy, as narrator, pauses here to marvel that the white-haired woman he knew, who was "always near to smiling, sometimes to laughter,"[28] and whom everybody loved, had once been a girl of seventeen. The day her father killed Ben Feltner, Martha Elizabeth had trekked all the way into the neighboring town to be with her father in his jail cell. She stayed with him as long as she could that evening and all the next day, ministering to him, coaxing him to eat and drink.

When Thad first felt his daughter's presence in the cell, he covered his face. "He put his hands over his face like a man ashamed," Andy's grandmother said. "But he was like a man, too, who had seen what he couldn't bear." She spoke slowly now, searching her grandson's face to see if he understood.

> "Maybe Thad saw his guilt full and clear then. But what he saw that he couldn't bear was something else."
>
> And again she paused, looking at me. . . . The old house in that moment seemed filled with a quiet that extended not only out into the whole broad morning but endlessly both ways in time.
>
> "People sometimes talk of God's love as if it's a pleasant thing. But it is terrible, in a way. Think of all it includes. It included Thad Coulter, drunk and mean and foolish, before he killed Mr. Feltner, and it included him afterwards. . . .
>
> "That's what Thad saw. He saw his guilt. He had killed his friend. . . . But in the same moment he saw his guilt included in love that stood as near him as Martha Elizabeth and at that moment wore her flesh. It was surely weak and wrong of him to kill himself — to sit in judgment that way over himself. But surely God's love includes people who can't bear it."[29]

How could Martha Elizabeth love him when he did not deserve it, when he despised himself and his own life? Yet she stood before him, as

28. Berry, "Pray Without Ceasing," pp. 47, 48.
29. Berry, "Pray Without Ceasing," pp. 49-50.

if bearing the dreadful mercy of God. To be in Martha Elizabeth's presence was to recognize the abyss of his own guilt and shame and yet to know the unfathomable love of God. Andy's grandmother finishes the story:

> "It's a hard story to have to know," my grandmother said. "The mercy of it was Martha Elizabeth."
>
> She still had more to tell, but she paused again, and again she looked at me and touched my hand.
>
> "If God loves the ones we can't," she said, "then finally maybe we can. All these years I've thought of him sitting in those shadows, with Martha Elizabeth standing there, and his work-sore old hands over his face."[30]

Ben Feltner's daughter-in-law had pondered Thad Coulter's anguish for years. She had thought of him in the shadow of his jail cell, unable to bear the shame of who he had become. How had this woman come to understand Martha Elizabeth as the presence of God's harsh and dreadful love? How had she been able to discern it? Andy reports near the beginning of the story that he found her sitting in a chair by the window in the small bedroom where she did her sewing. Her arthritis was bothering her, so she sat with her hands in her lap, turning things over in her mind:

> She sat still and let the pain go its way and occupied her mind with thoughts. Or that is what she said she did. I believed, and I was as sure as if she had told me, that when she sat alone that way . . . she was praying. Though I never heard her pray aloud in my life, it seems to me now that I can reproduce in my mind the very voice of her prayers.[31]

So the reader is left to wonder about those prayers. Yet Grandmother's very capacity to tell the story as she does seems to arise from a practice of "praying without ceasing." In this way Berry merely hints at the life of prayer that would enable someone to weave together such complex and multiple threads into a gracious pattern of meaning *sub specie aeternitatis.*

30. Berry, "Pray Without Ceasing," pp. 50-51.
31. Berry, "Pray Without Ceasing," pp. 9-10.

As her grandson in turn meditates on the story over the years, he catches a glimpse of the spiritual legacy he has received. He knows his existence is bound up with practices that have spanned generations. Mat Feltner had been able to forgive his father's murderer and eventually to befriend the Coulter family. The impossible possibility to forgive had a far-reaching impact. Andy concludes,

> Though Coulters still abound in Port William, no Feltner of the name is left. But the Feltner line continues, joined to the Coulter line, in me, and I am here. I am blood kin to both sides of that moment when Ben Feltner turned to face Thad Coulter in the road and Thad pulled the trigger. The two families, sundered in the ruin of a friendship, were united again first in new friendship and then in marriage. My grandfather made a peace here that has joined many who would otherwise have been divided. I am the child of his forgiveness.[32]

Conclusion

The innermost meanings of human life, which often remain elusive or obscure, are discerned in and through habits of prayer. Through intercessory prayer, Christians glimpse the interwovenness of their lives with those of others. In praying for them — their friends and family, strangers far and near, even enemies — they become aware of the hidden ways that God knits people together into a single fabric of meaning. As they intercede for friends, they confess their anxiety for their friends' welfare and ask for God's daily sustenance. They relinquish their need for control, trusting God's work in the lives of those they love. As they intercede for the poor and the persecuted, they not only seek their good but also ask for the guidance they themselves need so that their prayers will not be in vain. Interceding for the sick, they call upon God for healing and restoration, and for forgiveness when their compassion falls short. Those who pray for their enemies might be granted a perception of their solidarity with them or the grace of

---

32. Berry, "Pray Without Ceasing," pp. 58-59.

unlooked-for care. If they are also granted a forgiving heart, they recognize it for what it is — a gift from God.

Apart from the light of the Gospel, caregivers cannot begin to identify these patterns in their lives. Although much may remain obscure, prayer enables them to see the world as suffused and yet to be suffused with divine light. They receive an intimation of God's great cloud of witnesses, in time and eternity, and a fleeting glimpse of their own place among them. Pastoral caregivers who pray with and for others will themselves be strengthened and encouraged as they pray. They will be borne up by Christ, even as they consent to share in Christ's sufferings in the world.

Seven Prayers of Lament

Prayers of lament arise *in extremis*. When the people of God undergo trial and cry out for deliverance, lament is faith's alternative to despair. It is a peculiar form of petitionary prayer, one that springs from unrelieved suffering. When healing fails, lament is the hopelessness that refuses to give up hope. When injustice prevails, lament is the protest that digs in for the long haul. When humiliation abounds, lament is the self-respect that cries out to a hidden God, "How long, O Lord?" Lament bends anguish and anger into ardent supplication. Sometimes it is no more than an inarticulate cry.

Lament is fueled by human desires, whatever they may be. Why does one woman lament over her inability to conceive a child, while another can accept that a child is not given? Why does one member of a family still grieve for a beloved but lost brother, refusing to be consoled? Why does a man of faith persist year after year with the same plea to God, refusing to let go of a dream that seems within reach but is nevertheless withheld? Those who cry out to God in lament refuse to quench their desire. They are like the nuisance in Jesus' parable who wrenches his neighbor from a warm bed in the dead of night to ask for three loaves of bread for his visitors. They are like the importunate woman who so wears down the judge that he gives in just to be rid of her. Jesus admonishes his disciples never to give up hope but to persist in their entreaty to God, that their petitions may be heard. For if even an unjust human judge gives in to such importunity, how much more will the righteous Judge of the universe listen to their cries?

Yet how long can lament persist? Over time, hope and despair seem to hang in the balance. The more fervent the hope, the more insistent the whisper of despair. Lament risks everything on God. It refuses the shell of cynicism that would protect its vulnerable heart. Instead, it remains open, alive, desiring, and therefore suffering. Think of Hannah in her longing for a son. Despite the ridicule of Eli, the priest, and the protestations of Elkanah, her husband, Hannah refuses to relinquish her desire. Though she has a husband who loves her tenderly, she weeps and refuses to be comforted. Recall the details as related in First Samuel. Elkanah has a second wife, Peninnah, who has been blessed abundantly with both daughters and sons. She flaunts her children, puffing herself up and shaming Hannah for her childlessness. Month after month, year after year, Hannah remains barren. When the family undertakes their annual pilgrimage to Shiloh to offer sacrifices, Peninnah taunts Hannah so that Hannah burns with desire for a son. The temptation to repress the desire must surely be present. But Hannah persists. Her husband protests, "Hannah, why do you weep? And why do you not eat? And why is your heart sad? Am I not more to you than ten sons?" (1 Sam. 1:8). No matter how sincere, Elkanah is powerless to change his wife's heart. She yearns for a son.

Hannah brings her lament to God when she offers her sacrifice in the temple. She weeps bitterly, prays in distress, and vows that if she is granted a son, she will offer him back to the Lord, to serve in the temple all his days. When Eli sees her lips moving, he reprimands her for drunkenness. But she protests; she is not drunk, only praying in distress. Eli answers, "Go in peace, and the God of Israel grant your petition which you have made to him" (1 Sam. 1:17). Trusting in the promise as spoken through the priest, Hannah is no longer sad. As promised, the Lord opens her womb and grants her a son, whom she names Samuel. As the Lord is faithful to her, so Hannah keeps her vow to the Lord. After weaning her firstborn, she returns to the temple in Shiloh and dedicates him to a lifetime of service.

We are familiar with Hannah's song about God's faithfulness in hearing the lowly. Hymns of joy supplant long nights of sorrow. The joy is proportional to the suffering that precedes it. "Weeping may tarry for the night, but joy comes with the morning" (Ps. 30:5). Yet how long does the night endure? A professor once described the eight years it took to write his dissertation as "an unhappy moment in my life."

The endless prospect was in retrospect a brief time. How can such "moments" be borne?

Holy Scripture trains the church in hope. The Bible is very largely a story of hope emerging from hopelessness, of new beginnings arising from bitter endings. With the resurrection of Christ as the interpretative key, Scripture testifies that God comes to those who have lost all hope. Waters spring forth in the lifeless valley of Baca (Ps. 84). Rejected people are claimed for the work of God. Against all odds, slaves and prisoners are set free. Joseph is delivered from the pit, and the brothers who abandoned him are forgiven.

Lament means directing one's anguish toward God. Left to its own devices, the church is vulnerable to losing sight of hope. It is prone to forget the Creator who gives life itself, the Redeemer who forgives sin, and the Spirit who sustains it in hope. Jesus Christ releases his people from the burden of harm, both given and received, that would otherwise ensnare them in consequences beyond repair. God redeems the past by using what was meant for evil to bring good (Gen. 50:15-21). This is the tacit knowledge that sustains lament. Lament presupposes the majesty of God, his power to bring new life, and his compassion on all he has created. Lament is the last refuge of the courage that hopes in God.

Psalms of Lament

In Psalm 88, arguably the most hopeless of the lament psalms, the psalmist writes, "Thy wrath lies heavy upon me, and thou dost overwhelm me with all thy waves. Thou hast caused my companions to shun me" (vv. 7-8). Yet if God has so afflicted him, why does he cry out day after day to this very God? "O LORD, my God, I call for help by day; I cry out in the night before thee" (v. 1). The psalmist not only laments the troubles of his life, the nearness of death, and his forsakenness by friends and companions. He tells all this specifically to God, whose wrath afflicts him sorely. Then in a series of ironic, almost mocking questions, he addresses God as Lord of the living:

> Dost thou work wonders for the dead?
> Do the shades rise up to praise thee?

Is thy steadfast love declared in the grave,
or thy faithfulness in Abaddon?
Are thy wonders known in the darkness,
or thy saving help in the land of forgetfulness? (vv. 10-12)

The questions are hardly a request for information. They push God to remember his identity. Is he not the One who works wonders, whose steadfast love is declared daily in prayer, liturgy, and song?[1] Surely God has not forgotten himself. The complaint reminds God that he is the Savior of Israel, the protector of his people. Though God has visited calamity upon them, his is the power of deliverance. The God of judgment is nevertheless the God of grace. There is nowhere else to turn.

Psalm 13 shows how a psalm of lament is structured. In only six verses, it sets forth the major elements of lament:[2]

How long, O LORD? Wilt thou forget me for ever?
How long wilt thou hide thy face from me?

How long must I bear pain in my soul,
and have sorrow in my heart all the day?
How long shall my enemy be exalted over me?

Consider and answer me, O LORD my God;
lighten my eyes, lest I sleep the sleep of death;

lest my enemy say, "I have prevailed over him";
lest my foes rejoice because I am shaken.

But I have trusted in thy steadfast love;
my heart shall rejoice in thy salvation.

I will sing to the LORD,
because he has dealt bountifully with me.

The psalmist constructs his lament in three sections: the introduction, the body, and the conclusion. He begins by invoking God with

---

1. Patrick Miller, *They Cried to the Lord: The Form and Theology of Biblical Prayer* (Minneapolis: Fortress Press, 1994), p. 70.
2. See Miller, *They Cried to the Lord*, pp. 99-102.

urgency: How long will the Lord forget him? Will it be forever? One is not left to wonder about the complaint. All the lament psalms plunge one into the immediacy of abandonment. "My God, my God, why hast thou forsaken me?" (Ps. 22:1). "Why dost thou stand afar off, O LORD? Why dost thou hide thyself in times of trouble?" (Ps. 10:1). At the same time, a level of intimacy is presupposed. The verbs in the imperative ("Consider and answer me, O Lord my God; lighten my eyes") are not ones that would be used with a stranger or a mere acquaintance. They imply an existing relationship. They address someone accessible. So here with God. The imperative form presupposes a God who is known, loved, and expected to help.

The body of the lament specifies the psalmist's distress, usually followed by a petition. In Psalm 13, pain and sorrow, triumphant enemies, and the nearness of death are the complaints. The psalmist importunes an answer from God: "Consider and answer me." Other laments urge God to action, protest innocence, or remind God of past saving deeds. The psalmist vows fidelity to the God who delivers him.

The conclusion indicates answered prayer without showing how the psalmist moves from suffering to release. Mysteriously, the prayer is heard. The occasion for sorrow has become an occasion for joy. Here the psalmist proclaims, "I will sing to the LORD, because he has dealt bountifully with me." Something has shifted dramatically, for the psalmist has turned to song. The trial is over. The psalmist turns from the past toward the future in thanksgiving for the Lord's bountiful grace.

Psalm 13 is structured in a form known as chiasmus. In the ancient world, thought was not always structured syllogistically in a linear fashion, as one would expect today: If A and B, then C follows, with C representing the culmination of the argument. In chiastic form, A is paired with A′ at the beginning and the end of the constructed unit. B is paired with B′ moving in toward the center, with C at the cross-point in the center. The Greek letter *Chi* (as in *chi*asmus) looks like the letter *X*, which is the centerpoint of the construction. If the psalm follows such a chiastic structure, one would expect to see paired words or themes at the beginning and at the end of the piece, with the most important point being made in the middle. Psalm 13 pairs three themes through the repetition of words before coming to the cross-point.

A: How long, O **Lord**? Wilt thou forget me for ever?
How long wilt thou hide thy face from me?

   B: How long must I bear pain in my soul,
and have sorrow in *my heart* all the day?

      C: How long shall *my enemy* be exalted over me?

         X: Consider and answer me, O Lord my God;
lighten my eyes, lest I sleep the sleep of death;

      C′: lest *my enemy* say, "I have prevailed over him";
lest my foes rejoice because I am shaken.

   B′: But I have trusted in thy steadfast love;
my heart shall rejoice in thy salvation.

A′: I will sing to the **Lord**,
because he has dealt bountifully with me.

The psalm begins and ends, in A and A′, with the psalmist's attention on the Lord. At the beginning, he cries out in supplication; at the end, his cries have turned to song. What begins as lament ends as praise. In B and B′, the psalmist's attention is on his own heart. In B, he has sorrow in his heart, whereas in B′, his heart rejoices. In C and C′, as the psalmist moves toward the center, the focus in on his enemy. In C, the enemy is exalted over him, whereas in C′, the factual shifts to a hypothetical; no longer a fact, the enemy now would prevail only if the Lord fails to answer. The center verse is in the imperative: "Consider and answer me, O Lord my God; lighten my eyes, lest I sleep the sleep of death." The center of the lament is the direct, desperate cry to God for help. The psalmist calls upon him as "my" God, making a claim of intimacy and describing the extremity of his peril.

The time sequences shift. The psalmist asks his anguished question in the present, looking back over a long stretch of the past. The present pain and sorrow are a reality of long suffering, sweeping over a vast arc of time: "all the day." The present perfect (as the past continuing into the present) "I *have* trusted" then shifts in hope toward the future: "My heart *shall* rejoice." Then, in reverse order, the future is juxtaposed once again with the present perfect: "I *will sing* to the Lord, because he *has dealt* bountifully with me."

The shifting from present to past to future is a typical feature of the lament form. Psalm 126, for example, begins with the words "When the LORD restored the fortunes of Zion, we were like those who dream" (v. 1). Thus it seems that Israel is looking back in time, remembering their deliverance. The psalmist recalls how their "mouth was filled with laughter, and [their] tongue with shouts of joy" (v. 2). But then, suddenly, the tenses shift. No longer are they looking back with joy; rather, they cry out to God in the present: "Restore our fortunes, O LORD," they call, "like the watercourses in the Negeb!" (v. 4). They seem to be in a situation of trial, calling upon God's name. The perpetual shuttling among present desperation, past deliverance, and anticipated rescue is a characteristic mark of biblical faith that is structured into the very pattern of the lament psalms.[3] God can be trusted, this mode of depiction suggests, because he fulfills his promises; God comes when he will, even when all human possibilities are spent. Again and again the psalms instruct the church to wait upon God, to call upon the Lord in its day of trouble. Lament sustains it in hope because the prayer is a living membrane that connects the people to God and God's steadfast love.

Psalms of lament are both corporate and personal. There are laments for the entire nation of Israel (e.g., Psalm 137: "How shall we sing the LORD's song in a foreign land?") as well as for a single sufferer (e.g., Psalm 102, described as "the prayer of one afflicted, when he is faint and pours out his complaint before the Lord"). Liturgically, the most well-known lament may be Psalm 22, the prayer of Jesus from the Cross: "My God, my God, why hast thou forsaken me?" In this prayer, Jesus gives voice to all humanity's lament over God's absence in time of need. Hughes Oliphant Old expresses it this way:

> In his Passion Jesus himself prays the psalms of lamentation. When he offered himself up on the cross in that perfect act of worship, he presented to the Father the psalms of lamentation that Israel had prayed for a thousand years, and in those psalms were the cries of all humanity.[4]

Here the personal and the corporate are joined as Jesus conveys the human cry of anguish to the Father.

---

3. Miller, *They Cried to the Lord,* pp. 68-86.

4. Hughes Oliphant Old, *Leading in Prayer: Workbook for Worship* (Grand Rapids: Eerdmans, 1995), p. 80.

Worship is especially rich in prayers of lament during Holy Week, for here the innocent suffering of Christ joins collective human guilt. Through the Cross of Jesus Christ, God takes the sin of the world into himself and suffers its consequences. Jesus drinks the bitter cup of Godforsakenness by undergoing the worst human suffering imaginable — an unjust execution for crimes not committed, betrayal and abandonment by friends, derision from enemies, physical torture, and public humiliation. When the church enters into the solemn mysteries of Holy Week, it confesses its participation in the human sin that cost the Son of God so dearly. Prayers of lament knit human sorrow over sin together with the suffering of loss and abandonment. The church beholds Jesus on the Cross as both God and human being. He is the Son of God who suffers for the world in order to atone for its sin. At the same time, he is the Son of Man who suffers with the world the terrible plight of abandonment by God, persecution, and death. The Cross of Jesus Christ is God's response not only to the guilt of human sin but also to the terror and shame of human suffering.

At the heart of lament is a conflict felt by the person of faith who undergoes rending loss or extended trial. "If there is a just and loving God watching over his children, why doesn't he deliver them?" The prayer of lament does not avoid but rather enters into this tension between the experience of evil and faith's affirmation of the goodness of God. Lament takes this tension right to the breaking point, to a vision of God's eschatological rescue. Believing that the Lord is both loving and righteous, both mighty and gracious, the cry of lament cannot help but be a part of the landscape of faith because of the continuing presence of evil in the world. The loss of loved ones evokes anguish and incomprehension. Nicholas Wolterstorff, who lost his 25-year-old son in a mountaineering accident, writes movingly about this anguish:

> I have no explanation. I can do nothing else than endure in the face of this deepest and most painful of mysteries. I believe in God the Father Almighty, maker of heaven and earth and resurrecter of Jesus Christ. I also believe that my son's life was cut off in its prime. I cannot fit these pieces together. I am at a loss. I have read the theodicies produced to justify the ways of God to man. I find them unconvincing. To the most agonized question I have ever asked I do not know the answer. I do not know why God would watch him fall.

> I do not know why God would watch me wounded. I cannot even guess.[5]

Rationalistic explanations fail to do justice to the heart's anguished cry of "Why?" Lament alone gives hope. By God's grace, the prayer of lament enables one to keep the question alive. By keeping the channel to God open, lament enables the unendurable to be endured. Kathleen Billman and Daniel Migliore, authors of *Rachel's Cry,* elaborate:

> The prayer of lament is a vivid reminder that persons can survive the disintegration of their previously unquestioned theological frameworks. What endures beyond the collapse of the frameworks is the relationship with the living God, a relationship strong enough for the telling of truth. . . . It is the deepening of that relationship with the living God that is the goal of pastoral care, and it is to that end that the prayer of lament has its place in Christian life and ministry.[6]

Lament in the Book of Job

Job is afflicted by every kind of evil: physical pain, the catastrophic loss of loved ones and worldly goods, social ostracism and public humiliation, enemies who taunt him, and friends who accuse him outright of secret sins. Though his anguish is multifaceted, Job remains notably single-minded. Throughout the narrative, Job insists on hearing from God alone. He calls upon God repeatedly in the most intense lament in Scripture. He rejects his friends as "miserable comforters" who only compound his suffering. He knows that he has to do with God and God alone. His friends act as if they speak on God's behalf, which only exasperates Job. In the end God acknowledges that they did not "speak what is right" concerning him.[7]

---

5. Nicholas Wolterstorff, *Lament for a Son* (Grand Rapids: Eerdmans, 1987), pp. 67-68.

6. Kathleen D. Billman and Daniel Migliore, *Rachel's Cry: Prayer of Lament and Rebirth of Hope* (Cleveland: United Church Press, 1999), p. 140.

7. See Karl Barth, *Church Dogmatics,* IV/3 (Edinburgh: T&T Clark, 1960), pp. 383-88, 398-408, 421-34, 453-61.

The prologue makes clear that the calamities visited upon Job are not due to any sin of his, known or unknown. Therefore, when Job insists on his innocence — "There is no violence in my hands, and my prayer is pure" (16:17) — readers know that Job speaks truthfully, but his friends do not. Indeed, they are scandalized. How can he so blatantly insist on his own innocence? How can he accuse God? They cannot see beyond their conviction that the morally upright are blessed and the wicked are punished. According to them, the universe operates according to this inviolable law.

Job excoriates them in turn for being full of "windy words." If their roles were reversed, he would not preach pious platitudes or presume to speak for God. On the contrary, he would give solace to the afflicted. He turns from them in disgust and directs his lament solely to God. He knows that consolation can come only from beyond. God alone can address him in his affliction. Surely no one but God can answer his questions of "Why?" and "How long?" When Job appeals to God as his witness against God his persecutor, the pattern of prayer from the psalms reappears. Rather than fleeing *from* God as his enemy, he appeals *to* God as the One who will vindicate him. He appeals to God for help even though he believes God is persecuting him. He cries out, "O earth, cover not my blood, and let my cry find no resting place. Even now, behold, my witness is in heaven, and he that vouches for me is on high. . . . My eye pours out tears to God, that he would maintain the right of a man with God, like that of a man with his neighbor" (Job 16:18-21). The image of the witness in heaven comes from the ancient Israelite custom whereby a kinsman must avenge the blood of one killed unjustly. His blood, if left uncovered, will continue to cry out for revenge; his spirit will not rest until the death is avenged. Since there is no earthly kinsman to intercede for Job, who will take up his case and pursue justice? Who will demonstrate his innocence once and for all? Job boldly asks God to be his kinsman to defend his honor. Paradoxically, he calls on God to defend him against God.

As a man who fears God and understands his promises, Job knows that God is the defender of the defenseless, the protector of the innocent, and the lover of the poor. Therefore, God will be his witness, his defender, his redeemer. Despite all contrary evidence, Job casts himself on God as the only One who can vindicate him. Much the same thing occurs in Psalm 88 when the psalmist reminds God of his own character. He asks pointed questions about God's ability to work wonders, his praiseworthiness among the people, his steadfast love, and his saving help toward all who call upon him. Like Job, the psalmist appeals to God against God, reminding him of his essential identity.

All the dramatic tension builds toward the direct encounter between Job and God. Job insists on fighting his wife, his friends, and even God himself until he receives the answer he needs. The tenacity of his faith is fierce. Job relinquishes neither his claim to righteousness nor his insistence that the Almighty speak. The climax comes when, out of the whirlwind, God does in fact speak to Job. Sovereign and free, God vindicates Job. Yet his address is incomprehensible to the reader.

All that the reader sees in the foreground is a demonstration of God's power and might. The reader doesn't see the hidden work of the Holy Spirit. As in the psalms, so also here: the shift in attitude lies hidden in the encounter with God. Real change occurs. Beyond all expectation, Job is satisfied with God's response. Having insisted so relentlessly on his innocence, Job astonishes the reader with humble repentance. What is it, one wonders, that prompts Job to repent in dust and ashes? What does he hear from God that causes him to rest his case?

The transition that the reader sees in Job — from angry lament to humble acknowledgment of God's majesty — is reminiscent of that in the psalms when cries of anguish turn into shouts of joy. Though Job hardly shouts with joy, the shift in attitude is nevertheless dramatic. The transition is perplexing. One does not know *what* occurs in the spiritual encounter. One only sees *that* something occurs. The meaning of the encounter is shrouded in mystery. Yet this is so with each human soul and God. There is a holy inviolability in each person's encounter with God. Prayer can bring the sanctification of anguish even when one's plea is refused. Prayers for healing, when healing does not come, are then sustained by a "hope beyond healing."[8] Prayer points toward something mysterious that changes the human heart.

A poem that appears in Wendell Berry's *A Timbered Choir* hints at this mystery. In the poem a man is lying in bed in the dark, praying. Berry writes, "He is a man breathing the fear/of hopeless prayer, prayed/in hope." And then, mysteriously, something moves him. What "causes him

---

8. Dale Aukerman, *Hope Beyond Healing: A Cancer Journal* (Elgin, Ill.: Brethren Press, 2000).

to stir/like the dead in the grave" is love — "his own love or/Heaven's, he does not know."[9] In remembering love, everything changes. He finds himself surrounded by love, and his connection to God is restored.

Pastoral Care and the Prayer of Lament

The unique history that unfolds between God and Job is a paradigm for pastoral care. The decisive encounter is shown to be not between the caregiver and the afflicted, but between the afflicted one and God. When faced with Job-like suffering, caregivers are wise to avoid the judgmentalism of Job's "miserable comforters." They cannot be the judge of another's calamities or interpret them as God's punishment. The God who alone sees the human heart is the God who alone may judge. Rather than standing in the place of God, caregivers need to stand alongside the afflicted, helping them to articulate their lament: "Whether or not the cries of pain and protest are identified as prayer by the afflicted, when suffering is experienced in the presence of God, the prayer of lament is in the process of formation. The caregiver's role is to hear and help bring this prayer to voice."[10]

When evil is overwhelming, Eugene Peterson says, pastoral care becomes "an assignment to share experiences of suffering." The sufferer cannot simply put the tragedy behind him. One's life does not just go on. There is no convenient "moral of the story" to be sought. No meaning can be found until each detail finds its place in a meaningful whole. To illustrate his point, Peterson examines Israel's suffering as expressed in Jeremiah's Lamentations. These lamentations are not marked by an amorphous primal scream. Instead, actual events are recounted — the siege of Jerusalem, the deadly famine, the flight of the king, the looting of the temple, and the dreaded exile. Names, places, and dates are a way of "tethering suffering," lest the framework of history dissolve. "History is necessary," Peterson observes, "not to explain, but to anchor."[11]

When caregivers listen to those in distress, they are not there to explain the origin of suffering, as Job's friends sought to do, or to mini-

9. Wendell Berry, *A Timbered Choir* (Washington, D.C.: Counterpoint, 1998), p. 181.

10. Billman and Migliore, *Rachel's Cry*, p. 139.

11. Eugene Peterson, *Five Smooth Stones for Pastoral Work* (Atlanta: John Knox Press, 1980), pp. 114, 125, 126.

mize its impact. They are there simply to share it and to convey it to God. Peterson writes,

> Pastors have no business interfering with another's sorrow, or ma-nipulating it. Suffering is an event in which we are particularly vul-nerable to grace, able to recognize dimensions in God and depths in the self. To treat it as a *"problem"* is to demean the person.[12]

Peterson contrasts a "therapeutic" attitude with a "pastoral" attitude. The one looks at suffering as something to be fixed by an expert; the other sees suffering as something to be faced honestly, encountered fully, and shared in community. Hospital chaplains and hospice work-ers know that it is an honor to be asked to share in another's sorrow.

While enduring a two-year prison term near the end of his life, Oscar Wilde struck a different tone from the witty, light repartee for which he is known. Not published until five years after his death, his cry from "out of the depths" is powerful:

> If, after I am free, a friend of mine gave a feast, and did not invite me to it, I should not mind a bit. I can be perfectly happy by myself. With freedom, flowers, books and the moon, who could not be per-fectly happy? Besides, feasts are not for me any more. I have given too many to care about them. That side of life is over for me, very fortunately, I dare say. But if after I am free a friend of mine had a sorrow and refused to allow me to share it, I should feel it most bit-terly. If he shut the doors of the house of mourning against me, I would come back again and again and beg to be admitted, so that I might share in what I was entitled to share in. If he thought me un-worthy, unfit to weep with him, I should feel it as the most poi-gnant humiliation, as the most terrible mode in which disgrace could be inflicted on me. But that could not be. I have a right to share in sorrow, and he who can look at the loveliness of the world and share its sorrow, and realise something of the wonder of both, is in immediate contact with divine things, and has got as near to God's secret as any one can get.[13]

---

12. Peterson, *Five Smooth Stones for Pastoral Work*, p. 139.
13. Oscar Wilde, *De Profundis* (New York: Modern Library Classics, 2000), pp. 125-26.

Pastoral care counts for little if it is not a form of sharing in another's sorrow, and so of being in contact with divine things, a drawing near to the secret of God. Wilde's suffering gave him a new sense of what matters most in life — along with "freedom, flowers, books and the moon," the friendship that issues in shared suffering. Both the beauty of the world and its sorrow are meant to be shared.

When one shares one's suffering with others, one receives true consolation. By contrast, when one is isolated, one's suffering increases. To know that someone one loved was cherished by others, to weep with them and share the sorrow, draws one into human connection. The caregiver's role is to facilitate communication among those who grieve. Peterson speaks of moving from private lament to public acknowledgment, "transform[ing] what is individual into something corporate." He continues,

> Most cultures show a spontaneous comprehension of this. The suffering person is joined by friends who join their tears and prayers in a communal lament. They do not hush up the sound of weeping but augment it. They do not hide the sufferer away from view but bring him or her out into the public square.[14]

In the villages of Africa, communal lament is still the norm rather than the exception. When there is a death, the villagers crowd into the lanes, no matter the time of day or night, crying out, beating their breasts, and tearing at their garments. The family is given the gift of seeing their loss embodied communally. The cries that ring through the streets confirm the preciousness of the one who has died.

In North America today, it is not unusual for a person to die far from the place where he was born. Local people gather for the funeral, while family members fly in from miles away. Friends who learn of the death often must grieve alone, for they too live in far-flung places. At best, they may share their memories with someone who did not know the deceased. By comparison with African villages, these communities seem threadbare and fragile. They lack the continuity of generations and are held together only by committed efforts to stay in contact. Few stories belong to the community as a whole. One may not even know

14. Peterson, *Five Smooth Stones for Pastoral Work*, p. 142.

those people who share one's loss. One writer expresses the difficulty of connection this way:

> Given how often I have moved, my community is widely scattered. I have close friends all over the world; none of them know each other. We have only our own brief intensities of common experience to bind us, our telephone calls and letters. Friendship is tethered to loss, dependent on mental reconstruction instead of daily enactment. Sometimes I feel stranded at the center of a fragmented orb, my life divided into a series of experiences and places that can never be brought together — except in the solitude of memory. My family too is deposited all over the continent. Crucial junctures in our lives take place in hospital hallways or over bad coffee in airports.[15]

Yet human beings need the strength that comes through shared sorrow. Self-sufficiency melts away in the face of catastrophe and loss. Each person needs to be surrounded by the love that transcends death. "When the community joins in the lament, sanction is given for the expression of loss — the outpouring of emotion is legitimized in such a way as to provide for catharsis and then renewal."[16] The church may be one of the few places left where norms of community life are still valued. When the church joins in the prayer of lament, each member is upheld, and each person's sorrow matters to all.

Concluding Personal Reflections

In *The Timbered Choir,* Wendell Berry includes a poem dedicated to his granddaughters, who visited the Holocaust Museum on the day that Yitzhak Rabin was buried. The poem begins, "Now you know the worst/we humans have to know/about ourselves, and I am sorry." But it moves gracefully and powerfully from darkness to light: "If you will have the courage for love,/you may walk in the light. It will be/the light of those who have suffered/for peace."[17]

---

15. Deborah Tall, "Dwelling: Making Peace with Space and Place," in *Rooted in the Land,* ed. W. Vitek and W. Jackson (New Haven: Yale University Press, 1996), p. 107.

16. Peterson, *Five Smooth Stones for Pastoral Work,* p. 143.

17. Berry, *A Timbered Choir,* p. 192.

When I encountered this poem in the fall of 2001, not long after September 11, I remembered the inarticulate pain I had felt when I first had to tell our young daughter what had happened to Jesus. She was not quite four.[18] Christmas had come and gone, along with the several impromptu plays where Daddy had been instructed to play the part of "Jophus," I had been Mary, and she had been the baby Jesus. Now, with Holy Week approaching, I found myself mute. How could I tell her that Jesus, whom she loved in such innocence, was betrayed by one of his closest friends, deserted by the rest, handed over to be killed, and left to die on a cross? I couldn't bear the thought of seeing the hurt in her eyes or hearing her uncomprehending "Why?" I wanted to protect her from this story of inhumanity. But there it was, right in the middle of our faith, the Cross of Jesus, not to be evaded.

In the early days after September 11, I walked around in a daze, unable to concentrate. Images of fire and collapsing towers and human beings diving headlong to the earth went ceaselessly through my mind. At night planes flew overhead, and fear gripped my heart. Over and over again I imagined myself as a passenger on one of the planes that had crashed into the towers. I lay awake, imagining my way into the terrified hearts of the passengers, of the office workers at the World Trade Center, of those who jumped, or were burned or crushed, of those who escaped and those who failed to escape. The scene etched itself in my mind in a wordless horror, not unlike that of November 22, 1963.

Some pastoral counselors have been trained in what is called Critical Incident Stress Debriefing, a method of working with communities that have undergone a common trauma. As I listened to their stories after the events of September 11, a certain note was repeatedly sounded. Never before had these helpers felt so personally challenged. Never before in entering a traumatized community — where there had been a fire, a murder, or other tragic event — had they themselves been so impacted. Previously they had been able to provide a calm and stable center around which the community could give voice to its pain. Now the helpers themselves were reeling with grief. How could they be anchors when they themselves were stricken?

When a catastrophe of this magnitude is encountered, where are

---

18. Cf. Deborah van Deusen Hunsinger, "Vocation: A Joyous Task," in *Compass Points: Navigating Vocation* (Princeton: Princeton Theological Seminary, 2002), pp. 23-26.

words to give it form and voice? None of us is sustained by the chatter of newscasters or the stories of eyewitnesses and rarely by the reassurances of government officials. At such times, we need something more enduring.

In his poem "Loaves and Fishes," David Whyte says, "People are hungry,/and one good word is bread/for a thousand."[19] The bread that sustained me were four good words from the Apostles' Creed. Neither sermon nor anthem nor the great hymns of the church could penetrate the numbness that set in. But when we rose to say what we all knew by heart, I recited the Creed up to those four: "He descended into hell." Then I could not speak. Here was bread to sustain thousands: our Lord descended into hell. He himself loved each one who had met doom that day. The divine compassion knew no limit in what he was willing to suffer for our sakes. The psalmist knew this: "If I make my bed in Sheol, thou art there! If I take the wings of the morning and dwell in the uttermost parts of the sea, even there thy hand shall lead me, and thy right hand shall hold me" (Ps. 139:8-10). Our pain and terror and despair are knit into Christ's lamentation to God.

When Nicholas Wolterstorff lost his son, he entered a long night of grief. Questions about God's goodness, the mystery of evil, and the incomprehensibility of suffering assailed him. He wrestled, like Jacob, with God. When day finally dawned, Wolterstorff was led to see that "to believe in Christ's rising from the grave is to accept it as a sign of our own rising from our graves." He writes,

> Slowly I begin to see that there is something more as well. To believe in Christ's rising and death's dying is also to live with the power and the challenge to rise up now from all our dark graves of suffering love. If sympathy for the world's wounds is not enlarged by our anguish, if love for those around us is not expanded, if gratitude for what is good does not flame up, if insight is not deepened, if commitment to what is important is not strengthened, if aching for a new day is not intensified, if hope is weakened and faith diminished, if from the experience of death comes nothing good, then death has won. Then death, be proud.

19. David Whyte, *The House of Belonging* (Langley, Wash.: Many Rivers Press, 1997), p. 88.

So I shall struggle to live the reality of Christ's rising and death's dying. In my living, my son's dying will not be the last word. But as I rise up, I bear the wounds of his death. My rising does not remove them. They mark me. If you want to know who I am, put your hand in.[20]

As the church dares to love the world with an open heart, it will suffer for the world's sake. Yet, it is by sharing in suffering love that it finds its vocation in pastoral care. "For as we share abundantly in Christ's sufferings, so through Christ we share abundantly in comfort too" (2 Cor. 1:5). The mystery of participation, *koinonia,* is the mystery at the heart of this work. In its own small way, it attests to that greater suffering by which the world is overcome and made new. This is indeed a strange comfort, but it brings comfort where no other will do. There is no lament outside the bounds of this comfort, and no comfort that is not deepened by lament.

20. Wolterstorff, *Lament for a Son,* pp. 92-93.

Eight Prayers of Confession

When burdened by the wrongs one has committed, prayers of confession are a lifeline to God. How can one live with remorse and still find courage for the future? What can release one from the bondage of past mistakes? How does one escape from entanglement in guilt and shame? Prayers of confession, penitential practices, and prescriptions for restoration have a place of historic importance in pastoral care. William Clebsch and Charles Jaekle identify the "ministry of reconciliation" as one of pastoral care's four basic practices. Along with guiding, sustaining, and healing, they describe reconciliation as the practice of "helping alienated persons to establish or renew proper and fruitful relationships with God and neighbor."[1] It is the help given to those who wish to end their estrangement by repenting of the wrong they have done.

When we consider the centrality of Christ's atoning sacrifice, we might wish to claim the ministry of reconciliation as the fundamental pastoral task, assigning a more peripheral role to the other three. Eduard Thurneysen, for one, took this approach:

> Like the proclamation of the church generally, pastoral conversation has as its only content the communication of the forgiveness of sins in Jesus Christ. . . . There was and there is, therefore, no

---

1. William A. Clebsch and Charles R. Jaekle, *Pastoral Care in Historical Perspective* (Englewood Cliffs, N.J.: Prentice-Hall, 1964), p. 56.

other content of pastoral speaking with the church than forgiveness of sins. [It is] *the content and goal of all pastoral care.*[2]

Yet Thurneysen's argument had little impact in the United States. Seward Hiltner, who had much more influence on pastoral theology in America, did not even include "reconciling" in his list of essential functions.[3] Indeed, sin as a category of discernment eventually fell into such disuse that the psychologist Karl Menninger felt constrained to ask, "Whatever became of sin?"[4] Thirty years later, some churches have dispensed with confessing sin in common worship, believing that such a "negative" focus might lower self-esteem. Others have opted for prayers of confession that fail to grapple with the seriousness of sin. Consider this prayer printed in a church bulletin during the Advent season of 2001:

> God of grace, as followers of your Son, we are always on a journey. On our pilgrimage there is no time when we can afford to stop growing in love, in strength, and in our knowledge of you. So it is that when we gather to worship we would confess those places in which we need to grow. In preparation for the coming of Christ, hear us as we confess our need for growth, in silence prompted by your Spirit.[5]

Such a "confession" is a far cry from an acknowledgment of the desperately corrupt human heart, of which Jeremiah speaks (Jer. 17:9) and from which Paul cries out for deliverance (Rom. 7). Such a prayer suggests that a few more personal-growth seminars will take care of everything that ails us.

While the doctrine of "justification by grace through faith" continues to be of vital ecumenical interest, pastoral theology has largely neglected this conversation. Theologians and philosophers are now the ones discussing sin and repentance with an eye toward pastoral care.[6]

---

2. Eduard Thurneysen, *A Theology of Pastoral Care* (Richmond, Va.: John Knox Press, 1962), p. 147.

3. Seward Hiltner, *Preface to Pastoral Theology* (Nashville: Abingdon Press, 1958).

4. Karl Menninger, *Whatever Became of Sin?* (New York: E. P. Dutton, 1973).

5. *Bread for the Journey*, ed. Ruth C. Duck (New York: Pilgrim Press, 1985), cited by Marguerite Shuster in *The Fall and Sin* (Grand Rapids: Eerdmans, 2004), p. 99.

6. See especially Katherine Sonderegger, "The Doctrine of Justification and the Cure of Souls," in *The Gospel of Justification in Christ*, ed. Wayne Stumme (Grand Rapids:

As psychological modes of thought gained ascendancy and sin fell by the wayside, pastors struggled with the practical tasks of ministry. The dilemmas are illustrated by a pastor trained in the 1960s, now a seminary professor, who laments how little theological guidance he received in his pastoral core training. He recounts a situation from his early years of ministry. A husband and wife each came to him privately for pastoral counsel. Both were active leaders in the church, he an elder and she a deacon. Both of them invoked pastoral confidentiality as they proceeded to tell him that, unbeknownst to their spouse, they were each involved in an adulterous affair. Though the pastor had considerable theological acumen regarding doctrinal understandings of sin, confession, and forgiveness, he was unable to bring it to bear on this case, because his pastoral-care training had focused exclusively on what is known as "reflective listening," made famous by psychologist Carl Rogers.

Following the prescriptions of Rogers, the pastor felt constrained to show "unconditional positive regard," to enter empathetically into his parishioners' frame of reference, and to be "permissive" in his attitudes, bracketing any judgmental thoughts he might have. Yet, as he struggled to listen in this way, he became completely paralyzed. When he saw how their choices were destroying their relationship, he wanted to ask them how they understood their marriage vows in light of their Christian commitment, and how their behavior squared with their role as leaders of the church. But he feared this approach would be seen as judgmental and alienating. His training in listening had taught him how to be accepting but not how to share his own convictions. He stood by helplessly as their marriage was rent asunder and both of them left the church. As he related this story many years later, his distress was still palpable.

How to hold sinners accountable with firmness and love, a question grappled with throughout the history of the ecumenical church, was thus silenced by a theory of care that was neither theological nor ecclesial in its basis. Because pastoral theology has been taught with lit-

---

Eerdmans, 2006). See also Alistair McFadyen, *Bound to Sin: Abuse, Holocaust, and the Christian Doctrine of Sin* (Cambridge: Cambridge University Press, 2000); Cornelius Plantinga Jr., *Not the Way It's Supposed to Be: A Breviary of Sin* (Grand Rapids: Eerdmans, 1995); Diogenes Allen, *Temptation* (Cambridge, Mass.: Cowley Publications, 1986); and Gerhard Sauter, *Gateway to Dogmatics: Reasoning Theologically for the Life of the Church* (Grand Rapids: Eerdmans, 2003).

tle attention to differentiating pastoral care from psychotherapy, pastors have been hampered in their efforts. As Nancy Ramsay has written,

> To the extent that the therapeutic has "triumphed" in our culture, sin and the experience of redemptive transformation are often conflated as psychopathology and mental health, so that the more profound truthfulness of the ecclesial paradigm is trivialized while the more limited, albeit helpful explanations of a psychological/scientific paradigm are exaggerated.[7]

If it is to serve the church, pastoral theology needs to recover its theological bearings.

Sin as a Theological Concept

Prayers confessing sin take place in a context alien to psychotherapy, but central to a theological understanding. When sin is considered theologically, what can be said to orient us for the pastoral task? How can caregivers provide guidance to those burdened with unconfessed sin?

First, we must recognize that sin is spiritual in essence. It pertains primarily to God and only then to human relationships. The horizontal axis, so to speak, derives meaning from the vertical axis. For example, in Leviticus we read, "If any one sins and commits a breach of faith against the LORD by deceiving his neighbor . . ." (Lev. 6:2). Deceiving one's neighbor is regarded as a sin against God. Since our life is grounded beyond ourselves in God, any wrongdoing against a fellow human being makes us divinely accountable. The voice of Abel's blood, shed by his brother, Cain, cries out from earth to heaven (Gen. 4:10). Recall the traditional reading of Psalm 51. After David is confronted by the prophet Nathan and recognizes the gravity of his sin, he says to God, "Against thee, thee only, have I sinned" (Ps. 51:4). It would be mistaken to suppose that Da-

---

7. Nancy J. Ramsay, "Pastoral Assessment in the Congregational Genre," *Journal of Pastoral Theology* 1 (Summer 1991): 85. Thurneysen's *Theology of Pastoral Care* does clearly differentiate between these two universes of discourse. See also Deborah van Deusen Hunsinger, *Theology and Pastoral Counseling: A New Interdisciplinary Approach* (Grand Rapids: Eerdmans, 1995); and Nancy J. Ramsay, *Pastoral Diagnosis: A Resource for Ministries of Care and Counseling* (Minneapolis: Augsburg Fortress Press, 1998).

vid is thereby denying his sins against Uriah and Bathsheba. By murdering the one and taking the other in adultery, he has sinned against both of them. Nevertheless, the primary breach is in his relationship with God. For it is God who gave Israel the commandments not to kill and not to commit adultery, and God who has bound himself so closely to those who are wronged. Marguerite Shuster comments,

> When we speak of God's law, we understand that the sovereignty of the Lawgiver stands behind it, and the law is the way that the will of God confronts us. The law, therefore, is not simply a set of abstract, absolute, and perhaps disparate rules, but rather the revelation of the One who addresses, speaks to us, demands that we do certain things and refrain from doing other things. Thus, in giving the Ten Commandments, God does not say, "It is wrong to steal," rather, "you shall not steal" (Exod. 20:15) — in the form not of abstract principles but of personal engagement.[8]

Scripture teaches that disorder in our relationships with others is a symptom of estrangement from God. It is our connection to God that is primary and fundamental. When that is distorted, we cannot even relate to ourselves in a wholesome way. Think, for example, of Paul's observation in his first letter to the Corinthians that "the immoral man sins against his own body" (1 Cor. 6:18).[9]

Those who suffer from the burden of unacknowledged sin need to be brought before God. Prayers of confession cleanse and renew the soul. They prepare the way toward reconciliation with those who have been wronged. Acknowledging one's sin to another human being is not the same as acknowledgment to God, which is primary. Calvin writes, "The beginning, and even the preparation, of proper prayer is the plea for pardon with a humble and sincere confession of guilt. . . . It is no wonder if believers open for themselves the door to prayer with this key."[10] Every

---

8. Shuster, *The Fall and Sin*, p. 103.

9. In his letter to the Corinthian church, Paul argues that sexual immorality is a sin against one's own self, because the Holy Spirit not only dwells within one's mortal body but also joins one's humanity to Christ's.

10. John Calvin, *Institutes of the Christian Religion*, Library of Christian Classics, vols. 20-21, ed. John T. McNeill, trans. Ford Lewis Battles (Philadelphia: Westminster Press, 1960), 3.20.9, p. 860.

member of the church is accountable to God. Confession is not a self-help technique. There is nothing one can do to save oneself from sin's bondage and guilt. One must find the courage to acknowledge it, to pass through the narrow gate of repentance. Until one does so, God's judgment will burn, openly or secretly, within. "When I declared not my sin, my body wasted away through my groaning all day long. For day and night thy hand was heavy upon me; my strength was dried up as by the heat of summer" (Ps. 32:3-4). If one wishes to be whole and renewed, one can move forward only by confessing. Running from one's sin, closing one's eyes to it, rationalizing, minimizing, or denying it only prolong the pain.

Second, we must acknowledge that sin's origin is obscure even to faith. Anyone who has ever wrestled with the origin of sin will, along with the theologians of the ages, finally have to admit defeat. If God created the world and all that is in it, and pronounced it good, then whence came evil? If God did not want human beings to sin, and if sin is completely against the will of God, then why did God put the tempter into the Garden of Eden? If God created the serpent, and the serpent was evil, then isn't God the author of evil? How did good human beings have the capacity to commit evil, if that capacity were not given by God? Augustine's ruminations on this subject are unsurpassed:

> And I said: "Here is God, and here is what God has created; and God is good, mightily and incomparably better than all these; but of His goodness he created them good; and see how He contains and fills them. Where then is evil, and what is its source, and how has it crept into the Creation? What is its root, what is its seed? . . . Whence then is evil, since God who is good made all things good? . . ." Such thoughts I revolved in my unhappy heart, which was further burdened and gnawed at by the fear that I should die without having found the truth.[11]

Barth resorts to paradox in calling sin the "impossible possibility." Marguerite Shuster concludes, "The upshot is that we must insist once again that sin is inexplicable."[12] Sin is actual, yet baffling and absurd.

---

11. Augustine, *Confessions* (New York: Sheed & Ward, 1942), pp. 111-12.
12. Shuster, *The Fall and Sin*, p. 126.

Jeremiah points to sin's ineffability: "The heart is deceitful above all things, and desperately corrupt; who can understand it?" (Jer. 17:9).

Whenever we try to make sin more understandable, we stand in danger of underestimating its power. The temptation is either to blame God for sin or, alternatively, to find something that sin is good for. Rather than discerning that God brings good out of evil without making evil good, we are tempted to minimize the damage that our corrupt wills wreak on the world. In the Christian tradition, sin is understood as so radical that its remedy took nothing less than the death of the Son of God. Without the merciful intervention of God in Jesus Christ, we would be dead in our sins, having no hope of access to God. For God is holy and righteous, requiring all who seek him to be righteous as well. Again and again we read of God's righteousness in Scripture. "The LORD your God is in the midst of you, a great and terrible God" (Deut. 7:21). "For I was afraid of the anger and hot displeasure which the LORD bore against you, so that he was ready to destroy you. But the LORD hearkened to me that time also" (Deut. 9:19). "Thou . . . art of purer eyes than to behold evil and canst not look on wrong" (Hab. 1:13). We cannot begin to take sin seriously until we refuse to rationalize it. Faith acknowledges that though we deserve God's condemnation, God, in merciful judgment, has spared us by taking it upon himself.

Third, we must realize that sin's nature is known only through revelation. Anyone can observe strife and enmity among human beings and surmise that something is dreadfully amiss. Anyone can look at human history with its suffering visited upon millions of victims — of war and torture, enslavement and oppression, cruelty and hostility and neglect — and wonder why human beings treat one another so abominably. But to understand all this evil *as sin* requires a biblical framework. It requires the perception of faith. The truth about our own hearts needs to be revealed to us because it is in the very nature of sin to disguise itself. We don't recognize it or ourselves as its authors. Sin is notorious for its disguises. Max Scheler suggests that "one of the most mysterious ways in which [sin] works is that it provides its own concealment and blunts all sensitivity to its existence."[13] We presume to be

13. Scheler uses the word "guilt" here, though I believe that the concept of sin is even more accurate. Cf. Max Scheler, "Repentance and Rebirth," in *On the Eternal in Man* (North Haven, Conn.: Shoestring Press, 1972), pp. 61-62.

acting for the sake of good, and yet our motives, if we had the freedom to examine them honestly, are fatally mixed (cf. James 2:10).

On the basis of what we have observed or experienced of ourselves in the ordinary unfolding of our lives, who among us would describe ourselves as radically sinful, as godless or worthy of condemnation, unable to love God or neighbor? Perhaps we have thought that we were the exception to this rule of radical evil; our intentions are good, after all, and we are not really so bad. Yet Scripture, unlike our self-assessment, is unambiguous: "If we say we have no sin, we deceive ourselves, and the truth is not in us" (1 John 1:8).

We are instructed to understand ourselves on the basis of what Scripture tells us, even when it seems contrary to self-perception. Gerhard Sauter writes, "The inner grounding of confession of sin is recollection of the act of God. It is a sign of the beginning of knowledge of God and a recognition of the self."[14] The redemptive act of God is the justification and salvation of sinners. When we look away from ourselves toward God, we no longer have to worry about our lame rationalizations or the relative weight of our guilt compared to another's, or self-justification of any kind. We are free to confess everything to God. Dietrich Bonhoeffer expresses it this way:

> Christians are persons who no longer seek their salvation, their deliverance, their justification in themselves, but in Jesus Christ alone. They know that God's Word in Jesus Christ pronounces them guilty, even when they feel nothing of their own guilt, and that God's Word in Jesus Christ pronounces them free and righteous, even when they feel nothing of their own righteousness. Christians no longer live by their own resources, by accusing themselves and justifying themselves, but by God's accusation and God's justification. They live entirely by God's Word pronounced on them, in faithful submission to God's judgment, whether it declares them guilty or righteous. . . . Christians are dependent on the Word of God spoken to them. They are directed outward, to the Word coming to them.[15]

14. Sauter, *Gateway to Dogmatics,* p. 106.

15. Dietrich Bonhoeffer, *Life Together* (Minneapolis: Augsburg/Fortress, 1996), pp. 31-32.

Finally, we need to see that, contrary to what can be perceived by introspection, Scripture teaches that human sin is so evil as to be worthy of divine wrath. "The LORD will swallow them up in his wrath," says the psalmist, "and fire will consume them" (Ps. 21:9). At the beginning of the longest unrelieved passage about sin in all of Scripture, Paul writes, "The wrath of God is revealed from heaven against all ungodliness and wickedness of men who by their wickedness suppress the truth" (Rom. 1:18). And "by your hard and impenitent heart you are storing up wrath for yourself on the day of wrath when God's righteous judgment will be revealed" (Rom. 2:5). Nevertheless — and here divine grace is brought to expression — the good news is that God's righteous judgment against sin unexpectedly becomes a judgment of mercy. Delivered over to wrath and condemnation, we are astonished to hear that we are pardoned, that our sins have been judged and forgiven.

The Gospel message is this: that God himself has opened the way to a free and loving relationship with him. In ourselves, we cannot survive the judgment of a holy and righteous God. Nevertheless, in Jesus Christ, God has become human, a righteous human being. He has thrown a bridge across the chasm. Because he is fully human, Jesus alone is able to bear God's condemnation in our place, through his death on the Cross. Because he is fully divine, Jesus alone is able to stand in our place before God and clothe us with his righteousness. Our situation before God is completely made new in him. Through baptism we are united with Christ in his death and resurrection. By grace through faith, we are given access to God, that we might approach him in intimacy and trust. Because of Christ's righteousness, we do not have to fear coming to God with our confession. United with Christ, we are covered by his cloak of righteousness. His righteousness has become ours even as our sin became his.

Justification by Grace through Faith

The insight of Reformational faith, that we are justified by God in Christ and not by our own works, came to be known as "justification by grace through faith." Luther famously saw it as the doctrine by which the church stands or falls. When confessing our sins, whether in corporate worship or in private prayer or through pastoral ministry, we presuppose this doctrine. Human frameworks of knowing, it has been suggested, function like tools, "because they become assimilated to our bodies as instruments of perception and action. We 'indwell' them so as to understand and act through them."[16] The doctrine of "justification by faith alone" functions in this sense. It is the means of perception by which we are able to approach the throne of grace. We confess our sins, in other words, *already knowing* God's love and forgiveness, already believing in his desire to redeem us and bring us into spiritual communion with himself. James Torrance provides a helpful distinction between what he calls "legal repentance" and evangelical repentance:

> Legal repentance says: "Repent, and if you repent you will be forgiven!" as though God our Father has to be conditioned into being gracious! It makes the imperatives of obedience prior to the indicatives of grace, and regards God's love and forgiveness and acceptance as conditional upon what we do — upon our meritorious acts of repentance. Calvin argued that this inverted the evangelical order of grace, and made repentance prior to forgiveness, whereas in the New Testament forgiveness is logically prior to repentance. Evangelical repentance, on the other hand, takes the form: "Christ has borne your sins on the cross, therefore repent! Receive his forgiveness in repentance!" That is, *repentance is our response to grace, not a condition of grace.* The goodness of God leads us to repentance.[17]

This order is important to pastoral care. When grace is understood as the presupposition and not the consequence of repentance, it becomes clear that repentance itself is a gift of the Spirit. The freedom to approach God in prayer is the freedom God gives. Gerhard Sauter says, "Confession of guilt within the prayer of forgiveness is grounded in the freedom of self-knowledge. We cannot get behind this freedom. It is liberation for a new beginning."[18] Repentance arises from that "godly grief that . . . leads to salvation and brings no regret," in contrast

---

16. Christopher Jones, "Loosing and Binding," in *Forgiveness and Truth* (Edinburgh: T&T Clark, 2001), p. 36; Jones draws on Michael Polanyi's conception of practical knowledge.

17. James B. Torrance, *Worship, Community, and the Triune God of Grace* (Downers Grove, Ill.: InterVarsity Press, 1996), p. 44; emphasis mine.

18. Sauter, *Gateway to Dogmatics,* p. 110.

to the "worldly grief [that] produces death" (2 Cor. 7:10). Regret now becomes a harbinger of good, and godly grief promises renewal.

How are "worldly" grief and "godly" grief to be distinguished? Worldly grief places the self and its concerns, rather than God, at the center of our lives. What happens when we are called to account for something we have done (or failed to do)? Do we seek to deny responsibility and focus the guilt elsewhere? Is our first concern one of defending ourselves? How often do we ask, "What is my part?" or "What is the truth of this accusation?" Are we not instead disposed to ask, "How can I get the focus off me?" or "How is this person not living up to *his* responsibility?" Worldly grief takes offense at another's admonitions. It is not interested in the truth of the matter, and God's judgment is not sought. All our energy is spent on securing ourselves or rationalizing the offense.

Worldly grief can, by contrast, also take the form of sorrow that refuses to be comforted. Suppose that we acknowledge the truth of another's rebuke, feel convicted of sin, and experience remorse. But we are determined to be our own judge, and we refuse the consolation of the Gospel. In this instance we become paralyzed by the magnitude of our wrong. We torture ourselves over the sin into which we have fallen. We readily acknowledge our sin but refuse to receive God's forgiveness with humility. We secretly expect perfection of ourselves. We want to be justified by our own goodness instead of by the grace of God. We would rather be immobilized by self-recrimination (i.e., inverted pride) than face our wrongdoing, confess it, and be forgiven. Such worldly grief leads to death because it means life without God. It is determined to be its own judge.

When God occupies the center of the human heart, there is no need for self-justification or for hopelessness. Only that "godly grief" is needed that produces "a repentance that leads to salvation and brings no regret." The faith that knows its justification in Jesus Christ is a faith that acknowledges that no one stands beyond judgment. It knows that all human motives are mixed and that all our actions are tainted by self-seeking.

Godly grief is sorrow "according to God," whose will is to engender true repentance. God's love is poured into our hearts, deepening our desire for renewal. When we acknowledge the harm we have caused another, it is inevitable that we will feel grieved. As we allow that sorrow to be directed by God, we are led to actions which, by the power of the Holy Spirit, move toward the other's restoration and our redemption. The good news is that we no longer have to carry the burden of our wrongdoing. Because God is gracious and merciful, because God desires us to confess our sins, because God longs to set our foot in a broad place and bring us from the pit of arrogance or despair, we are free to repent. When our conscience is smitten and we feel the pain of regret, God is at work within us. He is Lord of the conscience and the source of all godly grief.

We are led to acknowledge our sins solely by God's grace. When we are brought to recognize our sin, we experience release. We no longer have to pretend. When faith is brought low, it sees things in their proper order. It sees our absolute dependence upon God and his saving work in our life. No longer do we have to waste energy trying to justify ourselves, assert ourselves, or hide from God. Faith looks to God as the giver of all good gifts, the sustainer of our lives, and the source of truth. It looks to God, trusting in his judgment and forgiveness.

Though never painless, true repentance has joy at its center. When faith repents, it does so in the context of grace. Because faith knows God's gracious judgment, because it knows that God wants us to live in freedom, we are enabled to repent. As God calls us to live in truth, we can abandon the lies that we tell in seeking to justify ourselves. Bonhoeffer underscores the meaning and importance of confession:

> Confession is grace, not law. It is not a work we do in order to become perfect Christians; it is a grace which leads to certitude, conversion, fellowship, and joy. Confession is divine sadness which leads to divine joy. . . . Where people lament that there is no life in the church, we might ask how that is connected to disregard for confession. In any event, new life in Christ, new obedience and service, and new joy in the Gospel all stem from confession.[19]

Confession and Preaching

The perception of ourselves as needy sinners is offered in common worship. As Scripture is read, the Gospel is preached, and the sacraments

19. Dietrich Bonhoeffer, *Spiritual Care* (Philadelphia: Fortress Press, 1985), p. 64.

are received, we learn to know ourselves as sinners whom God wants to restore to life. As we perceive ourselves in the light of the biblical narrative, we acknowledge the dark continuity between ourselves and some of the people we read about there:

- the prodigal son, who squanders all that his father has given — not just the material wealth that he wastes on things that corrupt his soul, but the immense love poured out for him, that he might make something of the life given him.
- the Samaritan woman, looking for a love that can satisfy the thirst of her soul, giving herself heedlessly to one man after another.
- Peter, who is so sure of himself that he brags about his faithfulness, certain that he would never deny his Lord. But when he fears for his life, he swears that he has never known Jesus.
- Thomas, who sees the risen Lord in doubt and longing. Hiding in the Upper Room, filled with shame and fear, he is astonished to be offered Christ's peace.
- the church at Corinth, boasting in their superior knowledge, sitting in judgment over others, and clinging to their cherished factions rather than recognizing their unity in Christ.

In the biblical story, we are repeatedly faced with a truth about God that is joined to a truth about ourselves. The truth about God is that he loves us with a severe mercy, with a depth impossible to fathom, and with overflowing generosity. Even when his rebuke is gentle, it involves a "no-nonsense" insistence on our facing the truth about ourselves. God's mercy entails judgment because we are sinners in rebellion. But the judgment is merciful because it puts limits on our tendency to be self-destructive.

It is God's judgment that brings the prodigal son to himself. After years in exile, he is set free to return to his father and confess his unworthiness. It is Jesus' judgment that does not skirt the truth of the Samaritan woman's sexual history: he "told [her] all that [she] ever did" (John 4:29). No longer burdened by guilt and shame, she is freed to begin her life anew. For Peter, the moment of judgment comes when Jesus looks at him as the cock crows. With remorse, Peter sees that his protestations of fidelity have been in vain. Thomas's fear ends when the

Crucified One appears alive before him and breathes his blessing of peace upon him. Paul calls the Corinthians to account, smiting their conscience toward a godly grief that produces repentance.

"It is a fearful thing," writes Max Scheler, "that we can win life only on the dark *via dolorosa* of repentance. But it is glorious that we have *any* way to life."[20] When Jesus appears alive in the midst of his disciples, he grants his gift of peace to those who had betrayed, denied, and deserted him. A love like this cannot be comprehended. In its light we recognize our shortcomings — our bickering, our pride, and our pathetic attempts at making ourselves important — for what they are. God's grace humbles us and gives us penitent hearts. When we are given the freedom to repent, we are paradoxically blessed with joy in the midst of sorrow. We are lifted beyond our sin even as we confess it. For we come to the act of confession by knowing of God's grace, mercy, and forgiveness.[21]

Pastoral Considerations

The pastoral challenge today is that people talk about these issues in every way imaginable. Some have no concept of sin, and many who do have an inadequate conception that does more harm than good. Certain features are almost always present: feelings of guilt and shame, or perhaps the denial of guilt and massive defenses against shame. Some people are riddled with regret; others know fear as their most prominent emotion, coupled with a compulsion to hide. The first task of pastoral caregivers is to listen to the person's self-understanding, hearing the multiple and complex strands: a whisper of regret in the midst of denial, self-blame that paradoxically seeks to avoid responsibility, a reluctance to trust, hesitation and doubt, remorse over the inability to change the past, shame that renders the tongue mute. The pastoral lis-

20. Max Scheler, "Repentance and Rebirth," pp. 61-62.
21. James Loder writes, "To be convicted of sin should be met with something like an 'Aha! so that's what's wrong! Praise God, there is an alternative!' . . . To be convicted of sin . . . would be unbearable, totally offensive, even unrecognizable if it were not that such a realization is preceded by the grace that makes such a realization not only bearable but profoundly generative of a new being." See James E. Loder, *Logic of the Spirit: Human Development in Theological Perspective* (San Francisco: Jossey-Bass, 1998), p. 116.

tener needs to be attuned to the human heart in order to speak to the specific situation with discretion and wisdom.

In this respect, pastoral theology has gained from its study of the psychology of his unconscious.[22] It has received new insight into the multiple layers, inner contradictions, and mixed motives of the human heart. Freud's "basic rule" of not withholding any thought or association, for example, has revealed the labyrinths of the human soul, for good and for ill. Freud also believed that dreams, which encode a person's emotional and spiritual situation, are like a confession that goes far beyond anything the person could consciously acknowledge. Carl Jung once likened the entire psychotherapeutic process to an extended act of confession. The psychotherapist, like the priest with the confessional seal, is pledged to confidentiality. Indeed, some have found relief in confessing their life story — all that is shameful and embarrassing along with whatever is laudable and noble — to their psychotherapist. Many have experienced an acceptance there that has delivered them from painful isolation.

Nevertheless, psychotherapy is still something quite different from the message of the Gospel, even if one draws an analogy between them or interprets the former as a parable of the latter.[23] It is something quite different to confess one's sin to a minister of the Gospel, when the promise of grace is already known, than to hope for a therapist's continuing regard despite actions that cause one shame. What can a therapist represent other than human acceptance, empathy, and respect? Though such a response is not to be underestimated in its power to heal, it is still different from the divine forgiveness that the Gospel has the power to convey. The theological context transforms the meaning of confession, as Bonhoeffer points out:

> The most experienced observer of humanity knows less of the human heart than the Christian who lives at the foot of the cross of Christ. No psychology knows that people perish only through sin

22. Cf. Deborah van Deusen Hunsinger, "An Interdisciplinary Map for Christian Counselors: Theology and Psychology in Pastoral Counseling," in *Care for the Soul,* ed. Mark McMinn and Timothy Phillips (Downers Grove, Ill.: InterVarsity Press, 2001), pp. 218-40.

23. Cf. Thomas Oden, *Kerygma and Counseling* (Philadelphia: Westminster Press, 1966), p. 51.

and are saved only through the cross of Christ. Anyone who has seen the meaning of the cross for but a moment is shocked by the godlessness of the world and by the awesomeness of his own sins; he will no longer be shocked by the sins of his sisters and brothers in Christ. The spirit of judgment is cut off at the roots. He knows the other to be accepted by God in the midst of his lostness even as he is accepted. He loves brother and sister under the cross.[24]

The pastoral encounter takes place at the foot of the cross. It points those who confess their sins toward the One who is able to forgive and bring comfort. Pastoral caregivers need to get out of the way. It doesn't matter what they think; what matters is God's action. Insofar as another needs assurance of their esteem, they can of course grant it, acknowledging that they too are sinners. They are not the other's judge, only a fellow supplicant.

Since confession of sin seeks something more than human understanding, caregivers need to be attuned to the Word of God. How can someone hear the "unheard miracle of grace," that they are forgiven for those choices that have harmed others, grieved the heart of God, and estranged them even from themselves? How can they receive the knowledge that they are no longer held captive to the sins and failures of the past, but are now free to make amends and seek the healing promised by God? These questions cannot be answered abstractly. Preaching the Gospel in the right way at the right time requires the gift of discernment. The questions themselves are finally a matter for prayer. Pastoral caregivers wait attentively until the right word is given, until they find their response to the movement of the Holy Spirit in the present moment. It is not simply a matter of juggling symbol systems or reading conceptual maps. Nor is it offering the most apt and insightful comment. It is instead an event that occurs between their spirit and the Spirit of God in the service of the Word for the sake of faith and healing.

When they stand alongside another, they know that they cannot set themselves in the place of God, nor can they act as if they know God's mind and heart. The mystery of each person's relationship with God needs to be respected. The best that they can do is to stand with

---

24. Bonhoeffer, *Spiritual Care*, p. 62.

the other under the authority of Scripture. In consenting to be the human vessel through which God's Word is spoken in times of vulnerability and need, they fulfill the pastoral task. When sin has been confessed, their task is to offer the Word of life:

> God has put this Word into the mouth of human beings so that it may be passed to others. When people are deeply affected by the Word, they tell it to other people. God has willed that we should seek and find God's living Word in the testimony of other Christians, in the mouths of human beings. Therefore, Christians need other Christians who speak God's Word to them. They need them again and again when they become uncertain and disheartened because, living by their own resources, they cannot help themselves without cheating themselves out of the truth. They need other Christians as bearers and proclaimers of the divine word of salvation.[25]

When caregivers offer the assurance of God's forgiveness to one assailed by doubt, shame, regret, or despair, they become a source of consolation as they comfort the other "with the comfort with which [they themselves] are comforted by God" (2 Cor. 1:4).

Protestants who affirm the "priesthood of all believers" believe that any Christian may hear another's confession of sin. Any Christian may act in this capacity, bringing word of God's mercy in Jesus Christ. Any Christian may act as companion and witness when another confesses sin before God. Protestants reject the idea that only ordained clergy may hear another's confession. Nor do they believe that only ordination qualifies one to mediate the forgiveness of Christ. Although no human being alone, priest or otherwise, is capable of mediating Christ's grace, any believer may be called upon to do so by a power given though never possessed. The mediation of Christ's grace takes place through earthen vessels or not at all.

Members of the church are instructed to confess their sins to each other and to "pray for one another" (James 5:16). The reflexive form "for one another" indicates that it is a mutual task. Yet where in the church today is such mutual accountability practiced? Hierarchical relationships often preclude such mutuality, as do most contem-

---

25. Bonhoeffer, *Life Together*, p. 32.

porary models of therapy and spiritual direction. Small groups that gather for mutual encouragement, accountability, and intercessory prayer seem to approximate most closely the New Testament vision. New Testament churches were small, mutually accountable groups who held all things in common. With our very different ecclesial situation and cultural assumptions, it is difficult to imagine such a common life. Thoreau's perception that most people "lead lives of quiet desperation" at times seems as true of the church today as of the population at large. Quiet desperation may come to those hiding behind a façade of their Sunday best. Bonhoeffer describes those unable to admit their sin:

> He who is alone with his sin is utterly alone. It may be that Christians, notwithstanding corporate worship, common prayer, and all their fellowship in service, may still be left to their loneliness. The final breakthrough to fellowship does not occur, because, though they have fellowship with one another as believers and as devout people, they do not have fellowship as the undevout, as sinners. The pious fellowship permits no one to be a sinner. So everybody must conceal his sin from himself and from the fellowship.[26]

The breakthrough to fellowship occurs when faith in Christ enables members of the community to take the risk of confessing their sins to one another. Mutual trust and openness pave the way for mutual respect and love to grow.

Confession and Twelve-Step Groups

The communal practice of confession and mutual accountability can be found today in the twelve-step groups of Alcoholics Anonymous. The first three steps for participants are to acknowledge their powerlessness over alcohol, to affirm that only a power greater than themselves can restore sanity, and to turn their lives over to the care of "God as we understand him." With the vertical dimension in place, the remaining steps turn mainly toward the consequences of choices made. Though the word "sin" is never used, the Twelve Steps expect partici-

---

26. Bonhoeffer, *Life Together,* p. 110.

pants in the program to take a "fearless moral inventory" (Step Four). They pledge to acknowledge the "exact nature of our wrongs" not only to God and themselves but also to "another human being" (Step Five). They also express a readiness to have God remove all "defects of character" (Step Six). Then they offer direct supplication to God, asking him to remove them (Step Seven). They acknowledge the people they have harmed and express a willingness to make amends (Step Eight). They take concrete action toward those they have hurt, except when doing so would cause further harm (Step Nine). They also continue to take "personal inventory" of their "shortcomings" so that they can "promptly admit" when they are wrong (Step Ten). Where in the church does mutual confession take such concrete shape? Where can people be seen as they really are and receive both the support and the accountability they need?

Though Alcoholics Anonymous was rooted in the Oxford Group Movement, it became more secularized as it reached out to the wider society. A "higher power" cannot simply be equated with a Christian conception of God, nor is the fellowship enjoyed in these groups the same as Christian community. Nevertheless, through twelve-step groups, many have rekindled a sense of what mutual confession might mean for the church today. Instead of denial, the twelve steps guide one toward acknowledging one's shortcomings. Instead of abstract or generalized notions of sin, the twelve steps encourage one to specifically confess one's misdeeds. A culture of acceptance in the knowledge of God's grace supports openness about one's actual struggles and failures.

While AA does not mention the name of Jesus Christ, it teaches something about the theocentric nature of community. Where divine grace and judgment are acknowledged (and both are implied in each of the twelve steps), right relationships are possible. Because persons are spiritual beings, the vertical and horizontal dimensions of their life together cannot be separated. When they rely upon grace for their justification, they cease their anxious striving to justify themselves in the eyes of others. As forgiven sinners they experience a solidarity that opens them to the other. None stands as superior to another in the eyes of God. All can be known and accepted in humility and also in gladness for who they are.

Conclusion

Reflecting on the "cure of souls" as a basic form of the church's ministry, Karl Barth writes, "Here in the cure of souls there can and should be confession with the promise of the remission of sins, and the invitation to the resultant amendment of life, not as an institution bound to certain clerical officials, but as an event."[27] Today mutual confession as a spiritual event is needed in the ministry of the church, not only among the laity but also among clergy. Mutual confession would undermine the competition and isolation that so pervade the clerical office. Church leaders would be free to acknowledge their need of one another, no longer laboring under the pretense of self-sufficiency. As the church practices mutual confession at the foot of the Cross, they may be given the Spirit's gift of true fellowship, *koinonia*. Together the members of Christ's body may trust in God's grace to renew and redeem their lives.

27. Karl Barth, *Church Dogmatics*, IV/3 (Edinburgh: T&T Clark, 1960), p. 886.

Nine Prayers of Praise, Thanksgiving, and Blessing

In the Eucharistic prayers of the church's worship, we learn how to praise God — first of all, for who God is as the Lord and giver of life, for the inexpressible glory reflected in all that he has created, and second, for his manifold gifts and blessings to us. In our life of gathered worship, we lift up our hearts to the Lord. We turn our focus away from ourselves and meditate on God and the wonder of his creative and redemptive work. All our attention is on the object of worship and praise — on this God who continually gives himself in love to us. As we pray the great prayer of thanksgiving, we contemplate the story of salvation into which our own little lives have been placed. Week after week, we are told of the wonderful works of God: the creation of the world out of nothing, the election of Israel out of all the peoples of the earth, their deliverance from the cruel bonds of slavery, the mercies of God's provision in the wilderness, and the miraculous gift of the promised land. Week after week, God's compassion and steadfast love are set before us as we contemplate the redemption of the world through the life, death, and resurrection of our Lord Jesus Christ.

Whenever we gather for worship, we are thus reminded that God is the One who gives us life, who preserves and sustains us, and that he alone has the power to sanctify and redeem us. We are reminded that God alone provides us with what we need each day: he gives us the earth in all its bounty and beauty; he gives us one another for companionship and mutual succor; and in Jesus Christ he gives us himself. Our prayers of gratitude therefore arise out of our meditation on God and the abundance of his blessings. We praise him for who he is. We thank him for all that he has given us. And we bless him as a way to mirror the blessings that he has bestowed on us.

Doxologies of praise and thanksgiving permeate the entire worship service. Opening hymns proclaim God's majesty and call the people together in one voice to praise him for his glory. Prayers of confession presuppose his goodness, for they rest on the assurance of his forgiving mercy. The sacraments of baptism and Eucharist include long recitations of the history of God's gracious provision and the church's response of gratitude. The reading of Scripture, the proclamation of the Gospel, and the offering of intercessory prayer are all suffused with thanks and praise. After Scripture is read, the liturgist often announces, "The Word of the Lord." When the congregation answers, "Thanks be to God," it acknowledges the gift that Scripture is, the very Word of God to us. With this exclamation of thanksgiving, the congregation acknowledges the outpouring of God's grace in and through this gift. Preaching lifts up God's grace again and again so that the congregation's gratitude becomes present and palpable. Finally, the service ends with God's blessing on his people, delivered by the minister of the community ordained to pass on this benediction.

Employing Scripture in Pastoral Prayer

As in our corporate worship, so also in pastoral care. When the people of God listen to those who need their care and in turn pray with them, they also turn their attention toward God and who God is. The incomparable gift of Scripture lies in its being so thoroughly God-centered. When caregivers' imaginations are shaped by Scripture and liturgy, they are unable to perceive another's life, or even their own, apart from the lens of faith. God's steadfast love that endures forever will shape all their thinking and hoping and praying. Consider the psalms. When the psalmist focuses on himself, he becomes mired in fear and hopelessness. Only as he turns toward God is his sense of hope restored. As he focuses on the particularities of his situation, he becomes overwhelmed by trouble, sorrow, and anxiety. Yet when he turns toward God, he sees everything in a new light: "But I have trusted in thy steadfast love; my heart shall rejoice in thy salvation" (Ps. 13:5). Even to recall the words "steadfast love" brings to mind the memorable phrase "for his steadfast love endures for ever." It hearkens back to the twenty-six verses of Psalm 136, where the line "For his steadfast love endures for ever" is repeated no less than twenty-six times. The repetition of the line is deliberate, ensuring that it will be deeply inscribed on the heart. It makes certain that whenever God's steadfast love is recalled, the rest of the phrase will continue to reverberate. Through this description of God's identity, the church is reminded of God's constant love, which transcends time and undergirds its trust in him.

When caregivers focus on who God is and what God has done, they may notice certain corresponding attitudes and affections rising up within: feelings of wonder and awe, thankfulness, joy, and peace. Gratitude grows when they ponder God's actual history with his people. It is important to remember, however, that a heart of gratitude cannot be gained simply by trying to will oneself into it. While the clichéd advice that one should "count one's blessings" surely contains a grain of truth, it can produce the opposite effect on the listener. Instead of hearing the blessing of the Gospel, she hears the necessity of the Law: she *should* be grateful; she *ought to* be thankful for all that she has. Being told that she ought to feel grateful may effectively mire her either in shame or in anger: shame if she judges herself to be ungrateful and selfish; anger if she takes offense at the judgment. By contrast, when she hears the indicative of grace — not the imperative of the Law — gratitude naturally wells up. When another takes the time to enumerate her blessings in the midst of adversity, gratitude returns.

Just as the psalmist mysteriously shifts from lament to praise, so too in the pastoral encounter as God's blessings are recalled. Instead of being exhorted to be grateful, in other words, the other receives the incomparable gift of actually hearing God's myriad blessings in her life. What is done in a communal setting in public worship is thereby done on a more personal scale in a pastoral visit. Instead of reciting the great sweep of God's salvation history, the pastoral caregiver has the more modest task of calling to mind the concrete blessings this one has received from the hand of God. Just as God's providence and love are recounted in worship, so now God's grace may be recounted as manifested in this singular life story. Those with eyes to see and ears to hear will perceive God's luminous moments of grace. The pastoral caregiver, as the interpreter and mediator of God's care, will weave the slender thread of this life into the larger fabric of salvation's narrative.

Patterns of meaning embedded in a life story typically emerge as caregivers meditate on it in the light of liturgy and Scripture. Theological meanings suggest themselves as they engage in intercessory prayer. In prayer, images shaped by the scriptural imagination begin to take shape. Caregivers may perceive the other as one wandering through a desert, waiting for the manna needed to sustain him through a single day's hardship. As God sustained the Israelites in the wilderness, so he will sustain those who call upon him for help. Metaphors of redemption come alive as longings for deliverance filter up into awareness. Scripture shapes the imagination toward myriad images of divine blessing: the cleansing and renewing waters of baptism; the release of captives from prison; the feeding of the five thousand; the royal banquet in the kingdom of God; the bride adorned in beauty for her bridegroom; the son returning home to the bosom of his father; dancing for joy before the ark of the Lord; the descent of the Holy Spirit, bringing forth passionate fires of praising; the water that wells up to eternal life, quenching each one's deepest thirst. Depending on the particularities of the concrete situation, one metaphor or another will speak more directly to the heart's longing. These images of redemption, liberation, nurture, comfort, and joy become the central axis of the caregiver's intercessory prayer. Through the prayer itself, the caregiver invokes God's blessing on this particular soul, even as she also blesses God for all the gifts of this person's life.

The art of pastoral prayer requires just this imaginative meditation and juxtaposition — interceding for another in light of the multivalent metaphors of Scripture, securing each life story in that rich, expansive net of meaning. In any specific pastoral care encounter, the caregiver has the freedom to name the particular blessings of the one she serves. A pastoral prayer on her behalf might recall the blessing of this person's mother, through whom came the gift of life; it might gratefully recall deliverance from the dangers of surgery or the ravages of illness. It might praise God for this particular life partner or cherished child, the gift of this community, or the joy of this particular calling, in each instance noting God's bountiful provision. Each time the caregiver recounts a blessing from God, she also blesses God for that incomparable gift. As the caregiver remembers how God has forgiven this one's sin, healed her sickness, sustained her through trial, and granted her good gifts, she weaves each memory into a pattern of faith by grounding her prayer in Scripture:

> Bless the LORD, O my soul; and all that is within me, bless his holy name! Bless the LORD, O my soul, and forget not all his benefits, who forgives all your iniquity, who heals all your diseases, who redeems your life from the Pit, who crowns you with steadfast love and mercy, who satisfies you with good as long as you live so that your youth is renewed like the eagle's. (Ps. 103:1-5)

Weaving back and forth between the particular life story and the scriptural text anchors the meaning of the person's life securely in the community of faith and its sacred narrative.

Even situations of grief paradoxically call for praise to God. There is healing in remembering the sheer goodness of what has been lost. When the church considers in prayer the immeasurable blessing of the life that has been taken from its midst, it may strike a note of joy as intense as its sorrow. Stories told at funerals are often punctuated with as much laughter as tears. Communities that take time to ponder the concrete gifts of one no longer among them experience genuine delight when each person remembers something inimitable about their friend's dear idiosyncrasies. The reminder of his humor or his gait, the recollection of his warmth or his perseverance — these things knit a strand of delight into the garment of sorrow. "Blessed are those who mourn, for they shall be comforted" (Matt. 5:4).

In situations of pastoral care, prayers of thanksgiving recall the essence of the church's relationship with God. "Grace and gratitude," writes Karl Barth, "belong together like heaven and earth. Grace evokes gratitude like the voice an echo."[1] Because it is God's nature to be gracious, the church's prayers of intercession, petition, lament, and confession will be interspersed with exclamations of wonder and praise, gratitude and awe. When caregivers intercede on behalf of another, they remember to thank God for all his blessings. No matter how great the person's present need, it is nevertheless surrounded by God's provision, if they have the eyes to see it. Even where difficult trial must still

---

1. Karl Barth, *Church Dogmatics*, IV/1 (Edinburgh: T&T Clark, 1960), p. 41.

be endured, they can recall God's blessings of the past, God's sustenance in the present, and God's promise of redemption, which gives hope for the future.

Since pastoral care encounters are usually intimate, with only two or three gathered to call upon the name of the Lord, caregivers have the freedom, and usually the firsthand knowledge, to allude concretely to the person's particular life story. The blessing of the past might be an earlier trial through which God preserved the other, or a friend who reached out in a time of need. The blessing of the present might be a clear sense of purpose in the midst of trouble, or the simple beauty of the natural world, which lifts the heart in hope. If the landscape, both literal and metaphorical, is especially bleak, caregivers can still pray with thanksgiving for the objective blessings of God: for God's steadfast love, for his compassion on frailty and weakness, for the forgiveness of sins, for redemption in Jesus Christ, for the strength and hope that Scripture offers, for calling the church to service in the world, for the gift of community — even for the gift of prayer itself. All these objective gifts are offered continually to the church as members of the body of Christ, even when some are unable to receive them. Though mired in suffering, the disconsolate can be reminded of God's ceaseless offering of himself in love.

The blessing of the future might be expressed as a fervent hope for the fulfillment of God's promises. What, after all, does anyone know of the future? None can penetrate its utter obscurity. Yet the church's imagination is fed and hearts are encouraged when it ponders the identity of a God intent upon redemption. As the church focuses once again on God's identity, God's purposes, and God's promises, hope and life return:

> For I know the plans I have for you, says the LORD, plans for welfare and not for evil, to give you a future and a hope. Then you will call upon me and come and pray to me, and I will hear you. You will seek me and find me; when you seek me with all your heart, I will be found by you, says the LORD. (Jer. 29:11-14)

Therefore, the community's thanksgiving becomes eschatological, oriented toward the future, as its wishes and desires are reconfigured through Christ. Does the community thirst for God's righteousness?

Does it long for God's kingdom to come? Does it suffer over the indignities that the poor must suffer daily? Does it live for the day when all creatures will have food and shelter and meaningful work? In prayer the church gives voice to the restlessness of hearts that long to rest in God; yet it gives thanks even for that disquiet. In this way the church's needs and its blessings are held together in light of the longing for God to "be all in all."

Hearts sustained by hope are grateful hearts. When a caregiver uses Scripture to give voice to a person's inmost longings, they are both freed from the narrowness of narcissistic desires and are knit into the great company of all those who have pondered Scripture as it gives rise to prayer. Consequently, they become aware that they never pray alone. They become aware how the Gospel has sustained whole communities in hope throughout the ages.

Finding the Right Words

Finding adequate words in a moment of great joy can be as pastorally challenging as speaking words of comfort in a time of grief. Since the greatest blessings of life are filled with solemnity, it can be difficult to strike just the right note. What greater blessing is there than the birth of a much-desired child? Yet birth is fraught with pain and danger even in today's world. A pregnant woman knows for nine long months that she will pass at least one night of travail before that baby will enter the world. Parents must gird themselves for the task at hand, bringing this helpless infant to mature adulthood, equipped for facing the challenges of the world. Yet even as they shoulder their new responsibilities, they cannot repress the joy that wells up within them when they behold this new life. What words might a pastor say that will give voice to the depth of their gratitude? What gestures or rituals capture its solemn joy?

Marriage, too, though intended by God for the mutual joy of husband and wife, is fraught with the myriad risks of human loving as well as the pain of separation from one's original family. Vows given and received in the community of faith are surrounded with the formal blessings of the church. Yet what words of blessing and thanksgiving should a pastor or friend pray on such an occasion? How might certain strands of the couple's personal history be presented with glad solemnity so that the wedding becomes an outpouring of praise to God?

Sheer endurance through times of despondency, separation, and trial eventually gives way to the quickening of new life, and even the event of death can become the occasion for acknowledging God's blessing. Even the daily utterance of the word "good-bye" contains a hidden blessing, a contraction for the wish that "God be with you." When a dying father solemnly says his last words on earth to a beloved daughter, what will his words of blessing be? When a mother sends her son off to college or marriage or war, what parting words of blessing will come to her lips? What does the church have to offer when natural eloquence fails? When someone shares a great joy, is it received with the dignity it deserves, or is it trivialized with paltry words of congratulation? Does the church have the kind of sanctified imagination that can discern the sacrifice, the faithful hoping against hope, the persevering struggle that prepared that person's heart for this longed-for day? Can caregivers enter imaginatively into the long night that preceded this day of splendor?

Here, as elsewhere, the church is best guided by Scripture. Experienced pastors know that generations of saints have been comforted with a recitation of Psalm 23 or the Lord's Prayer as death draws near. Psalm 90, with its harsh realism about the brevity of human life, gives comfort when one consents humbly to place all of life into God's hand:

> Lord, thou hast been our dwelling place in all generations. Before the mountains were brought forth, or ever thou hadst formed the earth and the world, from everlasting to everlasting thou art God. . . . Thou dost sweep men away; they are like a dream, like grass which is renewed in the morning: in the morning it flourishes and is renewed; in the evening it fades and withers. (Ps. 90:1-2, 5-6)

These words, so familiar from the graveside of loved ones, have been known to strengthen hearts with courage. Though all things mortal pass away, the Lord is from everlasting to everlasting.

In the autobiographical account of the last months of his life, Dale Aukerman writes of his daughter's request for a blessing. Knowing that his days were numbered, Aukerman wrote this entry in his journal just two weeks before he died:

Saturday, August 21, 1999

Maren requested that I bless her before she returns to California tomorrow. So this morning I asked for my Bible and a blank sheet of paper. I spent some time writing down blessings and scripture passages, resting several times. Shortly before noon, Maren sat down on a stool in front of the easy chair and I was able to give her my blessing, with Ruth helping to support my arm. Then I anointed her forehead with oil. What a gift that we could share this beautiful time yet. I think of this as a blessing for all three children.[2]

What could give more comfort to a child uncertain of her future than to be blessed by her father at a solemn moment of parting? This daughter had been raised in a family wholly familiar with the biblical pattern of parental blessing being passed from one generation to the next, and her request cannot be understood apart from this tradition. To find words that would be commensurate to the occasion, this father went to the source of all earthly blessings. However painful the parting, it could be faced openly because they knew One greater than death. When healing did not come, they still had hope beyond healing.

When Scripture molds the church's caregivers, a biblical imagination gives form to the prayers of their hearts. The psalms and prayers of Scripture become the caregivers' own as they come alive through daily meditation. At some point they are no longer reciting texts from memory but rather praying passages of Scripture "by heart." These passages have become a part of their own lived history with God. They have made these prayers their own as they have been woven into the various turning points of actual lives. Don Saliers expresses it this way: "Christian prayer and prayerfulness can be distinguished from the reciting of texts of prayers. . . . What makes our prayers *prayer* is whole-hearted attentiveness or attunement to God in and through the utterances."[3] Prayers of the church, prayers of the liturgy, words of Scripture, the hymns that are sung — all these become part of the caregiver's prayer when she speaks them with intention, with attentiveness toward God as she prays. In in-

---

2. Dale Aukerman, *Hope Beyond Healing: A Cancer Journal* (Elgin, Ill.: Brethren Press, 2000), p. 191.

3. Don Saliers, "Liturgy Teaching Us to Pray: Christian Liturgy and Grateful Lives of Prayer," in *Liturgy and Spirituality in Context: Perspectives on Prayer and Culture,* ed. Eleanor Bernstein, C.S.J. (Collegeville, Minn.: Liturgical Press, 1990), p. 64.

tercessory prayer, she may meditate first on the person's life situation, but then she will also turn and meditate on the grace of God. By the leading of the Holy Spirit, she will be led to bind together human need and God's grace into a single exclamation of praise.

Clearly such prayerful attunement requires one to slow down and ponder this particular life before God. Glib prayers are an insult both to God and to the person for whom one prays. One of the great blessings of pastoral care lies in its opportunities to slow down enough to nurture such meditation. One becomes aware of the gift of a single day, or even a single hour, only when one lingers long enough to enter imaginatively into what this day or this hour might mean to the person for whom one prays. A single day is a newborn's *entire* life; when one experiences it through the infant's eyes and ears, one may notice the extraordinary gift of an ordinary day. The day stretches out timelessly, as one becomes present to the experience of everything occurring for the very first time. Alternatively, a whole day (or hour) at the side of a dying friend can also be an inexpressible gift. Time mysteriously slows down in such liminal moments, and everything one does takes on special significance. "This may be my father's last meal. This may be our last conversation on earth. This may be the last time I can tell him how much I cherish him. This may be the last opportunity I have to ask his forgiveness or freely to grant him mine."

Every day, of course, offers opportunities to perceive the blessings of God, if we have the eyes to see them — the miracle that we awake each day to a new morning, that while we slept, God watched over and upheld us. Indeed, God sustained all of creation, including the trees and the oceans, the brooks and the meadows, the rain forests and the jungles, all the wonderful creatures of earth and sky and sea. Daily we have the opportunity to perceive signs of God's redemption of the world. God alone has the power to deliver us from evil, to redeem the past, to bring healing to our bodies and salvation to our whole life. God alone has the power to open up the future, to keep us receptive to what good may come. No matter how disheartened, stricken, or "stuck" we might be, God is capable of breaking in and catapulting us into a new situation. Though we feel absolutely stuck today, tomorrow might bring the miracle we have prayed for — or, if not an actual miracle, at least the first glimmer of light in a situation that has seemed completely intractable. "Behold, the Lord is at hand!"

If caregivers are shaped in their inner being by the prayerfulness of worship, they will approach their pastoral encounters with this kind of attunement to God's action, to hope in the midst of desolation, to patient waiting and expectant gratitude. If they keep their focus on God and God's action rather than on their own stumblings, they will keep hope alive, and gratitude will radiate in their hearts.

Illustration: A Pastoral Prayer of Thanksgiving

What is received through daily meditation on God's Word and what is in turn given to another in need obviously do not always fall into a neat one-to-one correspondence. However, if one is immersed in Scripture each day, fed spiritually by the Word of God, there will be ample sustenance when one turns to God in need. The pastoral encounter recorded below illustrates this point.

Amy had shared with John her longing for God's blessing. Having been traumatized by someone she loved, she had become acutely aware of how difficult it was for her to trust. She asked John to pray that God would bless her attempts to reach out toward others in trust.

Though John wanted to pray from Scripture, nothing had come to mind as he had listened to Amy. However, as he began to pray, he asked the Holy Spirit to quicken his heart and mind. As he waited in silence, images of blessing began to well up. Because he had a disciplined practice of being nourished by Scripture, it was there at hand when he needed it. His entire prayer was shaped by his daily engagement with the Bible as the living Word of God, as we can see:

> Loving God, send your Holy Spirit here now to guide this time of prayer. Move within us, have your way with us, make this time your own. Quicken our minds and hearts to receive the gift of your Spirit, as we come before you in prayer.

> [Silence]

> Gracious God, I give you thanks for the new thing you are doing in Amy's life. I thank you for sending your Spirit into her and stirring her up. . . .

[Silence]

I ask you, O Lord, to order this stirring — shape and direct it with your healing and holy hands. . . . Place your hands upon Amy; bless her now. Bless the work you have started in her, bring it to completion; bless the work you are doing. . . . Bless the trust with which she is venturing forth, bless and increase it; multiply this trust as she ventures into unknown and frightening territory, that she may be brought to the new life you are beginning in her. Continue to draw to her the people and the experiences . . . and all that she needs to continue this work of trust.

Shower your blessing upon her; let your blessing fall upon her like rain upon her head, like a stream of water . . . pour that water upon her head, pour it over her; let it be the water of her baptism, cleansing, renewing, nourishing, refreshing: Amy's new body and new spirit, which you are constructing: "Anyone in Christ is a new creation. See, the old ways have passed away, and behold, the new life is here."

I am in awe, O God, of your love for Amy. I am in awe of the love which has seen her through so much pain and trouble. I thank you for revealing your love for Amy which has seen her through so much pain . . . your love which remains when others fail. Your love does not end. . . . It is new every morning. . . .

[Silence]

Let the abundance of your love spill over into the lives of others. . . . Your love expands like a circle, touching more people through more people. . . . Use us, let us receive your love so that we may be part of that expanding circle . . . that you may be magnified and glorified and that the circle of your love may expand through us . . . [silence] . . . for we pray this in Christ's name. Amen.[4]

When John begins, he is aware only of coming to God with empty hands, asking God to fill them. And so *he waits* in silence, listening for

---

4. I thank both students involved in this assignment for their written permission to relate their experience.

God. Steven Chase underscores the importance of such silence: "While conversation involves elements of listening, waiting, attention, hearing, connection, communication, presence, and response, the two primary modes of prayerful conversation are word and silence. . . . Word and silence are not oppositional, but rather relational and dialogical."[5] As he listens to God in prayer, he recognizes the new thing that God is doing in Amy's life and thanks God for it. Notice the biblical resonances that begin to emerge: "Behold, I do a new thing!" God speaks through his word *as an event,* at a moment when John actually calls upon God for help. John prays for the Spirit to be present and then waits in trusting silence.

John prays for God's healing for Amy. The image of healing hands might have brought to mind Jesus healing the people with his own hands. Another scriptural allusion is evident when John prays for God to bless the work he began in Amy and to bring it to completion (Phil. 1:6). When he prays that God will bless and increase and multiply her trust, he may be alluding to the parable of the sower: when he sows the word of the kingdom on good soil, it brings forth a rich harvest (Matt. 13:18-23). Images of the showering of God's blessing become waters of baptism that cleanse, renew, nourish, and refresh, giving Amy a new body and a new spirit. Another explicit biblical allusion then comes to mind, clearly associated with this baptismal imagery: "If anyone is in Christ, he is a new creation; the old has passed away, behold, the new has come" (2 Cor. 5:17-18). As John meditates in prayer on all that has been made new in Amy, he is overwhelmed by the power of God's love in her life. He pours out his thanksgiving and awe for a God who has steadfastly seen his friend through so many trials.

Finally, the prayer returns to baptismal imagery: a drop of water that expands in circles now becomes the image for God's love that flows ever outward into wider and wider circles. It is an image of magnification, which then enters explicitly into his prayer — "that [God] may be magnified and glorified." The prayer trails off into an awed silence, and then John brings it to a close.

The prayer that John offers is memorable and meaningful because it is marked by a living encounter with God. The Word of God

5. Steven Chase, "Prayer as Familiar Conversation," *Reformed Review* 57, no. 3 (Spring 2004): 4.

comes alive as John prays. John turns with his full presence to God after taking to heart all that he has heard from Amy. He trusts that God, as living Lord, will respond not only to Amy's need but also to his own. God answers John's prayer by sending the Spirit to lead him to places he could not have anticipated when he began. John later wrote, "The images in my prayer felt like a gift of the Holy Spirit. I was overcome with a sense of God's presence. . . . It was something that continued to resonate with me in the days that followed. I hope it is something I will never forget."

Conclusion

In his first letter to the Thessalonians, Paul writes, "Rejoice always, pray constantly, give thanks in all circumstances; for this is the will of God in Christ Jesus for you" (1 Thess. 5:16-18). Such an admonition seems counterintuitive. How can we give thanks in *all* circumstances? How can we rejoice at all times? Christian prayer is interlaced from beginning to end with exclamations of praise and thanksgiving. This is so whether the church cries out in pain or pleads for mercy, whether it intercedes on behalf of another or boldly asks for its own needs to be met. Glad rejoicing can be part of every prayer because of the identity of the One to whom we pray, One who waits for us to call upon him in our need, One whose steadfast love endures forever.

Conclusion

This book has argued for the centrality of prayer in the work of pastoral care. When pastoral care begins in prayer and leads back to prayer, God is glorified, and God's people are drawn into rich spiritual communion. Listening to the Word of God, listening with care and understanding to each other, and learning to listen with an open heart to ourselves all contribute to pastoral care that is rooted and grounded in Christ. We listen first to God because we cannot live without God's daily sustenance. We listen to one another out of our love for God. Such listening deepens our compassion for one another in Christ. We learn to listen to ourselves with compassion, so that we may grow not only in trust but also in competence. We turn continually to God in prayer, acknowledging that our most fundamental need is for God himself. Prayer connects us to God and to all the needs that are fulfilled in him.

Following the prayer given us by Christ, we seek the hallowing of God's name, the building of God's kingdom, and the fulfillment of God's will on earth. Only then do we give voice to our needs for daily bread, forgiveness, protection, and deliverance from evil. As we come repeatedly to the wellspring of prayer, we realize that Jesus Christ is himself the fullness of life that we long for. As the Light of the World, Jesus Christ fulfills our need for hope, understanding, and inspiration. As the Bread of Life, he sustains us from his own substance each day. As the Water of Life, he both assuages and increases our thirst for justice. As the Cup of Salvation, he grants us fullness of joy. Worship and prayer keep alive the deep longing of our hearts: for lasting peace and justice, for true knowledge of God, for the beauty of holiness, for the miracle of forgiveness, for the richness of life lived in community. Worship sustains us in longing. Worship itself is the most fundamental need of the human heart.

While God alone can save us from sin and death, we are called to be companions to one another in this life. Though our suffering cannot redeem others as Christ's suffering does, we can accompany one another in love, offering the comfort that we ourselves have received. As members of Christ's body, we walk alongside one another, gladly bearing each other's burdens and sharing our own. As mutual caregivers, we offer each other the word of forgiveness, witness one another's lament, intercede in prayer for each other, and offer our thanksgivings together for the blessings of this life. Pastoral care becomes a place for giving and receiving genuine encouragement in the life of faith. As we encourage one another in faith, we call forth one another's gifts for the building up of the body. As a common body, we lift our hearts in praise to God, from whom all blessings flow. Living by those blessings and upheld by one another's love, we are given the courage and hope we need to reach out to the world with compassion.

Ideas for Engaging
and Teaching the Text

Every congregation has its own particular needs, yet all are called to pray. Some churches may want to develop a training program for deacons who want to be able to offer intercessory prayer with greater ease. Others may seek to involve the whole church in pastoral care groups who will pray together, offer each other mutual support, and study God's Word. Still others may desire to further their understanding of prayer in the Reformed tradition. I wrote this book with various aims in mind. In this final section, I want to suggest practical strategies for using the material presented in the previous nine chapters.

New concepts and skills cannot be learned simply by listening to a presentation or reading a book. For new material to be integrated, active engagement is needed. Studies estimate that only 20 percent of a lecture, for example, is retained in memory. By contrast, 50 percent of a discussion is typically remembered. (Ironically, one is more likely to remember what one says oneself than what another says.) The most significant learning occurs when one engages in a new practice, builds on newly acquired knowledge, or teaches what one has just learned. Knowledge is best integrated when concepts and skills are used as tools for building further knowledge. Good teaching creates space for the imagination. It is best when people are encouraged to bring their whole selves — their intellectual history, emotional needs, and spiritual longings — to the encounter. When something sparks their intellect or speaks to them emotionally or spiritually, they need an opportunity actively to engage it. Consider the "learning pyramid" that appears on page 193. By suggesting ideas for organizing small groups, creating role plays, and engaging

WHAT PEOPLE GENERALLY REMEMBER

An important learning principle, supported by extensive research, is that people learn best when they are actively involved in the learning process. The "lower down the cone" they go, the more they learn and retain.

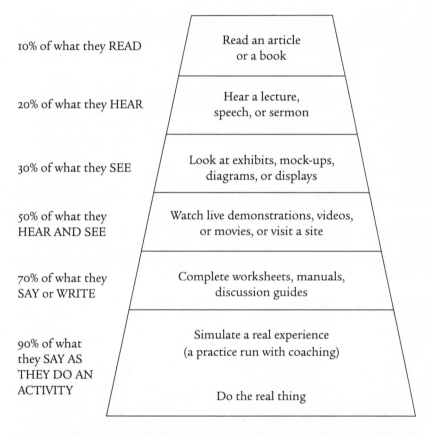

This learning pyramid was developed and used by the NTL (National Training Laboratory) Institute at their campus in Bethel, Maine, in the early 1960s when they were still part of the National Education Association's Adult Education Division. Earlier, a similar pyramid with slightly different numbers appeared in a book called *Audio-Visual Methods in Teaching* (New York: Edgar Dale Dryden Press, 1954).

members of the congregation holistically, this section aims at integrative learning.

Chapter One: A Theology of *Koinonia*

As I pointed out in Chapter One, *koinonia* is the essential means of all true pastoral care. Pastoral care groups are a particularly good way of enriching and expressing *koinonia*. To establish such groups, several key things need to be done.

1. *Decide on the organizing principle for the group.* Should members be organized by geographical proximity, age, gender, common theological perspective, or some other criteria? As the planning group considers the needs of the congregation, questions about the value of diversity become important. The intergenerational (and sometimes multicultural) nature of the church makes it one of the few places where people can meet those outside their usually narrowly defined cultural niche. Less homogenous groups may initially experience a higher level of discomfort, but they may ultimately provide a richness of experience unavailable to groups whose members are in agreement about essential matters.

2. *Define the central purpose of the group.* Having a clearly defined purpose is fundamental to the success of any group. The planning process should involve a wide group of interested persons for the sake of developing a common vision.

Here are several examples:

- Those experiencing adversity gather once a week to pray for one another. The purpose of the group is mutual support through empathy and prayer.
- A group gathers once a month to pray for discernment of the church's mission, to identify the gifts of the Spirit in the congregation, and to pray for each person's vocation in light of that mission. The purpose of the group is to discern God's call, to deepen commitment to the church's mission, and to support those who are actively engaged in these ministries.
- Interested persons with gifts of healing gather to pray for the reconciliation of individuals, groups, and nations. The purpose of the group is to offer prayer for those in special need of healing.

- Ministries that are already in place — for the addicted, the hungry, the poor, the bereaved — as well as groups that meet regularly for church business begin with a time of mutual listening and prayer. The purpose is to nurture spiritual sustenance for the church's mission by deepening its life of common prayer.[1]
- A group gathers solely for the purpose of *lectio divina*, focusing, and intercessory prayer. The purpose of such a group is to deepen one's life in the Spirit and develop closer spiritual ties in the church.

3. *Set up a clearly defined structure that enables personal freedom at the same time that it offers security and clarity of expectation.* A simple structure can be created that allows for both, as the following example indicates:

- The meeting begins with a time for gathering, collecting oneself, and observing silence.
- The group engages in *lectio divina*.
- Each person shares where God seems to be leading and asks for what he/she needs from the others.
- Prayers, both silent and spoken, are offered as each feels moved to intercede on another's behalf.
- The meeting closes with the Lord's Prayer or a song.

Basic ground rules also need to be discussed to develop clear expectations regarding length and frequency of meetings, membership constituency, and leadership. Discuss the following questions:

- How often shall we meet?
- How long shall each meeting be?
- How many people should be in each group? (It may be best to limit the size to four or five persons so that there is sufficient time for each person to share.)
- If someone needs to be absent, what is our expectation about informing others?

---

1. See Kent Ira Groff, *The Soul of Tomorrow's Church: Weaving Spiritual Practices in Ministry Together* (Nashville: The Upper Room, 2001).

- Will one person be designated leader for the whole series, or will there be rotating leadership?
- What are the leader's responsibilities? (These may include hosting the meeting, beginning and ending on time, choosing a Scripture passage to read, and initiating the closing prayer.)

Having a clear structure enables freedom within it. It reduces anxiety and enables each member to focus on what he or she wants to contribute.

4. *Be clear about the group's membership, which is essential for trust to develop.* Closed groups that open only at transition points typically grow in trust. For example, a group can agree to meet for eight (or twelve or sixteen or thirty-two) weeks. At the end of the agreed-upon time, new people are free to join and others to leave. When membership is left entirely open — with people free to come and go as they wish — group cohesiveness suffers.

5. *Establish a policy of confidentiality, which is also essential for developing trust.* Confidentiality means not discussing what is shared in the group outside the group. It also means not discussing it with others when only a part of the group is together in a different context. What is shared in the group essentially stays in the group. However, if one has a need to work through an issue related to someone else's story, one may discuss it respectfully (e.g., in one's marriage, friendships, therapy sessions) in terms of its meaning for oneself. The original story or comment that initiated one's disquiet may be mentioned, but the identity of the person should be disguised. The aim of the conversation, in other words, is not to discuss the person and his or her story but rather to clarify one's own feelings and needs in relation to it.

If two members of the group want to work through a conflict that concerns just the two of them, they should be free to do so. However, they might wish to ask for the group's support and guidance. In any case, they should report back to the group if they have resolved a conflict that developed in the group itself. Since each person is a vital part of the body, any conflict in the group will affect every member: "If one member suffers, all suffer together" (1 Cor. 12:26).

6. *Share stories that will inspire and unite the group.* Seldom do Christians have the opportunity to share the experiences that have shaped their lives of faith. Small groups give members an ideal situation in

which to edify one another by sharing how they have discerned Christ at work within and among them.

Here are some possible questions to consider:

- What prayers did you learn as a child? How have they been significant for you?
- Where have you sensed the mystery of God's providence in your life?
- How have you been sustained through times of illness, terror, or grief? What impact have they had on your life of faith?
- Who in your community inspires you by their words and acts of witness? Who exhibits Christ-like virtues worthy of emulation?
- What losses, traumas, or significant sorrows have you suffered? What do you need for healing to occur?
- Where have you received the pastoral care of others? What significance has it had in your life of faith?
- What gifts do you perceive in other members of the group? Are you able to acknowledge the gifts others see in you?
- What are the "natural patterns of care" in your congregation? Where do they need strengthening? What gifts might be developed if people were actively encouraged?
- Which of your prayers have been answered? Which did not seem to be heard? What effect has this had in your life with God?
- How would you express the lament of your heart? What are the origins of this grief in your life narrative?
- What story of hope or celebration inspires you? Share it with the group.

7. Engage in theological reflection. Questions can be posed regarding the theological ideas presented in each of the main chapters of this text. For example, in Chapter One I describe Jesus Christ as the one Mediator of God. How does this understanding inform or change your perception of prayer? Meditate on St. Patrick's prayer "The Eye of God" and notice what new insights emerge. (Keep a notebook handy to record them.) What does it mean to place the eye of God between yourself and the eye of another? God's hand between your own and that of another?

Karl Barth's understanding of humanity's "basic form" *(Mit-menschlichkeit),* as discussed in Chapter One, is directly relevant to how small groups in the church are conceived. I've summarized his ideas here for ease of reference:

- We are truly human when we allow ourselves to *see and be seen* by others in mutual openness. I am willing to let you see me as I really am, and you are willing to let me see you. We are inhuman when we withhold or conceal ourselves.
- We need to interpret who we are to others, for they cannot know us otherwise. We reveal ourselves in our uniqueness as we *engage in mutual speech and hearing.* Each of us is "a whole world"[2] and desires to be known in our wholeness.
- We are human insofar as we *render mutual assistance* to each other. None of us is self-sufficient. "My humanity depends upon the fact that I am always aware, and my action is determined by the awareness, that I need the assistance of others [and also to give my assistance to others] as a fish needs water."[3] Your humanity also depends upon this fact.
- Each of the above three steps are *done on both sides with gladness.* Thus we gladly see and are seen. We gladly speak and listen. We gladly offer each other assistance. This is "the living centre of the whole," a matter of mutual joy, "an active willing of this fellowship." We discover our own "uniqueness and irreplaceability" in this glad encounter: "And freely and from the heart [man] is what he is in the secret of the encounter with his fellow-man in which the latter is welcome and he is with him gladly."[4]

Louis H. Evans Jr. develops core principles for "covenant groups" that are compatible with the marks of humanity discussed by Barth. Derived from Scripture, these principles (some of which are evident in the major points being made here) can be altered, confirmed, or reworded according to the needs of the group.

- *The covenant of affirmation (unconditional love, agape love).* Each member commits himself or herself to love others in the group, and to remember God's love for the others in times of disagreement.

2. Karl Barth, *Church Dogmatics,* III/2 (Edinburgh: T&T Clark, 1960), p. 258.
3. Barth, *Church Dogmatics,* III/2, pp. 263-64.
4. Barth, *Church Dogmatics,* III/2, pp. 271-72.

- *The covenant of availability.* Each member of the group commits to give freely of his or her "time, energy, insight, and possessions" to any who has need.
- *The covenant of prayer.* Each person promises to pray for the other members of the group.
- *The covenant of openness.* Each person promises to strive toward greater openness, disclosing thoughts, feelings, and struggles. While each may obviously exercise discretion and choice about what to share, each promises not to "hide."
- *The covenant of honesty.* Each member commits himself or herself to "speak the truth in love," sharing personal perceptions as honestly as possible.
- *The covenant of sensitivity.* Each member promises to attune himself or herself to the needs of others and to draw them out to the best of his or her ability.
- *The covenant of confidentiality.* Each person promises to keep confidences shared in the group to further trust and openness.
- *The covenant of accountability.* Each member commits himself or herself to be accountable to the others in the group to develop the gifts given him or her by God.[5]

8. *Talk about the process.* Allow time at the end of each gathering to comment on the process, focusing on the "how" rather than the "what." Mutual sharing about moments of discomfort deepens trust and intimacy. When time is set aside for such observations, it helps ensure that the group will grow and change according to the actual needs of its members.

Though "process" and "content" cannot be separated from each other, they can be distinguished. As pointed out in Chapter Three, the content of a communication consists in *what* is said, while the process consists in *how* it is said. If the "what" and the "how" are not consistent with each other, incongruity arises. To use an example from that chapter, we find it incongruous when a person smiles while speaking of an ostensibly sad event. In a small group, it's important for members to get feedback about *how* they're saying *what* they're saying. Especially in

5. Louis H. Evans, *Covenant to Care* (Fullerton, Calif.: Victor Books, 1982), pp. 20-21.

the context of offering care, they need to know whether the contribution they intend to make is actually received by others. Each member needs the others' perceptions of both his gifts and the areas in which he needs to grow. As the group gains skill in giving and receiving feedback, they build a cohesive, mutually trusting group.

Process observation is important because individuals tend to learn best when they are free to comment on what they observe. They gain clarity and ease when they are free to communicate about their communication. Unhealthy families tend to have rigid unspoken rules — for example, "Don't talk. Don't trust. Don't feel." Individuals need to become aware of old habits before they can learn new patterns of interaction. As they gain ease in talking about what was formerly taboo, they grow in trust. They find the freedom to share their needs and to ask others about theirs.

Murray Bowen, a family systems therapist and theoretician, stresses the importance of opening up relational systems so that people are free to talk about whatever concerns them. He writes,

> An "open" relationship system is one in which an individual is free to communicate a high percentage of inner thoughts, feelings, and fantasies to another who can reciprocate.[6]

Churches create zones of healthy interaction when they encourage members to work through their anxiety rather than retreating when they encounter something threatening. Process observation gives tools for talking about one's discomfort in a safe and structured way.

One person may be designated as the process observer for each gathering. Ten to fifteen minutes before it is time to close, he or she can comment on notable process issues in the group that day. The following list may prove helpful:

- Body language: each person's posture, gestures, and eye contact or lack of it.
- Anything notable about tone of voice.
- Shift of focus in the conversation. Did it serve to deepen the emo-

---

6. Murray Bowen, "Family Reaction to Death," in *Family Therapy in Clinical Practice* (Northvale, N.J.: Jason Aronson, 1978), p. 322.

tional connection, or did it bring the level of sharing up toward the surface?

- Signs of anxiety. Did the process observer notice a rise in tension in himself at any point? What did he observe in himself and in others?
- Patterns of participation: Did anyone speak far more than the others? Was anyone silent throughout?
- Uses of humor: Was there a member of the group who brought humor into the interaction? Did it serve to relieve anxiety or perhaps to avoid it?
- Overall flow of the time together: What did the process observer notice about levels of interest? Was there a sense of closure? How did the group work together as a unit?

What needs of the group were met by the process that was followed? Does the group wish to make any changes for future meetings?

Of course, not everything that is said in a meeting can be "processed" afterward. Usually it is helpful to comment only on those things that seemed especially to contribute to group trust and cohesiveness or especially to detract from it. There is an art to making process observations that can be developed over time. The crucial point is to use this time to open up conversation about things that otherwise might pass without comment, but would fester and contribute to unease over time. If left unattended, certain interactions might lead to the eventual dissolution of the group. This is a time not for evaluating the group process but for raising issues that need attention. Some individuals are gifted in picking up the unspoken tension in a room. If they can be trained to comment on what they are observing when they notice the tension in their own body, they will make an invaluable contribution to the group as a whole.

Chapter Two: Listening to God

In an effort to truly listen to God, small group members might agree to undertake an individual practice of *lectio divina*. Even a small investment of time pondering a single sentence from Scripture can give shape to the day. With God's Word in one's heart, one may hear the

Spirit of God in new ways throughout the day. *Lectio divina* can also be used in groups as a way of grounding one's relationship with others in a rich communal web of faith. The three-way bond among self, neighbor, and God is made more secure whenever Scripture is pondered together and used as a basis for intercessory prayer.

Lectio divina was discussed thoroughly in Chapter Two, but a brief review of the practice that suggests how it could be implemented in a group may prove helpful:

1. *Lectio:* The leader reads aloud a short Scripture passage (no more than 8 to 10 verses), slowly and with clear intention. Silence follows. Members then share, without explanation or elaboration, the word or phrase that particularly struck them.

2. *Meditatio:* The leader reads the passage a second time. Again silence follows. Each member ponders the specific word "spoken" in relation to the events in his or her life. Members are asked to share where they hear God speaking the word they especially need.

3. *Oratio:* Members offer intercessory prayer for one another. A structure may be suggested, such as going around the circle and praying for the person on one's right or one's left. Alternatively, the group can decide to pray as the Spirit leads.

4. *Contemplatio:* Members take the received "word" into the coming week, using it as a basis for prayer and as a lens for spiritual perception. They seek further insight as they live with this word from God. When the group meets again, each member can share the "cream" of his or her contemplation with the group.

This practice contributes to the development of a community narrative as persons share their struggles in the context of their common faith.

Covenanting to memorize Scripture together is another endeavor that can be undertaken by groups. Each member might first rememorize any psalms once committed to memory. It's important to choose texts that are especially cherished, that capture something true. It's also important in memorizing to say the words aloud and meditate on their resonances in one's personal web of associations. In this way one weaves one's story into the biblical story. Patsy Rodenburg comments on the connection between individual word and larger text:

To speak convincingly, we have to dare to know a word and make contact with it throughout our bodies and breath. What do I mean by "know"? I am not talking about knowing the word from the dictionary but intuiting the word through a connection to our emotional life and sensual being. The intriguing thing about needing words is that they make rivulets and bridges between head and heart. Great texts reinforce that connection.[7]

One practice that contributes not only to ease but also to building community is to memorize Scripture with a partner. A pair of friends who usually take a morning walk together can spend a portion of their time memorizing a common passage together. One might recite the first line of a psalm, the other might recite the next line, and so on. When one is reciting, the other is also actively involved, since both are working on the same psalm.

Wayne Oates, a pastoral theologian, once remarked that all pastors should commit certain passages to memory. The texts that sustain the pastor will also sustain the parishioners. Consider which of the following passages might be worth learning "by heart":

- Psalms 1, 15, 23, 37, 46, 51, 79:8-9, 90, 91, 103, 139
- Isaiah 40:28-31
- Matthew 6
- John 14
- Romans 8
- 1 Corinthians 13
- 2 Corinthians 4:15-18
- Ephesians 3:14-21[8]

It's important to develop a pattern of life that includes specific times for prayer. Just as patterns sustain one's marriage and friendships, so one's relationship with God also requires daily attention. As couples look forward to their evening meal, to Saturday morning coffee, or to their weekly "date night," so one can set aside and anticipate specific times to deepen one's intimacy with God. Like any relation-

---

7. Patsy Rodenburg, *The Need for Words* (London: Methuen, 1993), p. 71.

8. This list was orally communicated to me during my first unit of Clinical Pastoral Education.

ship, one's relationship with God needs to be free at its core. One needs the freedom to give oneself spontaneously in prayer whenever one is moved to do so. Such spontaneous prayer, however, is sustained by a regular pattern of daily prayer and depends upon it as plants depend upon nutrient-rich soil.

In the morning, Psalm 5 can inform prayer: "O LORD, in the morning thou dost hear my voice; in the morning I prepare a sacrifice for thee, and watch" (Ps. 5:3). The sacrifice the community is called to make is the sacrifice of a grateful heart. Anthony Bloom elaborates:

> They are called to prepare themselves for the Lord's work in the day at hand. Awake in the morning and the first thing you do, thank God for it, even if you don't feel particularly happy about the day which is to come. "This is the day which the Lord has made, let us rejoice and be grateful in it." Once you have done this, give yourself time to realize the truth of what you are saying and really mean it — perhaps on the level of deep conviction and not of what one might call exhilaration. . . . Come to God again with two convictions. The one is that you are God's own and the other is that this day is also God's own, it is absolutely new, absolutely fresh. It has never existed before. . . . This day is blessed by God, it is God's own, and now let us go into it. You walk in this day as God's own messenger; whomever you meet, you meet in God's own way.[9]

An evening prayer could be Psalm 4, with its admonition to "commune with your own hearts on your beds, and be silent" (Ps. 4:4). The community is called to recollect itself at the end of each day, to remember who they are in God's sight. Each evening they ask God for forgiveness for the oversights, sins, and limitations of the day. They lift up all those whom they love, confess their anxiety, and ask to be released from vain worry. As sleep approaches, they give themselves into God's keeping, knowing that their lives depend upon God's watchful care.

Deciding on a daily pattern is not done once and for all. Like any relationship, one's relationship with God changes over time, according to one's varied needs. Parents with small children have different needs than widows who live alone. One of the functions of the small group

9. Anthony Bloom, *Beginning to Pray* (New York: Paulist Press, 1970), pp. 75-76.

would be to help each individual discern the gifts and possibilities as well as the limits and liabilities of each juncture in life. The group can help in discovering a pattern of prayer that keeps one's relationship with God open and vital.

Chapter Three: Listening to Others

Training programs in pastoral care, whether in the church or in seminary, consider listening skills to be fundamental. Any program wishing to teach these skills needs to include opportunities for practice, followed by disciplined reflection. The two most widely used methods in pastoral care are role plays and the verbatim report. Because both methods address the whole person, they can be located near the base of the learning pyramid described at the beginning of this section.

Because role plays require a certain level of emotional exposure, it is helpful for the leader first to demonstrate the listener role for the group. Openness to the group's observations during the "processing" time increases group trust and models expectations of how to give and receive constructive feedback.

In setting up a role play, the leader needs to remember that the length of the role play should be related to the length of processing time. A five-minute role play, for example, generally needs ten to fifteen minutes of processing time. Concrete feedback by the participants, in which they describe what they have observed without offering explicit evaluation, is helpful.

When training groups are in their early stages, it is effective to set up several simultaneous role-plays in pairs. This way, no one is exposed in front of the whole group, and everyone is actively engaged. After each pair has processed the conversation by giving each other specific feedback, it is helpful to gather the whole group together and ask each pair to share one thing they learned from the exercise. This simple structure maximizes learning, enabling each member of the group to learn from their peers. Each pair in effect teaches what they have just learned, thus integrating the learning further.

It is important to give clear, easy-to-follow instructions in setting up a role play. The following steps will help a leader set up and direct the role play:

1. Divide the group into pairs. In each pair, designate one person as the speaker and the other as the listener. After one complete round, these roles will be reversed with the same partner.

2. Describe the role play in simple terms. For example, the listener is a deacon bringing flowers to the speaker, a hospitalized church member who has undergone serious surgery.

3. Allow five full minutes for the role play. When the time is up, stop the pairs, even if some of them are in mid-sentence.

4. Now allow ten to fifteen minutes for processing, for giving each other feedback. Begin with each speaker giving feedback to each listener. Have the speaker begin by commenting on something he or she found helpful. Perhaps the listener had a friendly smile or maintained good eye contact or conveyed caring through her tone of voice and body language. Have the speaker specify the impact it had. What needs were met by what the other person did in her role as pastoral caregiver?

5. Each speaker in each pair can then specify a juncture in the conversation where he felt that the listener might have missed the significance of something he said. The more he is able to describe the other's actual behavior in specific terms, the better. Perhaps the listener became distracted and looked away; perhaps he began moving his foot nervously or cracking his knuckles unconsciously. If he can correlate the other's behavior with what he felt in response, he will be giving the listener valuable feedback. Here it is important to stay at the level of behavioral description and not fall into evaluative comments. For example, the speaker might say, "I noticed that you laughed after I said such and such." An evaluative comment would interpret this behavior positively or negatively — for example, "Your laughter cheered me" or "You were amused at my expense."

6. Now it is the listener's turn to process her experience. Where was it hard for her to listen? What was she aware of regarding her level of anxiety? Was there anything she felt especially good about in her response to the other? Was there anything she especially regretted?

7. Next, gather the group as a whole and discuss in turn what each person learned from the role play and also from the feedback.

8. With this first stage completed, have each pair switch roles so

that the speaker becomes the listener and vice versa. The same scenario may be used, but it will develop differently according to the imagination of the one role-playing the hospitalized person.

The pair is the simplest form of role play and may be sufficient to meet the purpose of the group's work. One might also want to set up a role play in groups of three. The first person would be the speaker, the second person the listener, and the third the process observer — that is, someone who gives the others concrete feedback about what he or she observes.

In our subsequent discussion based on Chapter Seven, I will suggest a role play in which the listener's purpose will be to open up communication among several family members. This requires more advanced skill and should not be attempted until the group has attained relative ease in its pairs work. In a seminary classroom where future pastors are being trained, this more advanced step is essential, since so much of their work will be with families and groups.

Another effective training tool for developing listening skills is to reflect together on verbatim material of pastoral conversations. The key to giving effective feedback on another's written verbatim report is for each person to focus on two or three aspects of it. Breaks or shifts in the conversation initiated by the listener often indicate unconscious anxiety. These places should be noted and explored. Verbatims can be given as homework assignments for the members of a training group as well as for seminary students. The format in Appendix A can be used as a model. It is worth taking the time to study each component. Each adds a further level of complexity to the meaning of the conversation. The sociological context, psychological dynamics, and theological meanings all need to be considered. It is also worth reflecting on one's feelings and needs as the pastoral caregiver.

When a verbatim report is being used in a training group, each member should have at least forty-eight hours to read and ponder the report before gathering to discuss it. A small group could profitably spend forty-five minutes to an hour discussing it, with a focus on the particular needs of the one presenting.

Chapter Four: Listening to Ourselves

Konstantin Stanislavsky was an actor who was possessed by a passion to understand what was involved in outstanding acting. Why was it that sometimes his performance was creative and deeply satisfying, not only for the audience but also for himself? Alternatively, what were the factors involved in those times when he felt dead inside, not present in spirit? He was asking these questions at the age of forty-three because he found that his joy in his work had mysteriously disappeared:

> [I felt] dissatisfaction and anxiety. . . . Dissatisfaction with myself as an actor, and the complete darkness of the distances that lay before me, gave me no rest, took away my faith in myself, and made me seem wooden and lifeless in my own eyes. . . . I would spend my mornings on a cliff that overlooked the sea, taking stock of all my artistic past. I wanted to find out where all my former joy in creation had vanished.[10]

As he emerged from this brooding period, Stanislavsky was determined to discover the capacities that excellent actors consistently exhibited. He not only wanted to become a better actor himself but also wished to develop a method that would guide others toward consistent excellence. After observing exceptional actors for several years, he felt that he could identify those traits that "create[d] a favorable condition for the appearance of inspiration."[11]

The three capacities these excellent actors consistently demonstrated in their work were *relaxation, concentration,* and *imagination.* These same capacities may aptly describe what is necessary for all creative work. In the work of pastoral care, insofar as one's listening, understanding, and interceding on behalf of another are truly creative work, these features are also present. A brief discussion of these capacities will show how this is true (and also show that Stanislavksy's ideas intersect with Eugene Gendlin's ideas about focusing).

Relaxation: A great part of an actor's training consists in working with physical movement designed to make him aware of his body.

---

10. Stanislavsky, quoted in *Actors on Acting,* ed. Toby Cole and Helen Chinoy (New York: Three Rivers Press, 1970), p. 490.
11. Stanislavsky, quoted in *Actors on Acting,* p. 492.

When actors exhibited the "creative mood," Stanislavsky noticed that they exhibited a marked physical freedom, an ease in movement, and a "lack of all strain."[12] Personal awareness of one's body is also necessary for the pastoral caregiver. Because one's work is completely embodied, one needs to be aware of what one's body is communicating. There are many avenues that one can explore in order to develop free, relaxed, and open movement, from t'ai chi to yoga to Feldenkrais. Training in dance improvisation, voice, theater, and massage all offer tools that can help one become attuned to one's body.

In physical health the human body exhibits not only strength and flexibility but also balance and endurance. Each of these four attributes signifies capacities of the mind and heart as well. Thus one needs both physical and emotional strength, physical flexibility and psychological resilience. Just as an athlete develops balance, so one needs to become aware of imbalances in all aspects of one's life. And one also needs endurance, which is a capacity markedly different from sheer strength, requiring patience, hope, and trust. A relaxed and energized body is needed for an open mind and heart. In order to truly listen to another, one needs to be free to let one's own associations to what the other says rise up into awareness. This is the "evenly hovering attention" that Freud found so valuable. Staying relaxed keeps one from taking on the other's problems as if they were one's own and becoming anxious to "fix" them.

As one becomes aware of one's body and its capacities, one develops a respect for its wisdom. One may notice how physical tension corresponds to emotional or spiritual imbalance. For instance, when one feels heavily burdened, one may find oneself sighing repeatedly. By paying attention to the body, one discovers that one's lungs are not working to full capacity. One is not taking in the life energy available through breathing deeply. Perhaps one's shoulders are slumped forward and one's midriff is collapsed, further constricting one's capacity to take in a full breath.

Pastoral caregivers may become vulnerable to taking another's emotional pain into their bodies by holding their breath. In order to "take in" the other's hurt imaginatively and empathetically, they need to learn how to stay relaxed and centered in themselves. In this way, the other person's energies will pass *through* them rather than remaining *in*

---

12. Stanislavsky, quoted in *Actors on Acting*, p. 493.

them. It is essential that caregivers integrate into their daily lives the practices that will help them open the flow of breath, take in life's energies, and remain in a relaxed and open state.

Concentration: Stanislavsky found that "the entire physical and spiritual nature of the actor must be concentrated on what is going on in the soul of the person he plays."[13] An actor needs to uses his senses, thought processes, emotions, and will to understand the character he is portraying. Similarly, pastoral caregivers need to use all their faculties in order to understand the persons they seek to help. Like the actor, the caregiver needs to become acutely observant of the other's body language. What are the meaning of the other's gestures, facial expressions, and tone of voice? The well-trained caregiver learns to differentiate among nuances of feeling and expression.

According to Stanislavsky, "The key to acting is to apply your inner life to the circumstances of the character. In this way, you do not just play yourself, you *use* yourself in the service of the part."[14] Similarly, as the pastoral caregiver listens to another, he focuses on the concrete particulars of the story that is unfolding and pays attention to each detail and its meaning for the person. He uses his own self-knowledge in helping the other to differentiate between feelings and needs. Like the actor, the caregiver does this by concentrating not on the feelings themselves but rather on the circumstances that give rise to the feelings. Just as the actor pays close attention to the circumstances of the character's life, so the pastoral caregiver concentrates on the circumstances of the life he seeks to understand. For example, a caregiver would not ask a vague, generalized question about the nature of another's grief. Instead, he would help the grieving person recall the exact circumstances and its sensory details to evoke the feelings associated with them. At the same time, he would enter imaginatively into those circumstances by concentrating his awareness on how the person might have felt.[15]

Exercises to improve one's powers of concentration and develop skill in uncovering another's emotional state are especially interesting to do in small groups. A group can be divided into pairs. In each pair,

---

13. Stanislavsky, quoted in *Actors on Acting*, p. 494.

14. Richard Brestoff, *The Great Acting Teachers and Their Methods* (Lyme, N.H.: Smith & Kraus, 1996), p. 38.

15. Brestoff, *The Great Acting Teachers and Their Methods*, p. 52.

person A imagines a situation in her life where she felt something intensely (e.g., anger, fear, grief, joy). As she remembers the situation and feels the emotion associated with it, person B observes her facial expression and tries to determine what she might be feeling. Fine-tuning is possible in this exercise as individuals become able to differentiate among irritation, annoyance, anger, and fury. Similarly, differentiations can be made among delight, joy, exultation, and contentment. This is an interesting game to play with children as well.

In *Beginning to Pray*, Anthony Bloom provides an example of the need for concentration in one's communication with others:

> In the beginning, when I was a physician, I felt it was most unfair to the people who were in the waiting room if I was slow in seeing the person who was with me in the consulting room. So the first day I tried to be as quick as I could with those in the consulting room. I discovered by the end of my surgery hours that I had not the slightest recollection of the people I had seen, because all the time a patient was with me, I was looking beyond him with clairvoyant eyes into the next room and counting the heads of those who were not with me. The result was that all the questions I asked I had to ask twice, all the examinations I made I had to make twice or even three times. When I had finished, I could not remember whether I had done these things or not. . . .
>
> Then I felt this was simply dishonest, and I decided that I would behave as if the person who was with me was the only one who existed. The moment I began to feel "I must be quick," I would sit back and engage in small talk for a few minutes just to prevent myself from hurrying. I discovered within two days that you no longer need to do anything like that. You can simply be completely concerned with the person or task that is in front of you, and when you have finished, you will discover that you have spent half the time doing it, instead of all the time you took before; yet you have seen everything and heard everything.[16]

Imagination: "The training of the imagination is a discipline just as important as the training of the mind."[17] So states Jungian analyst Rob-

---

16. Anthony Bloom, *Beginning to Pray,* p. 88.
17. Robert Bosnak, *A Little Course in Dreams* (Boston: Shambhala, 1986), p. 73.

ert Bosnak, who has spent his career teaching people how to hone their imaginative powers. Dreams are the sap of psychic life that may be boiled down into the concentrated syrup of metaphor. Metaphor is a form of speech or imagery that enables one to perceive connections among various parts of one's world of meaning. Anything alive with metaphorical power — from a Rorschach inkblot to poetry, from a fairy tale to sand play, from acting, dancing, or painting to focused dreamwork — can serve as a training ground for the development of the imagination.

For Stanislavsky, the imagination is essential to the actor, enabling him to enter the life of the character he is portraying. He imagines all the details: the pace of his walk, the sound of his voice (fast or slow speech? an accent?), the expressions on his face, the slope of his shoulders. To develop these details, he would use every memory, observation, and relationship he could recall, the totality of his life experience imaginatively elaborated. Laurence Olivier once said,

> I've got a memory for little details. I've had things in the back of my mind for as long as eighteen years before I've used them. And it works sometimes that, out of one little thing you've seen somebody do, something causes you to store it up. In the years that follow you wonder what it was that made them do it, and ultimately, you find in that the illuminating key to a whole bit of characterization.[18]

Pastoral caregivers who explore another's world also use their own life experience and imagination as a guide. Like actors, they keep a dual consciousness — of the other and of the self — so that their own stories and feelings do not intrude but rather enliven their imagination, enabling them to stay attuned to the other.[19]

Chapter Five: Prayers of Petition

In Chapter Five I discussed Ron DelBene's book *Into the Light: A Simple Way to Pray with the Sick and the Dying*. Although, as the subtitle indi-

---

18. *Actors on Acting*, p. 410.

19. Theater games, dance improvisation exercises, and poetry readings can all be used for developing the imagination. Robert Bosnak's *A Little Course on Dreams* is a splendid resource for learning to understand the language of dreams.

cates, it was written to help the very ill and those who love them, the breath prayer that DelBene describes in the book is for anyone who wishes to live his life to the fullest. Those at ease with their own breath prayer can teach the method to others.

In working with a group, spend at least one session helping each person find his breath prayer. This can be done easily by having the leader start with a relaxation and centering exercise, perhaps beginning with Gendlin's technique for focusing. Then, when members have achieved internal quiet, the leader can read through the following steps, giving each person the time he needs to discover his own breath prayer:

> *Step One:* Sit comfortably and be calm and quiet. . . . Remind yourself that you are in God's loving presence. . . . "Be still, and know that I am God" (Psalm 46:10).

> *Step Two:* . . . Imagine God calling you by name. Hear God asking you, "[Your name], what do you want?"

> *Step Three:* Answer God with whatever comes honestly from your heart. . . . Maybe no more than a single word, such as peace or love or forgiveness. . . . Whatever your response, it will be at the heart of your prayer.

> *Step Four:* Choose your favorite name for God. . . .

> *Step Five:* Combine your name for God with your answer to God's question of "What do you want?" and you have your prayer. For example, . . . "God, let me know your peace."[20]

If the group has established bonds of trust, members might want to consider sharing their breath prayers with one another. How does the breath prayer articulate each person's particular need? Members of the group may then pray with and for one another throughout the week by praying each other's breath prayer.

---

20. Ron DelBene, *Into the Light: A Simple Way to Pray with the Sick and the Dying* (Nashville: The Upper Room, 1988), pp. 33-34.

Getting access to the life of the soul requires what I call a "dreaming consciousness." One might ask the following questions to uncover hidden wishes: "What is the longing of my heart? How do I become attuned to what is most important to live out this day? How do I get access to the underground stream of desires that usually lie outside my awareness?" One can imagine lying under a tree on a summer's day watching clouds drift by. As thoughts flow through one's mind, one can notice where they go. What themes seem to recur? Noticing one's dreams — dreams of the day and of the night — may unearth hidden longings.

Chapter Six: Prayers of Intercession

As the discussion in Chapter Six indicates, intercessory prayer can be difficult to offer in the right way and in the right spirit. Appendix B presents a case study based on the life experience of a man called Don Jacobs.[21] It presents his dilemma, as he characterizes it, between acting according to his own integrity and his desire to be helpful to his Aunt Alice. In facing the prospect of losing her husband of sixty years, Alice pleads with Don to "pray for a miracle." Because Don understands prayer differently from his aunt, he doesn't believe that he can fulfill her request. The case raises important questions about the efficacy of intercessory prayer, unresolved grief, and the interpersonal tensions that develop in the context of traumatic loss.

A group can definitely benefit from studying this case. It can be

---

21. The case-study approach has been developed for theological communities primarily through the life's work of Robert and Alice Frazer Evans and the organization they founded, The Association for Case Teaching (see their web site at http://www. caseteaching.org). Although the particular case discussed here is taken from the *Casebook for Christian Living* by Louis and Carolyn Weeks and Robert and Alice Evans (Atlanta: John Knox Press, 1977), pp. 81-84, numerous books and individual cases have been published over the past twenty-five years. They can be located at the Case Study Institute Clearing House at Yale Divinity School. Modeled after the case approach developed by the Harvard Graduate School of Business, these cases are all based on actual events and persons and pose a dilemma or problem that remains unresolved. The unresolved nature of the issues serves to draw readers in as active participants in group discussion. Each summer the Case Study Institute offers a week's intensive training in teaching and writing cases. For a selected annotated bibliography by Alice Frazer Evans, see http:// caseteaching.org/case-teach-biblio.html.

assigned beforehand, or it can be read aloud in a meeting. Actively engaging the case will help members of the group consider their own attitudes toward intercessory prayer.

In Appendix B I've provided some suggestions for teaching the case.[22] With slight alterations, these suggestions can be used to discuss a variety of cases.

An alternative way to engage a group with the issues involved in intercessory prayer would be to give the group the assignment to read Wendell Berry's short story entitled "Pray Without Ceasing" (which was discussed in Chapter Six). Here are some exercises the leader might use to help the story resonate more deeply with group members:

- Close your eyes and remember the story. What image comes to mind? Read that image as the centerpoint of the story. What leads to it? What emerges from it?
- What is your visual memory of the story? What stays with you?
- Choose a paragraph that speaks strongly to you. Find its key words. How does the momentum in the paragraph build toward those words? Why are they so important?
- What is your favorite sentence? Why? What does it disclose about the meaning of the story?
- How would you describe the forces at work in this story? Where are the lines of tension?
- Why do you think Berry entitled the story "Pray Without Ceasing"? What is the function of the character Miss Della Budge in the story?
- What theological doctrines illuminate this story for you?
- What does Berry suggest about the mystery of time and eternity in his opening paragraphs? How does this beginning function as a framework for understanding the story as a whole?[23]

22. Stanley Saunders of Columbia Theological Seminary and I planned and taught this case together at the Case Study Institute in Estes Park, Colorado, in July 1995.

23. These questions arose in conversation with Marilyn Chandler McEntyre, who teaches English at Westmont College in Santa Barbara, California.

Chapter Seven: Prayers of Lament

It is important to understand the rich and complex texture of prayers of lament. Studying prayers of lament in a group can be particularly rewarding. The following exercises may prove helpful.

1. Have each member of the group memorize a lament psalm that is personally meaningful. Then have them share with the group or with a single member in the group the personal significance of this psalm. The lament psalms can be categorized as communal laments and individual laments. Communal lament psalms include Psalms 44, 74, 79, 80, 83, and 89.[24] Individual lament psalms include Psalms 3 to 17 (with the exception of Psalms 8, 9, and 15); Psalms 22 to 28 (with the exception of Psalm 24); Psalm 31; Psalms 35 to 43 (with the exception of Psalms 37 and 40a); Psalms 51 to 64 (except Psalm 60); and Psalms 69, 71, 73, 77, 86, 88, 94, 102, 109, 120, and 130.[25]

2. In Chapter Seven of this volume, I quoted from Nicholas Wolterstorff's *Lament for a Son* (Grand Rapids: Eerdmans, 1987). Have the members in your group read the volume and discuss which passages resonate with their experience of grief in the life of faith.

3. Engage in a role play involving the death of a family member. Divide the group into pairs or groups of three (pastoral care provider, suffering person, and process observer) for a role play. Choose one of the scenarios below:

   a. A caregiver visits a widow or widower whose spouse died last week, three months ago, or a year ago.
   b. A caregiver visits a parent whose child died suddenly in a car accident or died after suffering from cancer for several months.

In this scenario, the listener needs to draw out the grief-stricken person's narrative so that he or she feels fully heard and understood. Those in the listener role need to be aware of the temptation to divert the person, offer premature reassurance, or minimize his or her pain. When does that occur? Those listening might reflect on how their

---

24. Claus Westermann, *The Psalms: Structure, Content, and Message* (Minneapolis: Augsburg Publishing House, 1980), p. 29.
25. Westermann, *The Psalms*, p. 53.

minimizing might be related to unresolved issues in their own lives. Allow 10 to 15 minutes to do the role play and at least 20 minutes to debrief, first in pairs and then in the whole group.

4. Engage in a role play that involves several family members. The scenario is this: A caregiver visits a woman in the hospital who is near death. Nevertheless, she is lucid and wants to talk about unresolved issues in her family. They are resistant to hearing what she has to say, focusing instead on their "hope" and "faith" that she will soon be well. The caregiver, who is trusted and respected by the family, believes that they are in need of more open communication. How might the caregiver proceed?

In preparing for this role play, consider the comment quoted above (in part) by family systems therapist Murray Bowen:

> An open relationship system is one in which an individual is free to communicate a high percentage of inner thoughts, feelings, and fantasies to another who can reciprocate. No one ever has a completely open relationship with another, but it is a healthy state when a person can have one relationship in which a reasonable degree of openness is possible.
>
> The closed communication system is an automatic emotional reflex to protect the self from the anxiety in the other person, though most people say they avoid the taboo subjects to keep from upsetting the other person.[26]

Bowen worked with a woman whose family became so anxious when she broached the subject of her impending death that they wouldn't allow her to speak of it. He saw his task as one in which he needed to help control the family's anxiety and reactivity so that the "taboo subject" of death could be openly discussed. Here is how the woman described her situation:

> This is the loneliest life in the world. Here I am, knowing I am going to die, and not knowing how much time I have left. I can't talk to anyone. When I talk to my surgeon, he says it's not a cancer. When I try to talk to my husband, he makes jokes about it. . . . I am cut off from everyone. When I get up in the morning, I feel terrible.

26. Bowen, "Family Reaction to Death," p. 322.

I look at my eyes in the mirror to see if they are jaundiced and the cancer has spread to my liver. I try to act cheerful until my husband goes to work because I don't want to upset him. Then I am alone all day with my thoughts, just crying and thinking. Before my husband returns from work, I try to pull myself together for his sake. I wish I could die soon and not have to pretend any longer.[27]

With Bowen's assistance, the woman was finaly able to express these feelings to her family.

Those who are dying need an opportunity to give and receive love, to pass along whatever legacies they have, and to offer and receive forgiveness. They need assurance that their loved ones will be able to get along without them. The purpose of this role play is for the pastoral caregiver to become more skillful in opening up communication patterns in a family.

Chapter Eight: Prayers of Confession

Studying prayers of confession can help us realize the full scope of what we need to confess. The following exercises could produce rich rewards in a group.

1. Have the group consider this list of the "seven deadly sins": pride, sloth, envy, malice (anger), avarice (greed), lust, and gluttony. Have each member work through this exercise:

> Where does the list evoke unresolved issues in your own life? Are you aware of ways in which these sins distance you from God? Ponder the influences in your life that may have set you on a certain trajectory. Are there certain patterns of sin evident in your family of origin? Take 20 to 30 minutes to journal about these issues.

2. Discuss how sins and secrets function in an individual's life. Have each member work through this exercise:

> Are there secrets from your past with which you are burdened? Have you confessed these secrets to God and received the assurance

27. Bowen, "Family Reaction to Death," p. 330.

of God's forgiveness? If you still feel burdened by guilt and shame, is there someone with whom you might discuss these events? Consider consulting a professional pastoral counselor who could help you not only confess the sin but also understand something about its continuing power in your life. (See www.aapc.org.)

3. Examine the issue of scorn, and discuss how excessive scorn for another is often a clue for finding a lost or unclaimed part of oneself. Have each member undertake this exercise over time:

> If another's attitude is annoying, you might consider that you hold similar attitudes, though perhaps with different content — for example, opposite opinions held in an equally dogmatic or rigid way. Place the name of a person who irritates you excessively at the top of a page and then list all the attributes he or she has that annoy you. Put the paper away for a week. A week later, cross out that person's name and put your own name at the top of the page.

This exercise is intended to assist you in becoming aware of possibly denied or disowned parts of yourself. In a similar fashion, you can also draw up a list describing the excessively admired features of a person you idealize. When you put your own name at the top of the page a week later, you may find disowned characteristics that represent your latent potential. These may be qualities that you need to take responsibility for developing in yourself.

4. Have the group review Appendix C, which presents a case study that can be used to discuss complex issues in pastoral situations of confession. It is best to read it several times to prepare questions and observations.

Chapter Nine: Prayers of Thanksgiving, Praise, and Blessing

Studying prayers of thanksgiving, praise, and blessing in a group can help members realize all the ways, large and small, that they can offer thanks and give or seek blessing. Work through the following suggestions with group members, encouraging them to make a variety of these practices an ongoing part of their lives.

1. Meditate on Philippians 4:8: "Finally, brethren, whatever is true,

whatever is honorable, whatever is just, whatever is pure, whatever is lovely, whatever is gracious, if there is any excellence, if there is anything worthy of praise, think about these things." Spend twenty minutes journaling about those things that come to mind as you meditate on this passage. How is each one a gift from God? Write a prayer of thanksgiving based on your meditation.

2. If you have children, consider marking their forehead with a sign of the cross whenever they travel far from home. As a sign of their baptism, it becomes a nonverbal prayer of blessing, asking God to watch over them while you are apart.

3. A birthday can be a fitting occasion for a prayer of blessing. *The Book of Common Prayer* includes a prayer that can be used in the home:

> Watch over thy child, O Lord, as his days increase; bless and guide him wherever he may be. Strengthen him when he stands; comfort him when discouraged or sorrowful; raise him up if he fall; and in his heart may thy peace which passeth understanding abide all the days of his life; through Jesus Christ our Lord. Amen.[28]

4. Ponder Psalm 116 as you recover from surgery or serious illness. Consider the vows you want to make in the "great congregation" in thanksgiving for God's gift of healing. How might your gratitude be lived out as part of your vocation?

5. Reflect on the blessings in your life that correspond to the first five verses of Psalm 103. What sins has God forgiven, what diseases healed? Recount the ways God has redeemed your life from the Pit. Ponder the love, mercy, and goodness you have received and the ways in which life has been renewed.

6. In our uprooted culture, where so many people move every few years, consider developing a liturgy for a house blessing. Invite neighbors and friends to bless a new home and its inhabitants.

7. When invited to a baby shower (or a wedding shower), prepare a blessing, wish, or prayer for the new child (or new couple). Each gift can be accompanied with a prayer for the new life to come. When prepared in advance, these blessings make for a rich and meaningful event.

8. Memorize poetry that captures an experience of joy and

---

28. *The Book of Common Prayer* (New York: Oxford University Press, 1979), p. 830.

thanksgiving. (Paraphrased poetry is not equal to the task; time spent memorizing the exact words is well spent.) Consider memorizing "The Wild Rose" by Wendell Berry as a blessing for a couple celebrating their twenty-fifth or fiftieth wedding anniversary.[29]

9. Prepare for times of celebration or sorrow by meditating on the upcoming event (whether an anticipated birth, marriage, or death). Pray about it daily as you ponder Scripture. Prayers can be crafted on the basis of these meditations.

10. Take five minutes to offer a prayer of thanksgiving for something or someone you usually take for granted. Pray in gratitude for the gift of vision. Give thanks to God for the gift of hearing or of walking or of sexual expression. Spend five minutes pondering the gift of a spouse, a friend, or a child in your life and all the ways they enrich it.

Conclusion

These suggestions for meditation, journaling, discussion, role plays, study, and group interaction are offered in order to deepen engagement with the material presented in the text — and, more importantly, with one's fellow members of the community. Used creatively by pastors and church leaders, they are designed to enliven interaction, promote trust, and deepen learning for the sake of building up the body of Christ.

29. Wendell Berry, *The Selected Poems of Wendell Berry* (Washington, D.C.: Counterpoint, 1999), p. 153.

Appendix A Analysis of a Pastoral Conversation

Verbatim Account of Pastoral Conversation*

Name: Chaplain Alyce Richmond
Date and place: February 21, 2001; a nursing home
Length of visit: 40 minutes

A. PRE-CONTACT

Description:

Anne is an older lady in her late sixties or early seventies. She is petite and has cerebral palsy. Her cerebral palsy affects her speech, making it difficult initially for others to understand her. She is confined to a wheelchair but is very energetic. Her condition has not hardened her sensitive and gentle spirit. She seems to be well-liked by some of the staff. I have met Anne on two previous occasions. The first was during a worship service at the nursing home where we both introduced ourselves. The second time was when I visited Anne in her room. During the second visit we read from the book of Psalms. The purpose for this third contact is to follow up and to become better acquainted with Anne. The contact occurs in Anne's room. Anne shares a room with another resident who is present but silent during the visit. The room is small, con-

---

*I thank the student who wrote this verbatim for a class assignment and for her permission to use it here.

taining two beds, one bedside table, chairs, [with] one big window. There are several pictures of friends and family surrounding Anne's side of the room. Anne also has stuffed animals in a chair next to her bed.

My Role:

As the chaplain/representative from a local church, it is my role to visit the residents of the nursing home. In addition to visiting, I also lead worship once a month and organize fellowship activities. I believe that Anne sees me simply as a person from the church who visits and enjoys spending time with the residents. She seems to welcome the time that we spend together. I see myself less as a chaplain and more as a friend who enjoys being with the residents and listening to their stories.

Whose initiative:

I initiated the engagement under the circumstances of my regular nursing home rounds.

Known relevant information:

I learned from the Parish Associate for Pastoral Care at church that Anne had been born with cerebral palsy and this was the reason for her slurred speech and her confinement to a wheelchair. I do not know Anne very well. As was mentioned earlier, we have had two previous visits. During our second visit, I learned how hard it was to understand Anne's speech. At that time we did not have a conversation but we did read two psalms together.

Preparation:

I wanted to become better acquainted with Anne. I hoped to do this by reading more psalms with her at the beginning of our visit. By reading the psalms together, I would slowly become more adapted to her sounds and expressions. This then would better enable me to carry on a basic conversation with her. I was nervous as I anticipated the encounter. On our last visit I remember the awkward moments we had when I could not understand her words. We both were trying so hard to understand one another, but the verbal communication was not coming as fast as I wanted it to. In many ways I felt guilty that I couldn't understand Anne especially after she was trying so hard. These preliminary feelings and fears were very accurate. There were times when we both struggled for several moments trying to make out one word. These feelings and fears were modified slightly during our visit. Modification came when I realized the genuine respect and concern behind each of our attempts at understanding the other person.

B. CONTACT

Observation:

Anne lives in a very small space which she shares with a roommate. As I knocked on her door, I was very careful not to enter if she did not want me present in the little bit of space that she has left in the world. She has made her space special by putting photographs both on the window ledge and on the bedside table. In the chair next to her bed are some stuffed animals as well as her Bible.

Anne is very well-kept. Her shirt is neatly tucked into her pants. She is wearing a cross — the same one that she wore last time. Even though Anne cannot sit straight up, her body positions are always very gracious, showing her healthy self-respect. Because Anne's words are hard to understand, she uses a lot of body language. She will often move her arms/hands and head to convey what she is trying to get across. Her movements are very stiff and limited due to her physical condition.

The Process:

The visit lasted for about 40 minutes. The conversation began as we remembered our last encounter at Wednesday-night bingo. Then we read together out of the Bible. This act of reading connected us, thereby enabling Anne to share more of herself. The reading laid the foundation where we were able to more easily come together and from that point share more of ourselves. After the reading, Anne graciously and patiently tried to tell me that her mother taught her how to read when she was eighteen. Later, she shared how her mother carried her around until she got a wheelchair. The conversation ended when Anne needed to go to lunch. I thanked her for her patience in conveying her thoughts to me. She then thanked me as well.

> C1 [Knock on her open door, then wave]: Hi, Anne! I was wondering if I could come and visit you. [Pause]

A1: Yahhhh. [One big nod of head]

C2: [Still standing outside door] Would it be all right for me to come into your room?

A2: Yahhhh. [One big nod of head]

C3: [I go up and put my hand on her shoulder.] It's good to see you, Anne. How are you doing?

A3: Fine.

C4: Last time I saw you was on Wednesday night at bingo when you won the picture frame! How have things been since then?

A4: Okay. [Starts to motion towards the area behind her bed where there are pictures of small children on her wall — she says something which I don't understand.]

C5: The pictures on your wall?

A5: [She continues to motion and say something.]

C6: The flowers on your table? Valentine's flowers?

A6: [She continues to motion and say something.]

C7: The pictures? I'm sorry, Anne — I don't understand you. [I continue to look around to understand what she is saying to me.]

A7: [She proceeds to push herself away from the table. Then she slowly wheels herself over to the head of her bed. She opens the bedside drawer. Immediately I recognize the paper bag with the frame that she won at bingo.]

C8: Oh, the frame! Have you decided who you are going to give it to?

A8: Friend. [She backs up and returns to the table.]

C9: Anne, would it be all right if I take off my coat? It's kind of hot.

A9: [She nods her head, then looks out the window at the snow, saying something.]

C10: You think it's beautiful? [Meaning the snow]

A10: [Again, she motions outside of the window, saying something.]

C11: Warming up? Oh yes, the dripping water? [She smiles.] It must be heating up on top of the roof.

C12: [I kneel down to get more on her level.] I thought about you in church today. We sang the Twenty-Third Psalm and I remembered how you and I had read that together several weeks ago. I would love to do that again.

A12: [A few moments of silence — she begins to collect all the photographs on her table. She has a hard time lining them all up. She pushes the pile towards me and says what I think was . . .]

Here.

C13: [I ask her if they are special pictures, but I don't really understand her response.] Do you want me to put these up?

A13: [Nods her head and makes a deep affirming sound]

C14: Do you still have your book of psalms?

A14: [She looks down to the left side of her body. Her book of psalms is sitting next to her in the chair. She picks it up and puts it on the table. She says something and begins to motion to the other side of her bed.]

C15: [I follow where her hand is pointing.] The picture on your window?

A15: [She says something and motions with greater energy to the other side of the room.]

C16: The stuffed animals?

A16: [She continues to motion in the same direction.]

C17: Do you want me to get something for you?

A17: [Nods her head and makes a deep affirming sound]

C18: [I get up, walk behind Anne, and then walk over to the other corner of her bed. I look in the area to which she is pointing.] Oh, the Bible?

A18: [She smiles, her head pokes up and nods back.]

C19: Would you like me to bring it to you?

A19: Yahh. [One big nod]

C20: It looks like a new Bible — who gave it to you, Anne?

A20: Friend. [She pushes her book of psalms over to the side and opens the Bible.]

[Silence as she turns page]

C21: [I figured that she was probably going to turn to the psalms. I watched her open the Bible. Slowly and carefully she pushed the cover open with the stiff palm of her hand — then she stiffly fingered each page from side to side as if she were petting an animal. After a few moments, I found myself questioning whether I should help her. Finally, I helped her turn a few pages, but then I regretted what I thought to be an act of kindness. I had let my anxiousness and "fix-it" nature get in the way.]

A21: [To my surprise she stopped at First Corinthians. She pointed to chapter 1.] Read.

C22: Okay. But will you read with me too, Anne?

A22: [She makes a sound I can't understand, but I decide to start reading and see what happens.]

C23: [I read the first chapter of First Corinthians as she sits quietly but attentively, following every word.]

A23: [Then she carefully and slowly turns each page of her Bible until she arrives at Psalm 19. She points to the psalm.]

A24: Anne, would you mind reading this with me? I really enjoyed reading with you last time. [I slowly read the psalm. Anne comes in at the end of the sentences as if she is affirming what is being read.]

C25: Do you read the psalms often?

A25: [She answers but I don't understand — I do understand one of her words . . .] Read.

C26: Read another psalm?

A26: [She shakes the upper part of her body along with her arms. I gather that her answer is no. She repeats her words.]

C27: Read?

A27: [She shakes her body again and repeats her words with more intention.]

C28: [I'm getting a little frustrated. It's becoming tiring to have a simple conversation.] Anne, I'm sorry I don't understand. Would you mind repeating? [Diagnosis: How are Anne and I going to communicate?]

A28: [She repeats and her body movements become more exaggerated, as if she wants to break forth. I begin to sense her frustration.]

C29: [At this point, I'm very frustrated because I really want to understand Anne. How am I supposed to break through this language barrier? I don't want to highly frustrate her, but I also don't want to pretend that I understand what she is saying. Suddenly it dawns on me to ask Anne if she wouldn't mind spelling some of her words.] Anne, I'm sorry. Can you spell your words for me? [Intervention plan: Ask her to spell words.]

A29: "L"

C29: "L"

A29: "E"

C29: "E"

A29: "A"

C29: "A"

A29: "?" [I don't understand the letter she is saying.]

C29: "A?"

A29: [Her body movements tell me no. She pulls down a *Reader's Digest* from her table and turns it so that I can see the cover page. She points to the title.]

C30: Do you want to show me an article in the *Reader's Digest?*

A30: [She forcefully points to the title again and then says a word.]

C31: I don't understand, Anne. [I'm beginning to feel like I'm letting her down.]

A31: [She continues to forcefully and nervously point to the "R" in the title of *Reader's Digest.*]

C32: Oh!!! "R" [I smile and feel a little relieved.]

A32: [She smiles and becomes a little less tense.]

C33: "L" — "E" — "A" — "R"

A33: "N"

C34: Learn!

A34: Learn to read. [Holds up both fingers as if to express number ten]

C35: You learned to read when you were ten?

A35: [This is obviously the wrong answer. She shakes her body, holds up her hands again. This time she flashes her hands twice, saying something.]

C36: Oh, you were twenty?

A36: No. [Then she says another word which I don't understand right away.]

C37: Would you mind spelling that word for me?

A37: [She says the word and then she begins to spell . . . "E," "I" . . .]

C38: Oh, eighteen!

A38: [Smiling, she's pleased that we understand one another.]

C39: You learned to read when you were eighteen.

A39: Mother!

C40: Your mother taught you how to read?

A40: [Makes affirming sound so that I know her answer is yes. She is more calm now that I have understood her.]

C41: Wow!

[Anne then tells me how her mom carried her around until she got a wheelchair. This is another long conversation as we try to communicate to one another!]

[Anne points to her watch. It's time for lunch.]

C42: Anne, thank you for letting me visit with you. I enjoyed reading with you again. [I follow her out of the room as she wheels herself to lunch. When she arrives at the cafeteria, I say . . .]

C43: Anne, I'm sorry it took me so long to understand you. Thank you for being so patient with me.

A43: You. [She says "you" while pointing to me — I'm assuming that she is thanking me.]

C44: I'll come back and see you again. Have a good Sunday!

C. ANALYSIS

Theological Concerns

In thinking about this category of analysis, I can't seem to get away from the role that "story" plays in our lives. Anne and I began our time together by recounting the story of bingo last Wednesday night. We then progressed into reading the stories of the Bible. In both of these situations, we shared stories that were common to us and that gave meaning to our lives. Because we had established that foundation, Anne felt more comfortable sharing some of her own personal stories from the story of her life. It is story, after all, that makes community. It is my impression that Anne has probably always struggled — because of her physical limitations — with being a part of a community. From our brief conversation, I gathered that her mother was an integral and necessary part of helping Anne to be a part of a larger community (through teaching her how to read and to use a wheelchair). It was by our struggling together to figure out how we can hear "The Story" together and then how to hear one another's stories that Anne and I were able to become closer.

Theologically, Anne is probably also wrestling with what it means to get older and then to eventually die. The first psalm we ever read together (during our second visit) was the Twenty-third Psalm. In fact, we read it two times. She seemed very moved by the reading. As we read together during this third visit, I noticed that Anne was paying very close attention to every word. When we finished reading one page she would immediately look up to the top of the next page. During the reading, Anne did not move a lot. The reading had a peaceful, calming influence on her. (Note: I was trying to think about why Anne chose to open her Bible to First Corinthians and then later to Psalm 19. By the way she arrived at those pages, I tend to think that maybe she just randomly turned to those places. But upon further reflection, I think Psalm 19 speaks very powerfully to Anne's situation in that the psalm talks about the knowledge of God that is transmitted without speech (vv. 3-4).

Psychological Concerns

I think Anne daily deals with the tension of having the real and legitimate need to be heard. She deals with this tension very well, at least in terms of our relationship. I can easily imagine someone in Anne's situation deciding to stop communicating because it takes too long for people to understand. I applaud and greatly admire Anne for her determination, patience, and graciousness; she does not give up this daily battle. It would have been very easy for her to "shut down" a long time ago. The photographs around her room show how important it is to her to be in a relationship with other people. To be in relationship means to communicate, and that involves many frustrating moments for Anne — but thank God she is willing to go through them.

Sociological Concerns

Obviously, Anne's mother has played a significant role in her life by teaching her how to read and to use a wheelchair. If it had not been for Anne's mother, then she would not be able to communicate on this level with me. Based on the information Anne has shared with me, I would also guess that Anne's mother helped to instill a level of self-confidence and self-worth in Anne.

I wonder where Anne fits into the nursing home community. The one occasion when I saw Anne interacting with other people was during the worship service. She happened to be sitting next to a man who had recently lost his wife and had become very feeble. During the service, I noticed that she would help him hold the bulletin and follow along. Anne strikes me as the type who would probably reach out to the hurting. The man did not resist her helping gesture. I do not know, however, what her relationship is with her roommate or what her relationship is with the people in the photographs sitting around her room.

Reflections of Pastoral Caregiver

Looking back, I recognized and remembered the guilt I had for not being able to understand what Anne was trying to tell me (as if it were all my fault). I noticed that I apologized to her several times. It was very frustrating not to be able to comprehend her words. I was often afraid that she would give up before I finally could grasp what she was trying so hard to tell me. Not only was I afraid that she might give up, but deep down I was also afraid that I might call it quits and start functioning on the level of pretender.

I also recognize how powerfully freeing it was for me to say to Anne, "I'm sorry but I don't understand. Would you mind spelling the words for me?" That honest announcement to her was a confession of my frustrating and awkward feelings as a listener, as well as of my true desire to really understand Anne's thoughts and feelings. I think my honesty linked with her gracious determination paved the way toward developing better communication.

One thing that I know I don't want to do next time is to help Anne in any way to open her Bible and turn to the desired page. I will only help her if she asks for my assistance. Otherwise, the beauty of the moment is in sitting patiently with Anne as she contentedly turns each page, not frustrated by her own pace. The silence and the slowness is a gift. Peaceful patience has its rewards!

D. CONCLUSION

Assessment of Pastoral Opportunity

I believe that there are significant opportunities for further pastoral care in Anne's life. She seemed to really want to be in a relationship with me by virtue of the fact that she kept repeating her thoughts over and over and even spelled them out for me. She recognizes her human need to be in relationship by exhibiting her desire through hard effort. In my future visits with Anne, I would like to hear more about the significant people in her life — especially the people in her pictures. By my learning more about these people, Anne will be able to share the stories of her life, and in that sharing, her human and basic need to be heard will be met in some small way. During my visits with Anne, I want to be sensitive to the times when it's too hard for her to talk. In those moments, I need to remind myself to do several things: (1) not to take it personally if she gives up trying to clarify the words she is using — we all have bad days when it's a struggle to deal with our limitations; and (2) to remind her that we don't always have to talk — we can sit in silence together if she needs that; and (3) to affirm her worth and value as a member not only of the nursing home community but also of the larger Christian community.

Focus for Discussion

I chose this conversation because it was conversation that was difficult and awkward at times. (In some ways, I felt inadequate because I could not understand Anne.) It was also a conversation where I was honest with myself and with Anne in terms of not being able to understand her. Although the honesty was a bold and vulnerable step, it did help to bring a humanness and a genuineness to our time together. This was also a conversation where I very much felt God's presence.

In terms of feedback, I would like any suggestions as to what I could have done differently. What are some things that I did both verbally and nonverbally that might have been ineffective? While you are visiting someone, how do you deal with feelings of guilt and inadequacy at not being able to understand them? I would also welcome any ideas for creative interactions in the future.

Addendum: Questions for Reflection and Discussion

1. How would you address the chaplain's feelings of guilt and inadequacy?
2. What do you think the chaplain communicates to the resident in and through her words and attitudes?
3. Note the chaplain's responses in particular. What suggestions come to mind for what she might have done differently?

A Case Study

Pray for a Miracle

This case study is taken from the *Casebook for Christian Living*, edited by Louis and Carolyn Weeks and Robert and Alice Evans (Atlanta: John Knox Press, 1977), pp. 81-84. The volume provides a study guide for group reflection.

*   *   *

Don Jacobs rang the doorbell hesitantly. He knew Aunt Alice would answer in a minute. He could almost picture her coming from Alfred's bed through the hall toward the living room. He also knew what she would soon be asking him. "Pray for a miracle." Somehow that phrase stuck with her, from an evangelist or something.

Don wondered again how to respond. If he did what she asked, he would feel like a hypocrite of sorts. But if he denied her request, he would undoubtedly disappoint her. He tried to gather his confused thoughts as the encounter drew nearer.

Aunt Alice and Uncle Alfred

For forty-two of their fifty-six years of marriage, Alice and Alfred had been living right here on Sycamore Street. The clapboard house, now with its porch a bit askew, had been only a few years old when they moved in. They used to tell Don how small the neighborhood trees had been in those days. Now trees almost overlapped the street, and the sidewalks cracked with the pressure of big roots.

Together Alice and Alfred had shared work, a small grocery, and they had shared play, especially the good times with the family. They had been inseparable as Alice recounted it and as Don remembered. Seldom had either gone out alone, except to night meetings of Alfred's service club or sometimes to church. Alice had told Don, with tears in her eyes, just last week: "You see that bed Alfred is in? Until his illness, we had been together in that bed every night for two decades. We took some trips before that, but Alfred has never been away from me overnight."

Both Alice and Alfred were Christians. She had worked in Women's Guild and he as a deacon as long as Don had known them. Alice read the family Bible a lot now, and Don remembered her taking it out each Saturday night when he had been with them.

Don Jacobs

Don's own parents had died when he was eight. He had lived almost ten years with Alice and Alfred. Then he went off to college, and yet they kept in touch with him as though they were his real parents. Don had known other family members, cousins and such, through Alice and Alfred. And the bond had stayed a close one through the years. Don had married, and he lived with his family about twenty miles away. His kids considered Alice and Alfred as grandparents, and they lavished affection on all the Jacobs.

Don's own theology had changed over time. He had grown to think of prayer as important and as personally helpful. One prayed to be "in touch" with God, not to get anything to happen. He had read, among other works, a remarkable thing by Mark Twain about prayer. Mark Twain had made fun of selfish prayers, something about God responding to one man's request by saying a competitor prayed the opposite and the two prayers canceled each other out. That had made an impression on Don.

Yet he prayed. Sometimes he even repeated a word or two, in order to concentrate. He did not ask for things, though. After all, if God knew everything, what was the use? Mostly Don prayed "to get his life in focus" by pushing out all other things from his mind. That left a beautiful void that concentrated his energy afterwards on the task at hand, or on the needs of others. Don could not help but feel a bit suspicious of the evangelists who offered "good results" from prayer, a kind of manipulation of things in favor of the contributor. And he believed in the possibility of some kind of life after death, though he hoped natural events would not be absent there — wherever "there" was. As a scientist he felt strongly about the interdependence of all natural processes, and the beauty of nature appealed to him in a religious fashion.

Alfred's Illness

Uncle Alfred was now almost seventy-two as Don remembered the dates. He had lived a really full life, quietly and with dignity. About three years ago he had been diagnosed as needing surgery. Cancer had been discovered, and gradually evidence of a brain cancer had appeared. Alfred had been hospitalized from time to time, then allowed to "recuperate" at home whenever possible. His condition had deteriorated over the months of illness, so that recently he had been lucid only rarely. When he woke up, Alfred would begin to cry uncontrollably. He would seldom recognize anybody, Alice included. Mostly he just lay there, dying.

His weight had decreased over the months until he was just "skin and bones," as Alice described him. Other symptoms indicated that he would soon pass away, and the doctors had advised that Alice should place him in the hospital for an easier time of it.

Alice's Care and Prayer

Alice long ago had received some training as a nurse's aide. She wanted to care for Alfred as much as possible at home, "where things were familiar."

For the operations, she had stayed constantly at the hospital. At home she stayed right by Alfred's side almost all the time. Of late, she had been requesting all the persons visiting to "pray for a miracle." Rev. Wilkins had been there two days ago, and he had prayed about "God's will be done. . . ." Don had thought the prayer a good one, but after Rev. Wilkins left, Alice confided that she did not think that was enough. "He said that God's will be done to heal or bring Alfred to himself," Alice related. "I know Alfred can be restored to useful health. God will do it if our faith is strong enough."

Don tried to go to see them daily, either at lunch or in the evening. Yesterday Alice had become more insistent. "Pray for him, Donald. You're a good Christian man. God will listen to you." Don had prayed something like this, as he recalled:

> God, who makes and redeems each of us, we seek your presence with Alfred. Care for him, God, because we surely do. Be with him and help him. Help us too, God, for we need your love and care. Amen.

Don had tried to let that be that, but as he left, Alice had said something about "a miracle." It was a fixation with her right now. Don felt that he didn't even know what "restored to health" meant for Alfred. He felt that Alice was focusing on something that would not be helpful in her grief. But what to do about it? What should he do?

Addendum: Suggestions for Teaching the Case

Stanley Saunders of Columbia Theological Seminary and I developed the suggestions for teaching this case. We taught it together at the Case Study Institute in Estes Park, Colorado, in July 1995.

1. Begin the class with three passages from Scripture to provide a theological context for reflection:
   - Matthew 17:20: "If you have faith as a grain of mustard seed, you will say to this mountain, 'Move from here to there,' and it will move; and nothing will be impossible to you."
   - Matthew 18:19-20: "Again I say to you, if two of you agree on earth about anything they ask, it will be done for them by my Father in heaven. For where two or three are gathered in my name, there am I in the midst of them."
   - Matthew 26:39: "My Father, if it be possible, let this cup pass from me; nevertheless, not as I will, but as thou wilt."
2. Explore the case. Begin with questions about Don Jacobs:
   - What do we know about Don Jacobs?
   - What is his history with Aunt Alice?

- What is he most concerned about?
- What might he be feeling?
- What is he needing?
- What are his views on prayer?
- What kind of God do these views imply?

3. Next, ask questions about Aunt Alice:
   - What do we know about Aunt Alice?
   - What is her history with her husband, Alfred?
   - What is she most concerned about?
   - What might she be feeling?
   - What is she needing?
   - What are her views on prayer?
   - What kind of God do these views imply?

4. Now engage the class in role play:
   - Divide the group into pairs. One member of each pair plays the role of Aunt Alice and the other that of Don Jacobs. Alice and Don are at the kitchen table, where the family Bible lies close at hand. Alfred is lying gravely ill in the next room.
   - Give instructions for both roles. Alice is to share her deepest yearnings with Don, and try to determine what she wants from her nephew. Don is to try to determine what he wants to say to his aunt, and consider what he will say if she asks him to pray for a miracle.
   - Allow the pairs seven to ten minutes to develop the role play and ten to fifteen minutes to debrief with each other.

5. Debrief with the whole group: What happened? Were there any surprises? Which character did you most identify with? What do you admire in them? Of what are you most critical? What might you want to say to Alice or Don that you couldn't say in the role?

6. Close the meeting with these questions: Where is God present in this story? What would be a miracle for Alice? For Don? What in Scripture informs your understanding of where God might be present? What kind of prayer is most faithful to Scripture?

Clearly, these suggestions can be altered according to the needs and interests of the group.

Appendix C A Pastoral Conversation

This material comes from the *Casebook in Pastoral Counseling*, ed. Newman S. Cryer and John M. Vayhinger (Nashville: Abingdon Press, 1962), pp. 267-70.

* * *

John, who had been becoming more and more confused and frustrated — that was easy to see — knocked at the study door. During the interview that followed, he spoke with obvious feelings of pain. He was almost crying at times.

> **John 1:** Afternoon, Reverend L.
> **Pastor 1:** Hi, John! How are you today?
> **John 2:** Not so good. I called you earlier in the week. I thought I ought to come down and talk to you for a while.
> **Pastor 2:** Un-huh.
> **John 3:** I don't know exactly what it is, but I haven't been feeling too well.
> **Pastor 3:** Something's been bothering you?
> **John 4:** Well, it's pretty mixed up. Not only home and office; it's all over. I think I know pretty much what it is, but I can't seem to figure it out.
> **Pastor 4:** Things seem rather confusing? You almost think you know, but you're not quite sure?
> **John 5:** Yes. [Pause] Reverend, can God forgive people?

Pastor 5: I think he can. What do you think about it?

John 6: I don't know. I thought so too, but that was before. Now I don't know — I don't know.

Pastor 6: You have some doubts about the forgiving nature of God?

John 7: Yeah — maybe I better tell you. It was five years ago. I've never told anybody this. It's been bothering me so much I just had to tell somebody: I killed five men. It was during the Korean War. I just got married and was drafted and went overseas right away. One night when we were out on patrol, three of us and the lieutenant went out on a mission. I was the only one who came back. We started out and everything was okay. We got there and took care of our mission, and on the way back it happened — we were ambushed. I sort of got cut off from the others. I heard shots. I laid in the grass. They went on by; then I found myself behind the lines and couldn't get back. I wasn't too sure where I was, so I just started crawling. Then, I saw them: three pillboxes on one side and a river on the other. The only way I could get them was one at a time. So I did. Crawled up — couldn't shoot — too many — pulled out my knife, bayonet, got all five, one at a time. Didn't bother me much at first, even when I came back from the war. Didn't bother me too much. But then I got to thinking about it. All the time God says, "Thou shalt not kill." But I did. I killed — five of them, stuck a knife right through each one.

Pastor 7: This has caused you some amount of worry since you have come back?

John 8: Yeah. You know how I've been with the church. I started sort of worrying more and more all the time. God is supposed to be able to forgive people, but this is sort of different. This isn't the same thing as when you preach up there on Sunday morning. You sort of get up and tell about these people. The little things — cheating at business, a heavy finger on the scale, or something like that — but this is different. This is big business; this is murder.

Pastor 8: The experience in the army is a very big thing to you in relation to some of the things we preach about?

John 9: Not so much the experience, but the killing. I just killed these men. I know, it might have been them or me. Maybe it would have been better if it had been me. I don't know. I've just been waiting, waiting for something to happen. I don't think God can just come out and forgive this kind of thing. I don't know. Just seems — I don't know.

Pastor 9: Things have been building up inside of you, and you have begun to question God's activity in this?

John 10: Yeah, I guess, sort of. Well, God — he's running the universe, you might say. You just can't go around killing people right and left without being punished for it. God just doesn't sit there and let you stab people and let you get away with it. In our society, just like a man kills somebody, we kill him sometimes. This is almost the same thing. I mean, you take a life. You just don't go out and do this. You say, "Well, it's over with, it's part of the war"; but it's more than that. It's a man you killed. Just like if I killed somebody now, it's the same thing.

Pastor 10: Then you are wondering now how God can forgive one who has killed?

John 11: Yeah, that's about it. I don't know. I've been waiting; I've been hoping; I've even been praying. But I don't think he's forgiven me. He — I just keep worrying. Now I think I'm going to get punished; I don't know. I know he's going to punish me somehow. I don't know how, but I think this is it; this is what's bothering me.

I just keep waiting, looking every day. I wake up and I look out and think, Well, maybe today he'll punish me so I can go on living like I should. But he hasn't punished me. He just keeps me waiting.

Pastor 11: Waiting for punishment is a terrible threat.

John 12: Yes. You just don't kill somebody and get away with it. I mean, it's different; it's not like these little things. It is vital, vital to people. They got to live.

Pastor 12: In other words, killing is a rather large issue in the world today. More so than some of the other things, some of the smaller things you feel we talk about. This would make a very large problem; this would make one worry.

John 13: Well, killing is taking away life.

Pastor 13: Life seems important to you?

John 14: Yeah. I guess so. You can't live without life — what is there? I mean, I live; I got life. Why shouldn't the next guy have life? Why shouldn't he live the same way? You know — but I, I don't know. When you do something wrong, you have to pay. You just can't forget about it, cast it off, and not worry about it. You have to pay. God makes everyone pay.

Pastor 14: You feel that somehow God must have punishment for the wrong deeds of man?

John 15: Yeah. I know — I know we preach love all the time. Everybody says all we need is love. God forgives, loves everybody, everything is going to be okay. This is okay. But even with this love, sure, sure God loves us. He loves, he wants us, and everything; but you can't get away with this. There are certain laws, like the Ten Commandments. When you break them, sure he still loves you, but even then you still have to pay for these bad deeds which you do.

Pastor 15: The idea of love and hate, then, is a problem with you in relation to God?

John 16: God doesn't hate necessarily. But there are certain things when you do something wrong — you have to pay for it.

Pastor 16: Punishment rather than hate?

John 17: Yeah. Like when you add numbers up, you get so many and that's it. You add up punishment and you get so many and something has to happen. Then you wipe the slate clean. Take, for example, at home. I remember when I was small, my mother, she loved me, my father loved me too, and we were happy at home. They used to do everything for me all the time. I used to go out and play, and then when they'd call me I wouldn't come sometime. Like I remember one time, there was a field behind our house, and we always went out and played football. This one night I remember, I was out there playing. Mother called me for supper, but I didn't come. I heard her, but I didn't want to leave the game. I was playing, and it was important that we win. We had the ball; so I stayed there until the game was over. Then when I got home they knew I heard. I got a licking, went to bed. All they gave me was a glass of milk. It's the same thing with God. You see, they loved me too; but because I didn't come home, because I was bad, I broke the law of obeying a parent, I had to pay. I had to go to bed. And the next morning when I got up, everything was okay. But he's making me wait. I'm willing to pay, I'm willing to get sick or something — I don't know. He's making me wait. But the thing is bothering me. I can't wait any longer. I must — got to have something done.

Pastor 17: You feel that you have to be punished by God as you are punished by others; but the waiting for this punishment is bothering you a great deal — causing a lot of anxiety? It's the waiting that is important to you now?

John 18: I don't know when it's got to happen. It's got to happen pretty soon. I mean, I been out of the army five years. It never bothered me too much when I first got out. I thought about it; actually, I tried to push it to the back of my mind. I didn't want to think about it. I just left it go.

Pastor 18: The thought was rather painful then.

John 19: Yeah — Well, I didn't think about it. I blocked it out completely.

Pastor 19: You were hoping with time it would go away; but instead it began to grow larger, it began to be important in your life to see why this is?

John 20: Yeah.

Pastor 20: As time went on it didn't go away?

John 21: It got worse. I think what probably brought it back to a head was that last week I was a pallbearer at a funeral. Almost couldn't carry the man; too much. All I kept thinking of was that patrol over in Korea. Kept going back, back. I just don't know what to do. I know, even at home it's affecting things. The other day, my wife and I got talking. Nothing too bad. And I — I got nervous and hit her. I shouldn't do that; but it was like, I don't know. I just sort of lost control.

Pastor 21: All of a sudden something exploded that you couldn't control?

John 22: Yeah, I guess. Just out of nowhere. Wasn't her fault. I still don't know what to do. Why does he keep prolonging this thing? Get it over with. I just keep waiting, waiting.

Pastor 22: Waiting?

John 23: I don't know. I don't know! Even the kids notice it. I heard — the little boy, now five, born while I was in the army. My wife was about six months gone when I left, and then he came; and I got home to see him right before I left for Korea. And I heard him telling his mother, "What's wrong with Daddy these days? Why is he so cross?" I just sort of tried to forget about it; but he's right — I am cross. This business. I don't know what to do about it.

Pastor 23: The thinking of punishment is even affecting your home life, the punishment of God?

John 24: Yeah, un-huh. Afraid it does. I just don't know what to do.

Pastor 24: Just like waiting for something that doesn't come.

John 25: But it's going to come. I don't know when. But it will come. You can't kill a man and get away with it. God will — God will make it come. But I don't know what to do in the meantime.

Pastor 25: Well, John, I see that our time is about up for today. Let me suggest something. Perhaps you could come in to see me, and we could talk about this at the same time each week. Talk something as we are now. You will do most of the talking. We'll see together if we can work something out, if you would like to do that.

John: Okay, I'll come and talk.

Addendum: Questions for Reflection and Discussion

The pastor's strength is his careful active listening, but he offers little theological guidance. Discussing the following questions — augmented by any others the group might have come up with — should prove instructive:

1. The case presented is over forty years old. Given the development of the field of pastoral theology during that time, how might you respond differently today to John's concerns?
2. What are the relevant frameworks for understanding and assessing a pastoral course of action?
3. What specifically might you say theologically to help John with his dilemma?

4. How would your theological framework be informed by your understanding of ethics and psychology?
5. Specifically, what does John need to confess, and how might the pastor be most helpful to him in enabling such a confession?
6. What are the factors that need to be taken into consideration?
7. What do you see as the theological heart of the issue John is struggling with?

Acknowledgments

The author and publisher gratefully acknowledge permission to reprint the following materials:

Excerpts from *Casebook in Pastoral Counseling*, edited by Newman S. Cryer Jr. and John Monroe Vayhinger. Copyright © 1962 by Abingdon Press. Reprinted with permission of Abingdon Press.

Excerpt from "Loaves and Fishes" from *The House of Belonging* by David Whyte. Copyright © 1997 by David Whyte. Reprinted with permission from Many Rivers Press, P.O. Box 868, Langley, WA.

Excerpt from "A man is lying on a bed" from *A Timbered Choir* by Wendell Berry. Copyright © 1998 by Wendell Berry. Reprinted with permission from Basic Books, a member of the Perseus Books Group. All rights reserved.

Excerpt from "Now you know the worst" from *A Timbered Choir* by Wendell Berry. Copyright © 1998 by Wendell Berry. Reprinted with permission from Basic Books, a member of the Perseus Books Group. All rights reserved.

Excerpts from "Pray Without Ceasing" from *Fidelity* by Wendell Berry. Copyright © 1992 by Wendell Berry. Reprinted with permission from Random House, Inc. All rights reserved.

"The Eye of God" by Saint Patrick in *Cry of the Wild Goose: Celtic Prayers and Songs of Resurrection* by Kathy Eddy (copyright © R.M. Eddy and K.W. Eddy); original version in *Celtic Prayers*, edited by Avery Brooke (copyright © 1981). Reprinted with permission.

"Pray for a Miracle," excerpt from *Casebook for Christian Living*, edited by Louis and Carol Weeks and Robert and Alice Evans. Copyright © 1977 John Knox Press. Reprinted with permission of Westminster John Knox Press.

Index